r

EVANS, Jane

From behind the counter, 1896-1996

0001057457   £12.50

Please return this book by the last date shown above

The Lutterworth Press
P.O. Box 60
Cambridge
CB1 2NT

British Library Cataloguing in Publication Data:
A catalogue record is available from the British Library.

ISBN 0 7188 2958 1

Printed in Great Britain by Galliard (Printers) Ltd, Great Yarmouth

CONTENTS

Introduction

This book is a combination of many strands of social history, all of them linked by one family. It became clear as we researched through the family papers and the old scrapbooks of newspaper cuttings, and as we talked to members of the family, staff and family friends, that there was more to tell than the story of a shop.

Although linked by one family and their business, the story centres round many other aspects of the commercial, social and economic life of Northampton and Kettering. Within the framework of the family of Arthur and Hannah Watts there can be told stories of the growth of a business, the changing working conditions of its shop staff, the developments taking place in Northampton's Methodist churches, the efforts of a society struggling to return to normality after the Second World War, the developments in the wider commercial world – of tv advertising and giant multiples, buying groups and retail warehouses, and finally the onslaught of town planning on the small business both in Kettering and in Northampton.

The story depicts the ambitions, the struggles and the achievements of the various generations of the Watts family, and within the book we hope there is something of interest for all who know Northampton and Kettering, who remember or wonder about their past, and who are concerned about their future.

We gratefully acknowledge the help given by the following people:
Members of the Watts family, including Roy Harland, Francis Watts, Joyce Harland, Alan Harland, Jean Starmer, Eileen Dixon and the late Fred Perkins; present staff, retired staff and their families, customers past and present; David Walmsley, the late Arthur Walmsley, Tony Ireson, Spencer Gunn, David Miles, Cyril Darby, Philip Saunderson, Philip Harradine, Vivian Church, Stephen Church, Arthur Brown, John Whittaker, Harold Frost, Freda and Mildred Riches, Nick Evans; Marion Arnold and staff of the library of the Northamptonshire Studies collection, staff at the Northamptonshire Record Office, Judith Hodgkinson of the Central Museum, Northampton, Jane Percival of the South Midlands Co-op, the Northampton Chamber of Trade, the Northampton Borough Council, the Northamptonshire County Council, the Kettering Civic Society; all the people who so kindly allowed us to reproduce their photographs and newspaper items. The editors of the *Chronicle & Echo* for numbers 14, 27-32, 46 and 54, the *Evening Telegraph*, 34-5, the *Northants Post*, and the *Sunday Times*; Douglas Joll and the late Dorothy Grimes for their kind practical advice.

Illustrations

Maps

Foreword

I am glad to write this foreword for several reasons. A moment's reflection shows that with a bit of luck I too may be in the centenary bracket in 17 years time; this means that I have personal memories of most of the ground covered by the author.

For many years Francis and Jean Watts were nearby friends when they lived in Kettering. They served as mayor and mayoress, but later had to fight against the Council when it embarked on a redevelopment scheme destroying a splendid Victorian frontage of shops in which the friendly and welcoming Watts emporium was the centrepiece.

My home is Kettering – I have published five books in appreciation of it – but when researching my *Northamptonshire* I walked over every yard of central Northampton and fell in love with a wonderful town that embodies so much of England's history. I was renewing an earlier friendship, for I well remember my delight in riding Northampton trams as a youngster.

I have lived in a county famous for its industries, mainly shoemaking, engineering and making good clothes. Foreign competition has done much to damage traditional trades, and many of the changes sadden me. We are fighting back in many new ways, and must guard against spoiling our towns by losing civic pride, so long maintained by people like the Watts and Harland families.

I feel that we all have a duty to maintain Northamptonshire's traditions by our deeds, rejecting temptations to take easy ways out which in many cases have led to depressing results.

From Behind the Counter is a well-researched, generously illustrated and readable study of Northamptonshire life from an observation point giving unique insights. I hope the book will be widely read, and will stimulate discussion about old-fashioned values and the simple virtues and principles that the Watts and Harland families learnt and helped to propagate.

Tony Ireson

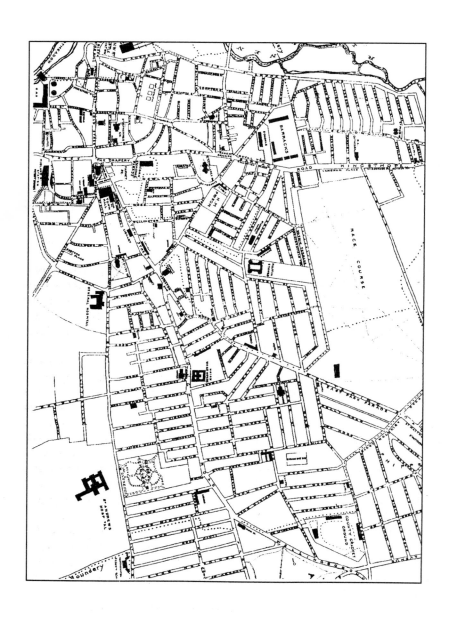

Chapter I
Arthur Watts 1896-1931

When Arthur Watts moved to Northampton in 1887, little did he realize that 109 years later his name would be a familiar one to old Northamptonians, that even a book would be published to celebrate the centenary of his business, A. Watts and Sons Ltd.

When he arrived, he took lodgings in Milton Street, comparatively new terraced houses built with all the latest conveniences and soon to be in the shadow of St Matthews Church. St Matthews was not yet built when he arrived in the town with his young wife, Hannah, and his two sons, Fred, aged 4, and Ewart, aged 1. He was to take up his promotion as district sales manager for the Singer Sewing Machine Company, whose shop was in Gold Street.

Northampton was a rapidly growing town that had expanded considerably during the nineteenth century. Yet when the Watts family arrived, Abington was still a manor outside the town boundary; Park Avenue North, where they were later to live was still fields and orchards. Victorian terraced housing for the new population of factory workers was still within only a mile radius north and east of the town's centre at All Saints Church. When Arthur's children were a little older, (Fred would have been 13) they must have delighted in the freedom to enter Abington Park, when it was given to the people of Northampton as a public park by Lady Wantage, in 1897.

Fortunately for Arthur and Hannah they were soon able to buy their own house at 36 Cowper Street , close to the bustling Kettering Road, which was considered one of the main shopping streets of the town, closely situated to where the majority of the town population lived. Abington Street was still largely residential. A stream ran down York Road, providing a pleasant walk out of town. Carriers with their horses and carts used the eastern end of Abington Street as a place to park.

The Wellingborough Road was also growing as a commercial centre alongside the Kettering Road, but it was considered by no means as smart, with a pub on virtually every street corner.

Arthur was known as a charming man, very kind and rather quiet. How did he come to establish such a flourishing business that would become known as one of the leading family firms of Northampton? It must be said that without

1. Arthur Watts, (1882).

Hannah, this quiet man might possibly have continued to pursue his career of selling sewing machines.

His roots were in the small town of Frome, situated just south of Bath, and where he was born in 1860. Arthur's family were weavers by trade. He was one of thirteen children, twelve of whom were boys. Arthur's grandson, Francis, can recall some of the family. One of them, Sydney, followed Arthur to Northampton and lived in Cedar Road. Another, called Charlie, had a general post office and an outdoor beer license in Swindon which Francis used to visit with his parents. A third brother became a sculptor in London and worked on the Albert Memorial, and lastly, one of Francis' Canadian cousins has discovered that her family is descended from another brother, Geoff, who became an artist. Coincidentally, Arthur's sister married a gentleman by the name of Orrell of Rochdale, and they had a furniture business similar to Arthur's. Although Francis has not been able to trace all his great-uncles, he has a Baptist minister friend in Frome who says that "In Frome we are full of Wattses!"

With the weaving background it was quite natural for Arthur to train to be a tailor. In this work he must have learnt to value the new sewing machines which had only been produced by the American, Isaac Singer, since 1851. As a young man, however, he suffered from ill health and was advised by his doctor to change his trade to one where he could spend more time in the open air. So it was that he became a representative for the Singer Sewing Machine Company.

In Cheltenham he met Hannah Slee who was employed as a housekeeper and came from South Zeal in North Devon. He married her in 1883, at the age of 23, and the wedding was held in the parish church of St Matthew, Cheltenham.

1884 was an exciting year for Arthur, as he and Hannah moved to Cinderford, Gloucestershire, and later that year was born their first son, Fred. As they settled into the pleasant surroundings of this small town in the heart of the Forest of Dean, and as Arthur went on his rounds selling the wonders of the Singer sewing machine, they could not foresee that their eldest son would one day grow up to be mayor of Northampton. Their second son, Ewart, was born in 1887, and in the same year Arthur and Hannah moved to Northampton to take up Arthur's promotion. Northampton, with its numerous shoe factories, was an important market for Singer, who used to manufacture and supply the heavy machines required in the production of boots and shoes.

Perhaps Hannah already harboured secret plans and ambitions for her quiet unassuming husband. Nine years later in 1896 Arthur was entering business, albeit on a small scale – one of the many Victorian entrepreneurs of that time. It is generally supposed that it was Hannah's driving energy which encouraged Arthur to embark on the idea of setting up his own business. She was a very forceful character. Their business was at 132 Adnitt Road, one of the new streets nearly adjoining Abington Park, the eastern section being called Wantage Road in deference to the town's benefactor, Lady Wantage of Abington. Here they are recorded as selling 'domestic machinery'. In fact this meant sewing machines, mangles, mailcarts and bassinettes. A mailcart was the equivalent to a pushchair and was defined as 'a light vehicle to carry children, being pushed or pulled by hand'. Bassinettes were oblong wickerwork baskets with a hood over one end, used as a cradle or as a form of child's perambulator. Sewing machines were much in demand by the outworkers of the clothing factories.

132 Adnitt Road was a small shop and during the course of the first twelve months of trading the business developed rapidly, no doubt helped by Arthur's hard work and perseverance and the growing market provided by the new 'estates' of terraced housing growing up around the area.

Only a year later the shop moved to 165a Kettering Road, the premises on the corner of Cowper Street and now occupied by Saundersons, the outfitters. This establishment offered a much better display area for furniture than Adnitt Road and was of course on the main shopping street – the Kettering Road.

One photograph shows Arthur standing proudly on the front step of his shop. It is still called 'A. Watts, Domestic Machinery Stores', but the catalogue and the photograph itself show the growing variety of goods offered for sale – bedsteads and bedding, floorcloths and furniture, even pianos and organs. The prams and pushchairs spill out on to the pavement; (it was a common practice in those days to display wares on the street). Toys already begin to feature in Arthur's selection of goods, as can be seen in the little doll's pram and horse on wheels at the front of the picture.

The catalogue showed the beautiful and intricate design of such commonplace items as sewing machines, mangles and baby's prams.

In 1901, after four years at no. 165a Arthur and Hannah knew that business had grown to such an extent that they were in a position to buy an even bigger shop and one with more storage space. The shop they bought was also in a prestigious corner position – nos. 80-82 Kettering Road, and this time they were able to have it altered to suit their precise requirements. In 1902 Browns, the architects, and Mr G.W. Souster, the contractor, altered the shop. It stood on the corner of Cleveland Road, a road no longer in existence. The shop and surrounding streets were recently pulled down to make way for modern housing near Abington Square.

The move to nos. 80-82 was not the only change in Arthur and Hannah's lives. While the shop had been on the corner of Cowper Street, they had lived in the flat above. Now they bought their own house. It was on the corner of Holly Road and Abington Avenue, a kind of half-moon house called Ingledene, still standing today.

2. Abington Street (1890) looking east, the site of the public library.

Their final move to Newton House in Park Avenue North came nine years later in 1911, when their eldest son, Fred, got married. The photograph on page 7 shows the impressive frontage with which Arthur could now advertise his business. On the right can be seen the lift that must have been invaluable for moving goods from the delivery carts into storage. The shop was now called 'A. Watts and Sons'. Fred had joined his father in the business in 1900, when he was just 16, and Ewart, a few years later.

Cork lino now formed a major part of the flooring stock, apart from carpets, and emphasis was placed on the large stock of prams and pushchairs. Goods still spilled out on to the pavement. Passers-by would see cane chairs hanging above their heads by the new-fashioned lamps, sewing machines opened out inviting inspection, mangles, prams, doll's prams; and inside, behind the upstairs windows, was crammed a variety of furniture from chests to china.

In October 1906 the building was altered once again to provide yet more space, and eventually the advertisements were boasting of 7,000 square feet of showrooms. In the issue of the *Northampton Independent* dated 18 May 1907, the reporter gives a detailed tour of the new shop, loyally supporting the business of this now well-established Northampton family.

On the ground floor an extensive window display of Prams and Mailcarts is made. These goods have always been a very special feature of this business. They are indeed specialists in Baby Carriages and accessories. On this floor will also be found a fine display of the celebrated Pfaff Sewing Machines. A testimony to the high quality and unsurpassable value of this machine is found in the fact that Messrs. Watts have sold over 800 of them, chiefly through recommendation. In the basement of the buildings are to be found a magnificent variety of 'Cork Lino' and inlaid Linos, including a lot of

Mr Arthur Watts · Northampton ·

in account with the

Stamford, Spalding, and Boston

Banking Company, LIMITED,

𝔇ʳ. Northampton ℭʳ.

1896						1896				
Sep 4	To Davies		1	16		Sep 1	By Cash	60		
15	Novelty Rack 6	4	5	6		12	do	15	-	·
17	Johns	3	10	3		Nov 3	do	18	10	
19	Novelty Rack 6		11	6						
25	London	2	15	-						
Oct 7	Ellis		11							
		23	18	3				93	10	

3. The first page of Arthur's business account book (1896).

very fine exclusive designs. Ascending to the second floor, there is to be found an admirable assortment of Bedroom and Drawing-room suites, including two special lines in Satin walnut Bedroom Suites, well worth inspecting. On this floor also, are a fine assortment of Bedsteads, and everything necessary for healthy sleep, including a fine stock of Northampton made 'Comfy' Bedding. You then turn into the Carpet Room on the same floor, and find a rare assortment of fine designs in Axminster, Brussels, and Tapestry Carpets, as well as some fine designs for Stairs. There are also to be noticed some tasty designs in Sheraton and Chippendale work, together with some very fine hand-carved solid oak Dining-room furniture. In the upper storey are the showrooms devoted to the lighter class of goods such as Bamboo and Wicker work, and the smaller articles necessary for home. It is impossible in a brief article like this to describe everything one sees at Messrs. Watts and Sons, but we can confidently recommend our readers to give Messrs. Watts a call. As to the secret of their success, Mr Fred Watts says: "It is to be attributed to my father's varied experiences in business all over the country, being applied to making his business go, as well as the hard work and 'stickability' which we have always had to put into it."

The prices of these prams reveal much about those times, for a good pram cost about half the price of a dining-room suite. How important a pram must have been to people in those days when without one, children could only be transported any distance if a horse and cart was available. Buying a good pram may have been as large a step as buying a car nowadays. Comparatively speaking, 4 guineas for 'The Durban' or 'The Glencoe' would have been a great deal of money.

4. 80-82 Kettering Road (1907).

The anecdotes of various people who could remember the couple, and Arthur's wife, Hannah, in particular, create a striking picture of an extremely forceful business-woman. For example, she would thrust catalogues into the hands of passers-by. Freda and Mildred Riches' father ran an ironmongers on the Kettering Road. Here is their tale:

'We always knew Mrs Watts as "old Lady Watts". We were brought up to think of her as Lady Watts. We believe she was the prime mover and drummer-up of business. She would be outside the shop on Cowper Street, watching all the girls going along. She'd get to know them a bit. She'd eye them up and down. My grandmother had quite a row with her because once she knew that my mother and father were courting, she stopped my mother and asked if she was pregnant. My grandmother, who was only a little person, went and had a row with her. She used to eye the girls up and down and even if they were quite respectable girls – if she thought there was any sign of pregnancy, she would stop and ask about booking a pram for them. She also kept her eye on the doctor's surgery and anybody coming out who might be expecting.

Before the First World War my father used to 'relax' after work by walking in the fresh air – instead of going home straight through the streets, he'd go down the Kettering Road to Abington Square and walk up the Wellingborough Road to home. Down the Kettering Road the shops were closing or closed and it was fairly quiet. There were about three public houses. He got to Abington Square and in Wellingborough Road, on every corner of every street was a public house – either noisy or just turning out. And he used to say "The difference between Kettering Road and Wellingborough Road!" Wellingborough Road was a shocking street in those days. Kettering Road was a respectable road of proper businesses, proper shops and only about three properly-run public houses.

In those days – pre-First War – the majority of young women in town worked at Crockett and Jones, the Brook, Sears, Manfields. The factories were the south side of Kettering Road, whereas a great many people lived on the other side of the Kettering Road. Our mother lived in Gray Street. Apparently every morning there was a tremendous amount of people going from Clare Street, Cowper Street, Hood Street, up St Michaels Avenue to Crockett and Jones, up Abington Avenue to the Brook, to Sears and to Manfields. The Brook Manufacturing Company was in Clarke Road. It used to be called the Pinafore Factory. It then went to a dress factory, and clothing and underwear. In Clarke Road all down one side it's all turned into flats now. It's still got the same frontage. That was the Brook. It employed loads and loads of women and girls.

Down Cowper Street it was what you might now call a rat-run, but they were walking of course. Our grandparents' house in Gray Street was built in 1879 and that was the third house in the street. They could sit in their back bedroom and watch the races on the Racecourse. Now of course you've got Burns Street and Colwyn Road. So you see that was a new housing estate round there then.

Our father's shop was an ironmongers and builder's merchants at 157 Kettering Road. He was apprenticed there in about 1898. It was George D. Taylor's. He was a Methodist at Kingsley Park. Dad became a partner and stayed there till 1939 after Mr Taylor died. He then took a shop at 108 Kettering Road, on the corner of Portland Street (which is now gone). He had paid one week's rent when the war started. If he hadn't paid the rent, he wouldn't have been allowed to start up, because all businesses were stopped. I think he actually opened on the day after war broke out. He just did ironmongery. He had virtually no money. I believe the shop was 10/- a week for the rent. When he was at Taylors, they used to work from early morning to late at night, – 7 o'clock normally, 9 or 10 o'clock on Saturdays. Kettering Road was extremely busy and with good shops. The other ends of the town – Far Cotton and St James and Kingsthorpe were almost foreign parts. You didn't go there then.'

The two sisters also have interesting recollections of another important aspect of the Watts family which has not yet been mentioned – their membership of the Methodist church.

Queens Road Methodist Church on the Kettering Road opened in 1887, the year of Arthur and Hannah's arrival in the town. It is likely that they attended the church from its early days. Arthur later became a Circuit Steward (an important position of responsibility for a layman). Freda and Mildred Riches have attended this church for many years and have noticed how often local shopkeepers were in fact Methodists.

'Nearly all the shops in the town were Methodist, and a lot of them were Queens Road. Queens Road was the church of shopkeepers. Along the Kettering Road Tom Clarkes, the grocers, were Queens Road. Perkins, the grocers, were Queens Road – Steve Clarkes the shoe shop, Caves the furnishers . In those days before the Second War the shop-owners were a bit upper class, a little bit above the shop-workers.

I do have quite strong memories of old Lady Watts when they arrived at

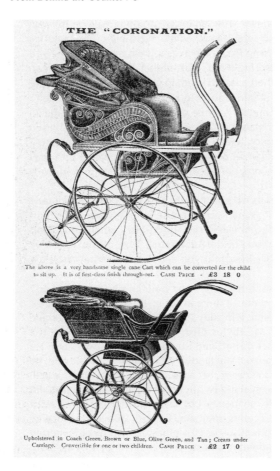

THE "CORONATION."

The above is a very handsome single cane Cart which can be converted for the child to sit up. It is of first-class finish through-out. CASH PRICE - £3 18 0

Upholstered in Coach Green, Brown or Blue, Olive Green, and Tan ; Cream under Carriage. Convertible for one or two children. CASH PRICE - £2 17 0

5. Prams in the 1902 catalogue.

Church. They used to sit fairly near the front, and she was always escorted in by Fred. It was like a procession. Old Lady Watts used to always wear black – very Victorian – and a jet bead cape. They were an important family: Fred and Ewart were leading lights in church and on the circuit. Ewart was Circuit Steward for many years. Fred was a local preacher.'

The two decades from about 1913 to 1931 were a time of enormously rapid expansion for the shop. However, the importance of the Kettering Road needs to be set in context. It was indeed a main shopping street, but it owed its existence to the growth of housing around the shoe and dress manufacturers in this north-eastern area of town. Few of the shops offered what might be called high-class goods. The local population could not afford them. At the turn of the century the prime shopping street was in fact Gold Street, to the west of the present town centre.

Here was located Jefferys the furnishers, with its elegant facade that is now a listed building. It is to be preserved as the rear of the premises is demolished to make way for a new retail development. (Jefferys were bought by Courts in about 1980.) In their time Jefferys were considered one of the more expensive furniture shops, along with Caves, catering for 'the county set'. The shop had been founded in 1874, having absorbed Phipps & Co. of Gold Street. The glass front of the lovely facade was a revolution in its day in 1887, and was put in to coincide with Queen Victoria's Jubilee. (The rococco windows were added in 1907.)

It is interesting to reflect that 1887 was the year Arthur Watts arrived in Northampton to take up his post not far from Jefferys, at the Singer Sewing Machine shop in Gold Street. When he first saw the elegant and prosperous furniture store of Jefferys would he have thought to himself: 'One day . . . ' ?

6. Arthur and Hannah (1910).

Even more interesting is what he might have thought if he could have foreseen that A. Watts & Sons Ltd would one day occupy these very premises, nearly 100 years later.

Other firms on Gold Street were Bells, selling fireplaces. They are still known for their high quality products and have survived to continue trade on Kingsthorpe Road. Swanns, the tailors, prospered on Gold Street for many years, closing down in recent times. Just around the corner from Gold Street was the Drapery, where Adnitts, the drapers, had opened up with one of the first department stores in the town. Staff lived in behind the store, on College Street.

The Adnitt brothers were another Northampton firm, and even today people can remember the upper-class refinement of the shop. On entering, customers were greeted by a shop-walker who would ask what they wished to see, escort them to the appropriate counter and introduce them to the assistant. Mr Spencer Gunn, who is related by marriage to the Watts family, can remember the last shop-walker, Mr Morton. He recalls:

> You weren't allowed to wander about – you were taken to the counter and introduced to the girl and served. There were chairs for ladies. One of Morton's old jokes was that a lady came in one day and said "Toilet rolls?" And he said "Yes madam – in the bottom department"'.

Old fashioned courtesy was commonplace in shops in those days. David Miles, who used to work in Jefferys, recalls that even in a grocers shop customers were bowed in and out.

> 'When I was young, you opened the door for customers. Woe betide you if you didn't! If you were selling fabrics, soft furnishings or textiles you immediately brought chairs out before you served.'

A major change in the shopping in the town occurred when Adnitts was bought by Debenhams in the 1960s. Debenhams was one of the first multiples to move into Northampton. No longer was this major department store locally owned.

7. Gold Street (c.1900) looking West.

Chain stores were of course slowly beginning to move into the town at that time, and the fact that they chose the Gold Street / Drapery area indicates the importance of the site. Woolworths opened up in Gold Street, as did Tesco. Marks and Spencers were a penny bazaar on the Drapery, later moving into Gold Street in about 1930. At its height Gold Street was the prime shopping street.

It is an interesting reflection on modern shopping trends that Gold Street in more recent times became one of the more forgotten corners of the town centre, (as did the Kettering Road), although now the new retail development behind Gold Street is set to revitalise this western area of town.

At all events, the post – First World War years saw A. Watts & Sons enjoying a rapid expansion with new branches being opened at Wolverton and Wellingborough. Two more sons had now been born to Arthur and Hannah – Gilbert and Stanley, but neither of them chose to work in the business.

Fred's son, Francis, recollects his father's attitude at about this time and how the brothers worked their affairs out:

'My father was pretty shrewd and he realized that there was not enough business for four boys, so father said to himself – 'Well, Ewart and I, and that's enough.' So Uncle Gilbert became the minister and then when Uncle Stanley came back from the Navy in 1918, the Wolverton branch was already established, so father turns and says "Look, there's a private house about two doors away from the shop. Why don't you start up?" He was getting on father's back a bit in a way, you know. "Why don't you start as a dentist?" So Uncle did. So then when he got married, he lived at an old house in Stony Stratford. And he remained there till he was 84.

I can tell you why they (Watts) went to Wolverton – because of the railway works and the printing factory. It was good business. I can remember quite well when I used to go to my uncle's surgery – 6 o'clock at night and Uncle Stanley's surgery was full because the works were right opposite. Oh

8. Frederick Watts (1905).   *9. Ewart Watts (1905).*

yes, it was fairly cute. The works were right opposite and they used to come off their shift and come into the dentist.'

Francis' cousins, Eileen and Joyce, remember the Wolverton branch as well. Their father, Ewart, would take them there.

'I remember going down there. You see Uncle Stanley had his surgery a few doors from the shop and we used to go down to have our teeth done while father was at the shop for the day. Well he never had time to do them, so we were very pleased about that. We used to make a nuisance of ourselves!'

Stanley was the youngest. The third brother, Gilbert, grew up to become a Methodist minister, a career of which his family would have been very proud. Fred and Ewart, however, were committed to working in the family business and so in 1913 'A. Watts' became 'A. Watts and Sons'. A partnership deed had been drawn up. Francis recalls

'In 1913 Grandpa Watts handed over the reins to the two brothers. He gave control to Uncle Ewart and my father on condition that they paid him rent for the premises. Of course Grandpa had a few houses in Cleveland Road anyway. He was only about 50. He went in on Saturdays to run them round a bit I think, but I can't ever remember my grandfather going into the shop on a day-to-day basis.

His main interest was the Methodist Church in Queens Road and playing bowls. He was a member of the Northampton and County Bowling Club for a long time. Uncle Ewart was a football and cricket man and my father – golf, bowls and snooker. Grandpa was a very keen supporter of the Men's Own, which met on Sunday afternoon at Commercial Street Baptist Church.'

The expansion of the business began in 1913 with the opening of a second shop. Nos. 80-82 Kettering Road accommodated the furnishing side of the trade quite well, but the baby carriage side of the business needed more space. Nos. 47a and 47b Kettering Road came on the market and provided a near-perfect solution,

10. "Babydom", 47 Kettering Road (1920s).

being nearly opposite the existing premises.

What should they call the new shop? A catchy name was needed to identify the nature of the trade being nursery goods rather than furniture. The name selected sounds odd to our modern ears – the shop was to be called 'Babydom'.

The photograph (taken in the 1920s) shows the comprehensive stock in which the firm invested. They could boast the largest stock of prams in the Midlands. The sewing machine department was transferred to no. 47 as well, and the shop front shows the bicycles and invalid carriages which were also on sale. The 'Repairs Dept.' sign reflects the after-sales service which was being offered.

Mr Spencer Gunn can still recall the impact made by the new shop:

'I remember Babydom. It was really posh – there were big words carved in gold letters on the front. It was a beautiful front of mahogany and curved glass. It had a big 50ft frontage with double doors and curved windows. The line of the shop, on the bend, is still there now.'

A picture taken at the display stand at the British Empire Exhibition shows a jumble of wheeled vehicles, and a careful look reveals the new-style 'push chairs' being offered, as well as scooters and doll's pushchairs. 'Tan-Sad' is a name which begins to feature as a make of push chair. The advertisement refers to one type as the 'Handy Car'.

Thanks to Mr and Mrs Dilworth of Moulton an invoice dating from 1916 was discovered during the research for this book and it provides an insight into the life of a newly married couple, the Rogers, setting up their home on Turner Street, near St Michaels Church.

Various remnants of lino, oilcloth, cocoa mats and slips (mats) were bought for the floorcoverings. Little carpet was purchased – 8 yards of tapestry carpet for twenty shillings, and three carpet squares for twenty six shillings. It is remarkable to note that the most expensive items were a 7 piece dining suite (7 guineas), an SW Dolly Pair (a manual washing machine perhaps – a dolly being the moving part) at £4 2s, and last but by no means least, a pram (£3 17s 6d) plus pram rug (4s 11d) and 4 corner shields for the pram hood (3s) – the total sum spent on the pram being a grand £4 5s 5d.

The invoice also reveals another aspect of Arthur and Hannah's flair for words – this time not in a catchy name for their nursery shop, but in choosing a Latin motto to head their stationery. 'Nil Sine Labore'. 'Nothing without Labour'. The whole family must no doubt have been brought up to recognize the value of hard work. 'Representatives would call by appointment', regardless of the distance involved, and goods would be delivered within a radius of 50 miles. As delivery was by horse and cart the latter offer was a considerable undertaking.

Here are some more of Francis' reminiscences of the Kettering Road days before 1920:

'My father started when he was about 13 or 14, you know, and father would drive the horse and cart. Don't forget the trade was built up outside Northampton, and when they had this branch at Wolverton he used to come home at midnight with the horse and cart. Father would go to sleep and the horse would bring him home.

At Newton House they had quite a spacious garage, and during the War of course when cars were prohibited, the pony and trap was kept in that garage and Grandpa Watts had a special trough in the corner. And I can remember going there to feed the horse – all those years ago.

Father used to be in the Special Constabulary in the First World War and I can remember him telling me how he used to watch for Zeppelins from the top of the roof in Kettering Road. He watched a Zeppelin come down in flames. And also he was coming home one day, about 1917, on his bike of course (no cars about), and he saw a plane come down on the race-course – a German plane. I remember going to see it as well.

In the First World War there was a company in Northampton called Wrenns Polishes and they made Wrenns boot polish here for years and years, and my father told me that these people, when they were in their prime and in the money, were good spenders. I can remember to this day Mr Wrenn coming into the shop – this would be in Kettering Road – producing a sack of golden sovereigns and saying "How much do I owe you? Help yourself". He'd say "Take it out of that". My father said it's absolutely true.

When I was a schoolboy I used to come down to Kettering Road and on Saturday morning my father used to give me one or two envelopes to go and pay the accounts in various parts of the town. There were a number of local suppliers they dealt with. One firm he used to send me to was Heymansons (who are now Rest Assured) in Bailiff Street. Father would have these suites delivered on the Monday. By Saturday he hoped to have sold them to have the money to go and pay Heymansons. They later became a national company called A.J. Tear. Dennis Heymanson was a lad of about 13 then and he was running the company – well, he had a lot of control anyway.

Not only that – I used to have to go round all the grocers – to Perkins on

11. Arthur and Hannah at Newton House (1931).

the Kettering Road, Tom Clarke in Gray Street, and of course everywhere I went I got half a pound of biscuits!

And then – you may think this a bit odd, father being a Methodist – but every Sunday morning – (in those days, 1918 I suppose, there was a Sunday post) – either before the service at Queens Road or after, I used to go with my father to the shop and open up. They had one of those gates in the arcade you move across, even in those days. And he used to go and open the post – on a Sunday morning! I thought it was a bit incongruous.

I can also remember – during the War obviously you couldn't go to the sea because you couldn't get transport – my father used to send us off to the country, to Bugbrooke, and we lodged with a man called Richardson and his wife – my mother, Freda and me. We used a pony and trap to get there.

In the end, in 1920, father got round Richardson and said "Why don't you come back in the town and work for us? You'll earn more than at the little market garden in Bugbrooke." As Grandpa Watts owned quite a number of houses in Cleveland Road at the time, they put him in this house next door to the shop in Cleveland Road and he was more or less the caretaker.

He was an absolute model old family retainer – a little walrus moustache and boots that turned up and squeaked. I know that Grandpa and Uncle Ewart made quite sure he didn't lack for money. And they stopped in that house until they died.

In those days the prams used to come by goods train in crates, kept together by string, and his job was to uncrate the prams. When he had done this, the crates were folded up again ready to send back by railway to the supplier. Also we sold a lot of ironmongery in those days and the ironmongery used to come in great big huge crates, all in straw. His job was to unpack all this ironmongery and send the crates back by railway, on a dray, back to their suppliers, so they could be re-used.

My father was the sort of man who would read us Charles Dickens' *A Christmas Carol* every Christmas, and he tried to keep up the pretence as long as he could that there was a saint called Father Christmas. So he used to get Mr Richardson one of those lovely white walrus moustaches. They used to sell Father Christmas outfits at the toy shop, and father dressed him up as Father Christmas. For three or four years he used to come to our side door at 'Epworth' on Park Avenue North on Christmas Eve with all the presents. And then from there he'd go to Uncle Ewart's at 18 The Broadway.

12. The White House (1931).

It was a long time before we found out there was no such thing as Father Christmas. This old man was wonderful.'

A small advertisement in a 1921 issue of the *Northampton Independent* gives us another catchy slogan with which the business might capture the attention of potential customers. Perhaps the same person who hit upon the name 'Babydom', also sat playing around with letters until they came up with WON (Watts of Northampton).

The business continued to flourish in the 1920s Francis attributes the success in part to his grandfather's astute business sense:

'You see you've got to remember that from about the 1920s. onwards the quality of the furniture we sold was rather on the – dare I say it – working-class scale, if you like. I mean you can imagine, can't you: Kettering Road's quite different from Gold Street where Jefferys were. So it was a different class of trade, because obviously where our customers lived (St Edmunds Road, Cleveland Road), they hadn't got much money. So Grandpa said "Right. We've got to sell stuff that people can afford." That's how he worked.'

In the 1920s a Baby Week was introduced into the municipal calender, when efforts were concentrated on educating parents in child welfare as well as celebrating the joys of babyhood. A. Watts and Sons Ltd eagerly took part in the spirit of the event and decided to offer a prize to every baby born in Baby Week ('signed notification of birth to be received at our office within 3 days of birth').

The advertisements appearing in the local press in this period of 1913-1931 remind us of another aspect of the expansion of the business. Arthur and Hannah were not content just to open up 'Babydom' across the road. Other branches were opening as far afield as Wolverton, Wellingborough and Kettering.

Was it Hannah's bold initiative that led them to open a branch in Wellingborough (at 59 Oxford Street) and one in Wolverton (at 26 Stratford Road) at the very time when the First World War was causing the population considerable hardship? A few years later they even felt that another branch

13. Inside Newton House(c. 1912).

could be opened in Northampton, and chose a site at 163 St James Road. How long would this boom be able to last?

Another aspect of this ebullient mood comes to light in one of the recollections of Francis. It would seem to point to a bold entrepreneurial spirit in Arthur, perhaps not often seen.

'A little aside here – it's not history, but it's speculation. Arthur Watts was very keen on going to Bournemouth. The brothers would go too. The year would be about 1920. I don't know how they managed to leave the business, but they did. Uncle Ewart, Grandpa and my father went to Bournemouth in 1920. I was there – I can remember that. I was only about 8. I can remember it ever so well. They came to what we call the Square in Bournemouth, near where the Winter Gardens are and there was a huge site there which was the old bus station. And Grandpa Watts – I can't imagine it, but he must have been the guiding light in it anyway – he said "Why don't we buy this site, move lock, stock and barrel, sell the shops in Northampton, and come down here and open up business?" That was cute, because he was just under 60 then and he was a very soft character really, but he must have had some flare somewhere. He wasn't as strong a character as my father was, but he'd got something. The fly in the ointment was Uncle Ewart. Father wanted it; Grandpa wanted it, and Uncle Ewart said (with some justification) he didn't think his health would stand up to it. And they abandoned it, but of course they'd have been millionaires if they'd gone there, because that site today is worth millions.

So Grandpa Watts had the foresight in those days – and he was 59 at the time. They kept going to Bournemouth for years. The sequel was that they went over to Sandbanks and bought a bungalow – about 1921 it would be. They had that bungalow until 1928. It's still there now.

That's just idle speculation – and I don't suppose anybody knows anything about that. So the fortunes could have been quite different.'

For a while A.Watts and Sons were able to boast that they had no less than six branches (including the three shops in Northampton) – an impressive number after no more than 27 years of trading. However, outside of Northampton it was only one of the branches that was to be able to continue for any great length of time, and this was at Kettering.

The Kettering shop opens up another chapter in the history of the firm which will be told later, but it is worth including here the story of the important day in 1923 when a customer called Mr Page cycled over from Kettering to see 'Mr Fred', as Fred Watts was known in the shop. Fred had noticed that Kettering was in need of a furniture shop and he was delighted to hear Mr Page's news was in need of a furniture shop and he was delighted to hear Mr Page's news that a property, part of a draper's shop on the High Street, was to let in the town. Fred took a 14 year lease on the premises .

At about the time the Kettering branch was opened, a major purchase for the business was made – one which would bring it more on a par with the competitors. No longer would deliveries be made by horse and cart; the first Watts van was acquired. A T-Ford chassis was bought and arrangements were made for York and Blundell of Wellingborough Road to put a body on it and paint it green.

Francis can still remember the very day that the van arrived:
'It came alongside Newton House in Park Avenue North for Grandpa to inspect. I was having lunch with him at the time. The first van!

At this time Kettering was just about to open. It was fed with stock from Northampton . (It wasn't always the right stuff either.) So what used to happen was – they used to go to Kettering about twice a week, and when they went they had a board specially made on the side of the van which clipped on with two hooks – '6 High Street, Kettering'. So when they arrived in Kettering, there was the address of this new branch , you see.'

Although he still worked in Northampton, with his parents and brother, Fred was responsible for this new development in Kettering, and within a few years, in 1928, set up the Limited Company of F.A. Watts and Co. In this same year Arthur also took the decision to make his own company limited.

So by the end of the 1920s A. Watts and Sons Ltd was flourishing, but the main two shops were still on the Kettering Road. At that time was this road still more important than Abington Street as a shopping area?

At least in its eastern end Abington Street was predominantly residential even up to 1922. It was, however, always an important thoroughfare and during the 1920s became one of the main shopping streets in town. The western end, below Fish Street, used to be extremely narrow, until it was widened in 1946. Here there used to be only a single track for the trams.

The blue-clad Corporation drivers would have to wait at the Wood Hill corner until they were sure it was clear, before swinging their clanging vehicles round the bend. At the opposite eastern end it was also awkward to swing out from Abington Square into the Wellingborough Road.

Until the early part of the century large houses with Colly Weston slated roofs lined the residential end. Here lived Lady Cockayne, Lady Throckmorton, William Kerr, a surgeon at the hospital, the Markham family, and Thomas Sternberg, author of *The Dialect and Folklore of Northamptonshire*. There were two warehouses, a brewhouse, a school run by Mr Henry Harday, and a very few shops.

The Notre Dame convent, built opposite the end of St Giles Terrace, was established in 1871. Then in 1910 the public library moved to Abington Street from the Old County Gaol buildings in Guildhall Road, (the old gaol still being used as the county library – as opposed to the borough). The library with its impressive facade was designed by Herbert Norman, the winner of the local competition to design the new building. It complemented the convent opposite, and local residents could only feel pleased at this addition to their neighbourhood. However, a short while later these same respectable residents of Abington Street

GREAT

PREVIOUS TO REMOVAL

LAST FEW DAYS

SALE

Tremendous Stocks of Furniture, Linos, Carpets, etc., to be Cleared

AT

GENUINE BARGAIN PRICES

A. WATTS & SONS, LTD.

FURNISHING SPECIALISTS,

80 & 82, KETTERING RD., Northampton

14. Advertisement for the Great Sale (1931).

were horrified by plans for a music hall almost next to the library. The site chosen was the quaint premises of Broome's library and Miss Law's haberdashery. This was the New Theatre, built in 1912 and a major new development in the local area (now the site of Primark).

After the First World War further developments in the street occurred – in 1919 the YMCA bought premises almost opposite the theatre. The Town and County Building Society was built in 1923 on the site of Gobion Manor (now the home of BBC Radio Northampton). In 1931 they doubled their frontage. The residential nature of the eastern end of the street was gradually changing.

The Northampton Co-operative Society (at no. 60) claimed in fact to be one of the principal influences in the growth of Abington Street as a shopping centre. Their advertisements in the local press made striking claims : 'The Opening of this Up-to-Date Store immediately brought several thousand extra shoppers into the Street. People go where People are.'

The Co-op was built in 1910 and by the late 1920s most of the shops that were in business in this middle section of Abington Street had been established since that date. In fact before 1910 there were hardly any shop fronts between Fish Street and Abington Square. The huge windows of the new Co-op store must indeed have attracted shoppers to the new principal shopping thoroughfare, much as a new shopping centre would today. The advertisements (after 1920) enumerate the various departments – tailoring, outfitting, drapery and furnishing, and 'on the other side of Groom's Yard', boot and shoe, confectionery and tobacco.

The photograph on page 21, of the early Co-op premises in the 1920s shows how Abington Street looked in those quiet early years of the twentieth century. In 1909 no. 60 Abington Street was bought for the Co-op as a lock-up shop (now the site of the furthest right-hand portion of the new Co-op store). A new palatial white building was erected in 1910 and already by 1913 expansion was necessary. Nos 62 and 64 (Hollingworth's carriage manufactory) were bought, enabling the palatial building to be extended towards the Library and opened in 1920. During the building the Co-op also bought nos. 66 and 68. No. 66 was a former house with a semi-private passageway at the side leading to Groom's Yard, a cul-de-sac where there were several dilapidated back-to-back cottages (two up and one down). These and other cottages on the Riding were eventually also bought by the Co-op who had them condemned. The passageway leading to Groom's Yard would eventually become the site of the present arcade. The whole site was replaced by the new Co-op in the 1930s, a building whose architecture was to match the revolutionary Thirties style in which Watts' White House would be built.

To complete the story of the development of the Co-op on Abington Street – the frontage on St Giles Street was bought in the 1930s, with the novel plan to link the two shopping streets by an arcade. This was started on in 1937, but building had to be stopped in World War Two. It is interesting to note that as demolition of the old properties began, Northampton people were surprised to see the Riding, now exposed to the public gaze. As the date on the present St Giles Street facade commemorates, the southern end of the arcade was opened in 1938 and the bridge built over the Riding. With great ceremony the new building was opened in the presence of a crowd of a thousand, gathered within the length of the arcade. Most of the departments were open by the time war broke out, but the magnificent Abington Street frontage was only completed after the war. It is thanks to our Council's new sense of heritage that this facade was preserved in all its 1930s glory when the Co-op was renovated in the early 90s.

(The Co-op arcade, or Ridings arcade as it is now known, is connected to Watts by more than its close proximity: In 1995 Watts was able to move into the shops between the Riding and St Giles Street, thereby much improving its display area in the centre of town.)

In the post-war period of the 1920s the idea of a departmental system was becoming a fashionable innovation. One of Watts' competitors, Phillips Warehouse, was situated at no. 15 Abington Street and in 1928 the store underwent considerable improvement and extension with the adoption of the departmental system.

The customer was now treated to a series of model rooms which would give the idea of how furnishings might appear in the home. (Phillips began in 1886, selling materials, floor-coverings, and house furnishings. It continued as a family business, just selling materials, until about 1990.)

What other shops were becoming established along the new shopping street? Near to the Co-op at no. 61 was Saxbys Leather Goods, founded in 1912. On the corner of Wood Street A.R. and W. Cleaver announced their new extensions in 1928, where they could house their grates and mantelpieces, baths and lavatories, electric fittings, wallpapers etc.

In 1926, nearly opposite the New Theatre, the private house of Dr Sanders was bought by the baker, W.Q. Adams, and the Wedgwood Cafe was opened, soon to become a fashionable meeting place. It changed its name when it was bought by a chain of restaurants, but interestingly enough has now reverted to being called 'The Wedgwood' as in the old days.

At no. 82 W.H. Johnsons had a business selling sports equipment, glassware, cutlery and gifts. The store was next to the New Theatre. At no. 80 there still stood one of the old houses, occupied by an insurance company.

In 1928 the street was becoming such a growing commercial centre that the idea of 'Abington Street Shopping Week' was created. The *Northampton Independent* devoted several pages to the promotion of this 'leading shopping

15. The old Co-op premises, Abington Street, to the right of the central library (1920s).

centre' in its issue of November 3rd. So the character of the eastern section of Abington Street had indeed changed by the end of the 1920s.

Just a few hundred yards away at no. 47 and nos. 80-82 Kettering Road, Arthur and Hannah with their two sons must have been brooding on the new developments.

Then as the 1920s drew to a close, a new site came up for sale on Abington Street – the insurance company office at no. 80.

Arthur celebrated his 70th birthday in 1930. He and Hannah now lived in a house specially built for them on Park Avenue North. They called it Newton House and it stood on the corner of Cedar Road. This they knew would be their final home and Arthur at least was not planning to undertake major changes in the business side of his life. He was a Circuit Steward and by 1930 a Trustee of Queens Road and other churches in that Circuit, his life was full and he was growing old.

Ewart and Fred were not, however, prepared to miss a business opportunity. With great excitement no. 80 Abington Street was purchased, a site right between the noble facades of the Public Library and the New Theatre. The new shop to be built would be a striking example of modern architecture. It might even have a name to make the business something special, as 'Babydom' had done. Plans were duly drawn up.

No. 80 was to be transformed. It had been an old insurance office where there had worked a man disabled in the First World War and whose son, Mr George Worth, was later to work for the new owners, A. Watts & Sons Ltd. George can still remember his impression of the old building as a child:

'My father used to work in the old building before it was altered to Watts. I was about 4 or 5 years of age. It used to be the Phoenix Insurance Company, as far as I can remember. I used to live in Wood Street. My father used to take me down to that place – 80 Abington Street, and it's always stuck there in my mind. In actual fact my father was a cripple from the First World War, with one leg. (Phoenix later moved to the Market Square.)

I remember the small window of 80 Abington Street (before Watts bought it). I always remember the 80 at the door, and you went into this passage and into one office. Then you went into the back office. The first thing I did when I was a little lad – I used to run along the passage into the back office. That was because you could see out into the garden. There were half-round windows, blue curtains – these big heavy blue curtains used to come down on to a ledge. I used to go looking round these curtains to find the big moths they used to get there. Oh it was funny. And there was a big lawn with a shed down the bottom, which I think Watts used afterwards, and that was for stabling the horse when they used to have a horse and cart.

I don't remember the White House being built, but my mother and I used to go to Slades at one time. It used to be two doors above. They used to have toys and books. Johnsons used to be next door to the White House. S. & W. Motors Garage was there round the back. You couldn't get through into the Riding.

The White House stood out a mile when they built it, because it was built before the Co-op. I can remember that being built.

Of course there's such a lot happened in Abington Street. I can remember the trams running up and down. The Labour Exchange used to be down the bottom, between Fish Street and Wood Hill, and Wiggins Coal Merchants and all those people. From Fish Street down to the Market Square was very narrow – just a single-line tram. When a tram went down, there was hardly any room each side for people to pass it.

Where the buses come out of the bus station – that's where I used to live, at the top of Wood Street, opposite the Fanciers Club. It's disastrous the way they've pulled things down – I mean Newland, Princes Street, Grey Friars Street, Albert Street, Wood Street, Union Street and Wellington Street – all those have disappeared. That's where I lived. They seem to have just taken where I lived out of it. The Temperance Hall Cinema – the tuppenny rush on the Saturdays. It's disastrous when you think how much they've taken out of Northampton. They've taken the heart out of it really.'

The wholesale demoliton and change of the 1960s and early 70s cannot be compared with the new buildings of the 1930s, and yet the architecture was radically new and often swept away the past. However, reactions to the changing face of Abington Street and other parts of the town seem to have been very positive sixty years ago.

There was a growing interest in the design of new shop fronts. Unlike the nostalgia of today, old shop fronts were dismissed as 'old-fashioned'. This excerpt from an article in the *Northampton Independent* of 3 October, 1931, illustrates the new attitude and even makes great claims for 'the tradesman as artist'.

A shopkeeper in these days is not merely a tradesman, he is an artist as well. If he is not, he stands little chance of success.

He has not merely to buy goods and sell them to his customers at a profit – he has to attract the customer by display of goods, and properly to display he has to call in the assistance of the experienced architect and of the lighting experts.

16. Hannah Watts aged 81.

A HUNDRED YEARS AGO

What a difference this is from the days when our shops had bow windows and small panes of bottle green glass, before the age of crinolines, when young ladies of Jane Austen's day stepped daintily along the streets on fine days and stopped seemingly to gaze in the windows, but really in the hope that some passing beau would notice her and remain unnoticed by the eyes of Mamma. There was no night shopping in those days. Even tallow candles did not provide much illumination, and besides, what young lady, even though escorted, would have dreamed of braving the streets at night time!

THE FIRST REVOLUTION

Then came plate-glass and that wonderful invention, gas. What changes there were in the shops. The art of window dressing had begun.

The last few years have seen rapid strides. The shopkeeper wants a building to set off his goods, and many of them, too, have even loftier aims – they want to add to the dignity and beauty of the street and the town.

AND THE SECOND

The day is coming – if not already here – when we shall take our visitors to see not only the glory of the architecture of St Peters and the Church of the Holy Sepulchre, but the magnificent architecture of our shops and the offices in our main streets.

One of the best shop fronts in Northampton is that of Knight & Son in Mercers Row, which was designed by Mr Leslie Knight's brother.' (This building still stands and remains a jewellers.)

Ewart and Fred chose local firms and craftsmen to design and build their new shop. The architect was Frank Allen F.R.I.B.A., and the builder, A.P. Hawtin and Sons; the electric light was by the Northampton Electric Light Co.; the central heating by Booth Horrocks, and the lift by Smith, Major and Stevens. The building was erected on the American steel-frame principle; the white stone front, in the 'Empire style'. The frontage was the inspiration for the name – 'The White House'. They would no longer be called 'House Furnishers' but 'Artistic Furnishers' and 'Baby Coach Specialists'.

The removal involved a great sale at the Kettering Road premises to clear the stocks of furniture, linos, and carpets.

The date of the move was set to coincide with the Chamber of Trade Display Week at the beginning of October 1931. We can only guess at the tension and excitement that was stirring the Watts household on the threshold of this important step in their history. The changes must have been overwhelming, especially for an old man as quiet and unassuming as Arthur. He had not been in the best of health, but had been able to walk about and take an interest in affairs. Then on Tuesday September 15th he fell seriously ill. He was nursed at his home, Newton House, but on Sunday afternoon, September 20th, at the age of 71 he died of a stroke.

The day after his death, his obituary appeared in the Chronicle, mentioning his prominent position as a Wesleyan Methodist as well as his chairmanship of a major local business. The reporter was quick to spot the romantic quality of Arthur's story, subtitling the article 'Romance of a Northampton Business', and relating his rise from a small sewing machine dealer in Adnitt Road to his position as chairman of Messrs. A. Watts & Sons Ltd.

The funeral took place at Queens Road Methodist church, and Arthur was buried at Abington churchyard, not far from his home. When Hannah tended his grave she could look across the park and see the street where she and her husband had first set up business 35 years ago. How times had changed.

Hannah outlived Arthur by ten years. Her 8 grandchildren remember 'Grandma Watts' with great affection. Fred's eldest daughter, Freda, would sit with her every Wednesday afternoon, when the housekeeper had her day off. Joyce and Eileen, Ewart's two daughters, remember her well, along with their grandfather, Arthur:

'He was a very quiet man. He was very much bossed about by Grandma. Well the shop wouldn't be where it is today, if it hadn't been for Grandma. She was the brains behind it really.

In saying that, Grandma was a very kind person, basically. I mean I could get anything out of her. She gave me 2d a week pocket money and my parents gave me 1d.

Arthur was a good businessman. He was honest, reliable, kind and people would like him.

Hannah didn't go down to the shop once Arthur had died, unless I took her down. I'm sure when Ewart and Fred came home, she would quiz them about it and want to know what was going on.'

Chapter II
Mr Ewart and the White House

The opening of the new Abington Street shop caused quite a stir in the town. The exterior was even floodlit at night. Mr Spencer Gunn, an old friend of the Watts family, can still recall the excitement at the time:

'The White House opening had the nobility, the Mayor and all those kind of people there. Let's face it, the Watts fraternity were well into local chapels and that. It was a great day. They had the original house and stables demolished and built the White House.'

The Chronicle reporter covering the story claimed that 'the shopping facilities (of this business thoroughfare) have now been greatly enhanced'. Great crowds took the opportunity of accepting the invitation to view the new showrooms with no obligation to buy. The facade was praised as 'a striking landmark' and would rank 'among Northampton's finest business establishments'.

NURSERIES IN WHICH KIDDIES WOULD REVEL
On the ground floor are the fine arcade windows and a large showroom containing a splendid display of general furnishings. Above are two other handsome showrooms, which have a depth of 82 feet.

On the second floor will be found an unrivalled new stock of baby coaches and cars by all the leading makers, and nursery furniture and cots for which Messrs. Watts are recognized specialists in the Midlands. There is also a charming selection of strong toys. Then on the same floor can be inspected a wonderful stock of carpets, rugs, linos, soft furnishings, bedsteads, bedding, with eiderdown quilts in lovely colourings and designs etc. The top floor is devoted to excellently designed and made dining, lounge and bedroom furniture and furnishing, ironmongery etc.

Messrs. Watts & Sons claim that there is nothing needed for furnishing the modern home that they cannot supply from their stores, and that the value is unsurpassed. The building is one of the most brilliantly-lighted shops in the county, and at night the floodlighting of the exterior will make it a conspicuous object.'

Responsibility for the White House now fell largely on Ewart's shoulders. He and his brother inherited an equal share in the shop, but Fred of course was also involved in the Kettering side of the business.

What kind of man was 'Mr Ewart' (as he was known by his employees)? He was certainly unlike his father in some ways, being gregarious and an extrovert. His parents, however, passed on to him their strict devotion to the Methodist Church.

Ewart was born in 1887 and named after the great Liberal Prime Minister, William Ewart Gladstone. He and his brothers attended schools at Vernon Terrace and Clare Street. From an early age Ewart showed that he was good with his hands and on leaving school served an apprenticeship in cabinet-making. This training must have been valuable to him when he joined his father's business.

In 1912 Ewart married a young schoolteacher, a talented pianist called Lilian Florence Read. They bought a house at 18 The Broadway. In 1913 their first child, Joyce Lilian was born, and over the next four years they had two other children – John Aubrey Ewart and Eileen. Aubrey grew up to become a surgeon in Kent, although he maintained an interest in the family business as a director.

The two daughters recall what it was like growing up in the 1920s and 30s, and their memories of their parents. Unlike their father who was very outgoing, their mother, Lily, was just the opposite. She was rather shy and was glad to have her two daughters at home.

In the end Eileen attended a Domestic Science course at the Technical College for 2-3 years, and Joyce worked at the Northampton General Hospital:

'Nothing was arranged for me when I left school, so I took myself down to Miss Dawkins, who'd got a commercial school, and signed on and told them to send the bill to my father! I wanted to be a nurse, but that wasn't allowed. But I ended up in hospital as a medical secretary, so that made up for it.'

Eileen married Edward Dixon and lived in Brighton for much of her life. Joyce carried on the family name in the shop, but that happened some time later.

How did the White House fare after the great opening in 1931? The 1930s brought with it the Depression years and it is no surprise that Watts became less profitable, just as every other business in town must have done. Ewart, however, continued to think positively, and in 1936 the firm acquired its first workrooms. These were in Albert Street (one of the streets that has now disappeared under the Grosvenor Centre), and included a big garage for the vans with workrooms above. The proliferation of branches did not continue, however. In 1932, for example, the shop at Wolverton was sold as a furniture business to Arthur Chamberlain. This must have been quite a difficult decision for the firm to make, as only five years previously the premises had been enlarged by acquiring the property next door.

In Northampton itself Watts had little competition. There was Hamps of Sheep Street, Jefferys of Gold Street and Caves on the Kettering Road . Hamps was a slightly different kind of furniture shop; as early as 1913 they were advertising goods 'direct from our own manufactory'. Also Jefferys and Caves tended to deal with the wealthier people in the county. It is interesting to note that Caves is even older than Watts and that it too has Methodist connections. Frederick Cave was a well-known Methodist preacher and a fine cabinet-maker and carver. He founded the shop in 1879, at 111 Kettering Road, a site which his firm still occupies today.

One customer from those days, Mr J. Savage, who is now 87 years old, remembers that in the 1930s Watts was "the only (furniture) shop in town". He was a farmworker at Upper Harlestone and when he married in 1933 he furnished his cottage from Watts. The 'dressing chest with triple mirrors' mentioned in the invoice, still stands in his spare bedroom.

At this time Watts were enthusiastically promoting their business by advertising in areas other than the normal newspapers and magazines. Ewart decided that it was worth buying advertising space on bus timetable frames. However, this medium posed a surprising number of problems.

In 1934 it was arranged to rent the required space and pay a promotions firm to install the advertisements. These were even to be placed on a private house in Great Brington, at Kingsthorpe cemetery and 'Mrs Dickenson's tea-shop' at Irthlingborough. Time had to be spent of course on checking that the advertisements were kept in place. It was with great consternation that the firm found that their space had 'gone missing' in 1936. This was shortly after the Strike, when rioting had led to several timetable frames' being destroyed and the advertisements' consequently disappearing. The irate correspondence between Watts and the bus company would indicate that this kind of promotion was just not worth the effort, and the United Counties Omnibus Company finally decided to do away with timetable advertising.

The idea returned in the 1940s, however, when the Watts advertisements re-appeared on nineteen bus stops around the town, as well as on the actual buses themselves. The firm even rented space on sub-post-office grilles to bring their business to the attention of potential customers and make 'A. Watts and Sons Ltd.' a household word to the Northampton public. Compared with advertising on bus stops, how much more grand and profitable would seem the special private showing held at the White House in 1932, complete with afternoon tea and music by Fraser Mackenzie Ltd. (a local music shop).

The advertisement in the *Northampton Independent*:

'extends an invitation to all ladies interested . . . in the very latest models in baby coaches, folding cars, cots, nursery furniture etc.'

The idea would seem to have been a popular one as the showing was repeated over four days.

Not only did Watts seek to look after their customers and potential customers, their staff were well provided for. It was quite a common practice to provide housing for ones employees, and Mr Philip Masters recalls how his father, Frederick, had joined Watts in 1919 and lived in one of their houses – no. 70 Lower Hester Street in Semilong. The Watts brass plaque on the door has long since been removed.

Frederick Masters was employed as a collector salesman. This was an important area of work for Watts. Their five employees would set off on their bicycles (and later, if they were lucky, their 250cc motorbikes) to travel as far afield as Guilsborough and Castle Ashby. Armed with their HP books and catalogues, they would visit previous customers who might be tempted by the latest catalogue, and also those customers who owed them HP instalments. Frederick, in common with his colleagues, did not like to miss a day's work, for there was one thing for sure: 'If you didn't call for your 1s one week, you wouldn't

17. Kenneth Harland in uniform.

get 2s the next.' Fortunately, most women were at home during the day and the salesmen's journeys were therefore not usually wasted.

Several payment books dating from 1923-34 and belonging to Mr F.G. Solomon of Bostock Avenue, were found among some old papers and they serve to give an insight into the way in which a working man might furnish his home. Everything from a vase to a pram quilt was paid for by instalments. The 1923 list of 'goods supplied' begins with a Baby Washer at 4s 6d and amounts to a total of £12 6s 8d. With frequent gaps (sometimes of up to 6 months) the weekly sum of 3s (15p) was paid off. As more items were purchased the bill rose to £104 5s 7d, until eventually the last entry – on 21 September 1934 – shows that £103 13s 0d had been paid. The family must have been relieved to have nearly paid off their debt at last.

Sam Johnson was another collector salesman who worked for Watts in the 1930s, from 1934-1939. His narrative tells us much about the way of life in the retail trade at that time. The late night opening of the 1990s seems nothing new. He highlights the variety of work with which Watts was then involved, from fulfilling contracts with the local authority to furnishing buildings such as the new Fire Station and Moulton Agricultural College, to 'providing a Spring-cleaning service' and repairing prams.

'When I joined Watts in 1934, Mr Ewart Watts was then in charge and Mr Ken Harland was an assistant.

They had quite a few collector salesmen. Although I initially went there as a French polisher I eventually became a collector salesman, and then I went into the shop. There were five of us. The whole area of the town and county was split up and we each had an area. We went round canvassing, bringing in business, and also to collect the instalments.

There was Mr Wallington, Mr Masters, Mr Fitzhugh, Mr Ward and myself. Also there was a Mr Brickwood, but he eventually went inside, as a salesman.

We did a lot of door-to-door canvassing. We had catalogues. You have to remember at that time when you went canvassing you'd probably go to 30 houses and there'd probably be 25 people in – which is totally different from today, because there weren't any married women going to work.

We were mostly concerned with the furniture, but of course if we did get an order for the pram department it went on our commission.

We travelled around on our bikes after reporting to the shop any orders we'd got from the previous day. We'd go to Cogenhoe and Castle Ashby – as far as that.

We used to offer a Spring-cleaning service for many years, lifting and turning carpets, cleaning them – things like that. Of course we'd repair furniture for the customers in those days. We'd give a real after-sales service. We'd mend prams, respoke the wheels, retyre them – we did the hoods and aprons too.

Then we had to do upholstery as well and we'd fit loose covers for customers in their homes.

The shop-hours at that time were Monday 9 o'clock in the morning till 7 at night. We never got away till half-past seven. On Friday it was 9 o'clock in the morning till 8 at night. On Saturday it was 9 o'clock in the morning till 9 at night. Of course that was common throughout the whole retail trade. On Abington Street at that time you'd go along at 9 o'clock at night and it would be buzzing. There'd be no end of people. The market was still on. We used to get a tea break of half an hour.

When the Fire Station was built, Watts had the job of furnishing it. We all had to help in this respect and they had a lot of wardrobes and that kind of thing. There wasn't a lift then. We had to cart all the furniture right up to the very top, which was quite a job in itself, I can tell you. It was very heavy furniture, you see. They also furnished the Moulton Agricultural College.'

At this stage in the company's history it was becoming obvious that the loyalty of many of the staff was exceptional. Some of them – Mr W. Wallington, Mr Alfred Adams and Mr F.G. Solomon – worked for the Watts family for over 45 years; others, for over 20 years. We are fortunate in being able to record some of their reminiscences in this book. Ewart realized the importance of his staff in making the shop what it was. Towards the end of his life, in 1951, he was asked the secret of his firm's success and replied: "Hard work, personal service and a loyal staff."

Apart from Ewart's commitment to the business, there were other important ways in which he made his mark on the life of the town. It is generally accepted that he would have liked to become involved with local politics. His brother had made his first attempt to win a council election as early as 1916. In fact Fred became Mayor of Northampton in 1945. However, Ewart became involved in other kinds of public affairs.

One of the most important ways in which he exerted his influence was in his church, Queens Road. Ewart had always been very active here. He was Senior Circuit Steward of the Gold Street Methodist Circuit (the highest office which a layman can hold). The Hester Street Methodist Mission elected him their treasurer and he guided them through a successful extension scheme. At the time of his

18. Ewart and Lily at Brixworth Methodist Church.

death he was secretary of the Queens Road choir and trustee of several other churches. Freda and Mildred Riches still remember the energy and enthusiasm which Ewart put into running a fellowship club at Queens Road.

'We had more to do with Ewart because he started the Guild of Friendship at Queens Road. If you say nothing else – I think that was the greatest thing he did. He started this meeting in 1940 and it was for any age – well from about 14 to 80. It was early war time and people were going off to the forces, and also there were a lot of soldiers about, coming into the town, and so it made a place for them. We used to have what was called a canteen, which meant cups of tea and buns afterwards. You had to have a license for it – you got coupons for the food. It was for troops, anybody who wanted to come, any Methodist who turned up in the Church. That Guild of Friendship kept on. Ewart was the prime mover of it and he was there all the time. It started on February 28th, 1940. We remember that because we used to have an anniversary every year. It was on Wednesday evenings.

During the War years the few of our regulars who didn't go away kept the Guild going with Ewart, for anybody who came and went. And afterwards Ewart still was there every week. At 9 o'clock every Wednesday evening in war time, we used to have what we called an Epilogue. Whatever else we'd been doing, whether we'd had a serious meeting or fun and games, we'd have this Epilogue. Ewart often used to take it. Anybody who was anywhere in the world would know that at 9 o'clock that was happening. We'd sing a certain hymn, 'Oh God, Our Father, Who does make us one.'

Now we don't get a very big congregation on a Sunday night, but sometimes we've had that hymn and you have looked round and nearly half the congregation were at those first Guild meetings and have kept together, partly because we were Church folks, but partly because of that Guild. The times you see people in town that you haven't seen for a long time, and they'll stop and say 'Oh, the Guild!"'

For a long time Ewart provided leadership for the Guild of Friendship. His hospitality helped to ensure the success of the group.

'Sometimes it used to be very much open house at Ewart's. The Guild would invite themselves over for one of the meetings. Ewart's family was one of the first we knew who had a television and I remember they invited us over to see it. We were all goggle-eyed at it. It was the very first live link from

France. We were all amazed. We used to make free of the kitchen and do refreshments.

They used to have servants. A lot of these wealthier people used to get country girls from the country chapels come in to be servants. They used to go round to the country chapels. There was more or less only service for the young girls in the villages, because there weren't the factories out there. It was agricultural work for the men. The Methodist folks in the villages were only too happy if the girl should go into service with a Methodist family. You see, they would live in, and the family would know that they were in a decent, respectable family where there wasn't going to be alot of drinking, swearing, and that sort of thing. So quite a lot of the country girls came in. I remember one who went to Fred's and her sister went to Charlie Perkins'

By the late 40s Ewart was nearing retirement age and a successor was sought to run the Guild of Friendship; someone was needed with a similarly outgoing personality.

In 1931 a young man had started work at Ewart's shop who was later to play an important role in the business. His first job description was 'dusting and unpacking', and after three months came promotion to being 'a packer and duster'. Kenneth Harland considered himself fortunate, however. He entered the trade when conditions were changing. Until then, young men, even those with educational qualifications, used to pay the firm each week for the privilege of learning a trade with an old established firm of repute such as A. Watts & Sons.

Kenneth felt pleased to have a job with a weekly salary of ten shillings (50p). Much later he looked back on this period of his life:

'This (ten shillings) just about covered my travelling from my home in Towcester. This was before Beadons ran a charabanc service. It was a case of catching the 7.25 train on the old Stratford T. and Mid-Junction Railway, and on reaching Castle Station hoping to board a tramcar for the New Theatre stop in Abington Street, and obtaining permission to leave the shop early to catch the 7.50 last train for Towcester at night.'

This same young man was not content with being a junior salesman. Within three years of joining Watts he was appointed by another furnishing company, Phillips Warehouse (Kettering) Ltd., to take charge of their Corby shop. By 1936 he was made manager of both their Corby and Kettering stores. However, all this time he maintained a link with the shop that had given him his first job – he had fallen in love with Ewart's older daughter, Joyce. In fact, shortly after the outbreak of the Second World War, Kenneth and Joyce were married at Queens Road Methodist Church. Then Kenneth had to go away to serve in the army, where he was awarded the British Empire Medal (Military Division). His closer involvement with Watts the Furnishers came a few years later.

As in Ewart's case, Kenneth Harland was closely involved with Queens Road and he seemed a natural successor to Ewart to run the Guild of Friendship. His personality was similarly outgoing.

'When Kenneth came out of the forces he came and virtually took over the Guild. We divided up into older and younger groups – Monday for Youth Club. We all met together on Wednesday nights. The youngsters just about

19. Ewarts' certificate for service in the Home Guard.

In the years when our Country

was in mortal danger

WILLIAM EWART KINGSLEY WATTS

who served   16.Jul.40 - 31 Dec.44.

gave generously of his time and

powers to make himself ready

for her defence by force of arms

and with his life if need be.

George R.I.

THE HOME GUARD

worshipped Kenneth. In a way during that time we had the back-up of Watts as a firm. For instance, we had a very good drama group and we could on occasion borrow things from Watts. For disembodied voices we borrowed Kenneth's new-fangled dictaphone. Also we'd occasionally use their van for an outing.

At Queens Road after the First War they had started the Men's Institute on Friday evenings. This was because there was a need for men returning from the War to have a place to go to for a bit of relaxation, but not pub-relaxation. They didn't want serious discussions and debates. It was a room for men – mainly from the church. Watts provided a 3/4 size billiard table. After the Second War the church realized it must keep it going for the men to come back to. The Institute lasted until the Church closed in 1960.

There was trouble during the years just after the Second War when our youth club was enormous, because we were rather taking over the Men's Institute. The young lads wanted to play table tennis on Friday nights and then they wanted to allow the girls in . We were all rather taking over.'

Another leader of the youth group at that time, Philip Harradine, recalls how Ewart was a great encourager of people and remembers another aspect of the youth work about which Ewart was very enthusiastic:

'In the early 50s there was a Milk Bar which opened on Abington Street, opposite the Co-op arcade. Ewart was very keen on it because of strong drink being a problem if it's abused. The Milk Bar was a splendid idea. They had them in America – they still do. Ewart was a great encourager of it. It was a little feature in the town. It got a write-up in the Chronicle & Echo as something very new. It was important. It was somewhere to go where young people could get an excellent range of milk drinks.'

So Ewart played an important role in the lives of many people connected with

Queens Road. Yet there was another side to his life which made further demands on his dedication and commitment. His first major position in public affairs was his election in 1936 as President of the Chamber of Trade. He had played a leading part in the Chamber for some time and was an active member of the Northampton branch of the National Federation of Furnishers.

On 1 January 1937 the *Northampton Independent* wrote an interesting article looking to the future, as far ahead as 1956, and more particularly asked some prominent individuals of the town what the Coronation Year of 1937 might hold in store for the local citizens.

Characteristically, Ewart diverted the question to a humanitarian issue, pleading the case for more old people's sheltered accommodation in the town. His colleague, Mr A. Dickens of the Chamber of Commerce, answered the question more directly by hoping for increased prosperity in the local manufacturing and retail industries.

THE SHAPE OF THINGS TO COME – WHAT OF 1937?
The old year of 1936 has drawn to its close, and as it ran to the end of the lap the new, energetic, and vital 1937 stood tense and eager to receive the torch to carry the light of life forward.

Northampton has run its course well and honourably in 1936.

The year has been a momentous one, full of happenings of local and national importance. To what can we look forward in 1937?

The answer is only to be obtained by asking Northampton itself – which is to say, her prominent individuals.

Mr A. Dickens (President, Northampton Chamber of Commerce):
'The year 1937 has every prospect of being one of general prosperity for this country.

The continued improvement of trade should be still further enhanced by the Coronation.

The British public will have much greater spending power, and Northampton must look to it that we get our share.

As regards the staple trades of leather and shoes, this can only be done by unity – by unity among our manufacturers to obtain reasonable prices for their products, and by harmony between the employers and their workpeople. All who desire the good of the town are anxious that this harmony, established for so many years past, may continue undisturbed.

Our townspeople consequently will have more money to spend, and our shops will be well advised to prepare for this. We have no doubt that they will meet the situation with energy and enterprise, and thus they ought to reap a good harvest.

May Northampton go forward and prosper in 1937.'

Mr Ewart Watts (President, Northampton Chamber of Trade):
'Your question as to how I would wish Northampton a Happy New Year is novel.

Northampton is, I think, unquestionably a happy town; its freedom from serious strife, both politically and in its labour problems, its love of sport, and its reputation for sobriety make it stand out as an example to the rest of the country, and in wishing it another happy year I am only reiterating the sentiments of every proud citizen.

During the last few years many great improvements have been made – public parks, playing fields, baths – and in many other ways our Council has endeavoured to provide for the enjoyment and happiness of its people.

But most of these have been for the young. What about those who have toiled hard in thought and work for this better Northampton which we now enjoy?

Recent years with great depression and increased taxation have not given them much chance to fill the stocking sufficient for the rainy time of old age. Often their last years have to be spent in one or two rooms in the house of a stranger, or the offer of the 'House' situated on the Wellingborough Road. Surely it is below the dignity of Northampton to allow this state of things to continue.

If we could, this Coronation Year, with public subscription build, say, fifty non-rated small homes similar to the Bethany and Methodist Homesteads, which could be let at a very small rental to suitable cases, it would be a tangible expression of our wish for a Happy New Year to Northampton.

We have had recent evidence that all the public-spirited 'Lord Nuffields' do not live in Oxford, and I would be delighted if this suggestion could be given support, to do anything that is in my power to further the cause to be achieved, and in doing so I am sure I can bespeak the sympathetic consideration of the members of the Northampton Chamber of Trade.'

Back in 1936 Ewart, as President of the Chamber of Trade, had also been asked by the *Independent* for suggestions on how to celebrate the Coronation. Apart from the grand municipal schemes which had already been suggested, such as an Old English Fair on the Market Square and a garden party in Abington Park, Ewart wanted to encourage individual street parties:

"I understand that in one street £20 has already been raised for a street festivity and a tremendous amount of bunting is being made by the unemployed men in the street out of old pattern books which have been given to them ."

Ewart's commitment to public affairs is illustrated by his growing involvement in a number of committees. He was Chairman of the Commerce Advisory Committee of the College of Technology, and a member of the employers' panel of the Ministry of Pensions and National Insurance Appeals Tribunal.

In 1950 voluntary posts included the Brixworth Rural District Council Safety First Committee, Chairman of the Northampton and District Council Fuel Saving Committee, the Labour Exchange Advisory Committee, the panel of the Labour Exchange Court of Referees, and the Local Industrial Savings Committee.

His other interests included the Rotary Club, the County Cricket Club (of which he became vice-president), and the Town Football Club. Well might the *Independent* reporter covering Ewart's election to the presidency of the Chamber of Trade ask 'What does he do in his spare time?'

Ewart and Lily had a beautiful newly built home at no. 13 Abington Park Crescent, 'St Elmo'. When the Second World War broke out they moved to the village of Overstone. The lack of buyers for their old home meant that it was requisitioned by the army – a dreadful fate for any house, for it was well-known that the interior would not be carefully looked after by the servicemen.

Ewart was 52 now and for his contribution to the war effort he chose to join the Home Guard, his service to which was honoured in certificates signed by King George VI and Lieutenant-General Cunningham.

He also served on the Northampton Salvage Committee and the Northampton Central Committee of Firewatchers. The Salvage Committee was responsible for saving unwanted goods to further the war effort.

As a local businessman Ewart was still involved with the Chamber of Trade, and in 1941 and 1942 he was elected their President again. As in his previous time of office Ewart gave a stirring New Year message to the residents of the town, praising the selflessness of the local tradespeople who chose to help the war effort in some way.

The advertisements for A. Watts & Sons Ltd. reflect the difficulties and restrictions faced by retailers in the War. It was clear to shops like Watts that the dwindling trade in furniture might be enlivened by offering for sale second-hand goods. So in 1945 they produced painstakingly detailed lists of the items on offer – ranging from an old Chinese cabinet to a billiards table to pillows and rubber-filled camp mattresses.

Then at last the war was over. The business looked set to flourish again and Ewart began to look forward to taking semi-retirement, although in the years 1947 and 1948 he again served as President of the Chamber of Trade.

Who was to succeed him? In 1946 he and his brother, Fred, had decided to make a complete break between the Northampton and Kettering businesses. Ewart, was to buy Fred's shares of the Northampton shop over a two year period.

In that same year Ewart was able to appoint a new manager to the White House, now that all the young men were back from the Services. He was well aware that his only son, Aubrey, was not going to be directly involved with the business, for he was enjoying a successful medical career. With what pleasure Ewart and Lily must have looked on the marriage of their daughter to Kenneth Harland, a young man with the experience as well as the family commitment, to make a success of the shop. The potentially awkward situation of finding a successor to Ewart could now quite easily be resolved.

So in 1946 Kenneth came back to work for Watts and was appointed Manager. Ewart had harboured this wish since 1942 when he made his will and appointed Aubrey, Kenneth and Horace Lacey Executors and Trustees. He had expressed his desire that in the event of his death his son-in-law be offered the position of manager of A. Watts & Sons Ltd.

One of the first problems that Kenneth encouraged Ewart to address was the inadequate rear access to no. 80 Abington Street. S. & W. Motors had the site directly behind Watts, stretching right across the Ridings and on the present day Ridings car park.

In 1949 Ewart wrote to Mr H. Shales of S. & W. Motors requesting access for loading and unloading at the rear of the shop – for the rent of £50 per annum. The reply from Mr Shales still conveys his outrage at what he deems Ewart's 'impudence' in offering such a small sum for such an important improvement to his business. The matter, was shelved till the 1960s and Kenneth and Ewart had to content themselves with some minor alterations, carried out in 1951.

The family name was now well-known to the people of Northampton, and many had cause to appreciate what Ewart had done for them personally, whether in the church at Queens Road, in the shop, or in his varied public affairs work. So when the *Independent* ran a series of articles entitled 'They Serve Northampton', it was no surprise that Ewart figured in the list of people covered. The particular article on Ewart appeared on 9 November, 1951. The scope of the business sounds most impressive:

Since the firm's thousands of customers cover a wide area of the Midlands, apart from the overseas connections, free delivery of goods by a fleet of modern vans is a feature of the Watts service.

Touring the large showrooms from end to end one finds nothing that is shoddy or unworthy of the best type of home, for the firm only stock high-class goods, though at competitive prices; and they insist that all items are guaranteed by the makers. In fact the firm's buyers personally visit warehouses and factories to examine all unfamiliar goods before introducing them into their range.

FULLY EQUIPPED WORKSHOPS

Apart from furniture and their distinctive baby coaches, the firm specializes in carpets and upholstery and there are fully equipped workshops, capable of undertaking any type of repairs, where expert craftsmen are also busily engaged on contracts for local authorities, institutions and many county houses.

Additionally there is a toy department which is a positive 'paradise' for children.

The firm of A. Watts & Sons Ltd. is one of the oldest members of the Northampton Chamber of Trade, Mr W. E. K. Watts having been President of the Chamber four times.

Thus does 'The White House' do honour to this series of articles devoted to those who serve Northampton.'

From the time when Kenneth became manager, Ewart was able to have more time off from working in the shop and indulge his love of watching cricket or football at the County ground. In 1953 he made arrangements to retire completely at the end of the year. He appointed Kenneth Managing Director as from 1954 and would then transfer to him some shares in the business.

On the 25 March, 1954, Ewart set out as usual from his home in Church Way, Weston Favell to attend a Cobblers football match. While watching the game he saw a man who was clearly feeling unwell and with his usual kindliness got up and started to help him up the steps towards the exit. At that very moment Ewart himself collapsed. He was immediately taken to the General Hospital, but died shortly afterwards. His death saddened not only his family and the staff of his shop, but many people in the town whose lives had been touched by his kindness and loyalty.

The sudden death of Mr William Ewart Kingsley Watts at the age of 66 has brought a painful shock to his many friends in town and county and the manifestation of mourning at his funeral provided impressive evidence of the widespread appreciation of his character and useful public work.
(*N.I.* 2/4/54)

Chapter III
Mr Fred and the Kettering Years, Before the Second World War

In the early 1920s in Kettering there stood an old building near the Market Square which was both a draper's and an undertaker's – Mr Frank Goosey's. At the back were stables, a large orchard and a spacious gravelled yard. Mr Goosey decided to lease half his premises and the 'To Let' sign was erected. This was the sign that set Mr Page thinking about a possible opportunity for A. Watts & Sons. He was a good customer of theirs and was aware of the lack of furniture shops in Kettering.

One day in 1923 he cycled to Northampton and went to see 'Mr Fred' in Watts' Kettering Road shop. It did not take long for Fred to see the exciting business possibilities. They had already opened a small shop in Wellingborough. Kettering would be a very suitable place for a new branch.

The High Street shop was old and would be expensive to maintain. The shop floor was only about 3-4,000 square feet and the frontage no more than 40ft, but it was a start. Fred was approaching 40 when he signed a 14 year lease with Mr Goosey. Ewart had little to do with the new business, and Fred must have felt a great sense of satisfaction at the challenge presented to him at this time in his life.

Fred had always been a man of great organisational skill and business acumen. Ever since the beginning of the century he had worked for his father and with his brother. He had boundless energy and had become President of the Northampton Chamber of Trade as early as 1916 when he was only 32. In the same year he had even stood for election as a councillor and had contested a ward in the town.

With his family he attended the Queens Road Methodist Church, where his brother was later to become so involved in working with young people. Fred had different leanings – he was very interested in John Wesley, the founder of Methodism, and had begun to make a collection of 'Wesleyana' – eventually devoting a whole study to his collection. He became a local preacher and worked in this field for 40 years, also serving the church as Circuit Steward several times. In 1929 he was the Treasurer of the Methodist Conference.

20. Hilda Tucker, her brother Courtenay and sister Madge.

Apart from these interests Fred also enjoyed music and was a keen member of his church choir. In fact in 1908 aged 24 he performed the bass solo in Stainer's 'Crucifixion'.

It was at about this time that he came to know the Reverend Tucker, the minister at Queens Road from 1906 to 1909. The Tuckers were living at 13 St Michaels Avenue. They had a daughter called Hilda, who was a strict tea-totaller and a very keen worker for the Methodist cause. She and Fred were soon to become engaged and they were married in 1911 at St Leonards-on-Sea, (for the Reverend Tucker had been transferred there in 1909).

One of Hilda's great interests was tracing her family tree and she eventually discovered that she was descended from none other than a king – Edward I (who is associated with Northampton because he erected one of the Queen Eleanor crosses at Delapre, marking a stopping place during his wife's funeral procession to Westminster).

Fred and his young wife had a house built for them at 75 Birchfield Road. The new estate was growing rapidly in this period before the First World War, transforming the area north of Abington Park – an area once consisting of fields and cherry orchards.

Hilda and Fred had four children – Francis (born in 1912), Freda, Douglas and Jean (born in 1923). Jean does not remember her parents' first home, for in the year she was born they commissioned A.P. Hawtin to build them another house, this time on Park Avenue North – one which would be called 'Epworth' in honour of John Wesley's birthplace. The house was on the corner of Birchfield Road, nearest Ashburnham Road. (The site is now a block of flats.) It was here that Fred was able to have a study almost entirely devoted to John Wesley, full of his books and with several of his portraits. With Fred, Ewart and Arthur all living so close to one another, they could enjoy a close-knit family life. Jean remembers how they used to go to her grandparents' for Sunday lunch – Hannah would always give them roast chicken followed by pink blancmange.

Jean inherited her mother, Hilda's, musical talent and eventually, during the Second World War, spent four years at the Royal Academy of Music in London. Although social life was limited from 1939-1945 with most men from 18 to 45 being called up for the war, Jean has happy memories of growing up in the 1930s.

Epworth had its own tennis court and Jean and Freda enjoyed giving tennis parties there. Jean recalls getting up very early at 7.30 to play tennis with the boy next door, and in the evenings the dance music of Sidney Munns' young band floated over the allotments from nearby Ashburnham Road, as they

21. The wedding of Fred and Hilda (1911).

practised in the small backroom of Sidney's home. The Salon ballroom had opened down on the Weedon Road and the two daughters were keen to go along and join in the dances. However, Fred found it difficult to adjust to the new style of young woman. He did not want his daughters to use make-up and disapproved when Freda wanted to go the Salon. Jean considers herself lucky, however, for as she was the youngest, her father treated her more leniently. Although women were not encouraged to go out to work after the Second World War, Jean became a piano teacher. It was 'quite acceptable' to teach piano pupils from home. She also became the organist at Spratton Church and taught singing to the boys of Spratton Hall School.

The family allegiance to Queens Road continued, despite the building of a new Methodist church on the corner of Park Avenue North and Abington Avenue in 1925. The new church, known as Park Avenue, followed the Primitive Methodist tradition and the Watts family preferred to worship in a Wesleyan Methodist service.

From the beginning Park Avenue Church was well attended by local wealthy families who ensured its strong survival in the early years. Even today it is a well-endowed, thriving church.

Set against this domestic background was the exciting decision in 1923 to purchase the lease of no. 6 High Street, Kettering. (The numbers have since been changed and it is now no. 21. In fact the site is now occupied by the Granada Theatre and being used as a bingo hall.) Francis, Fred's eldest son, was 12 at the time and he recalls the astute reasoning behind his father's decision:

'The impact of the adjacent steel town of Corby and the opening of the steel works was not lost on my father, for at that time there were few facilities and there was trade to be done. Corby was less than 1000 in population terms and little more than a village. . . .

For years and years we were suppliers to Stuart and Lloyds. They later became nationalized as British Steel. We supplied and laid rolls and rolls of A-quality plain brown lino for the offices. (In the winter it was not an easy

22. Fred and Hilda with Francis, Freda and Douglas

job to lay it either.) Then of course it led to other things. It was big business. We supplied the hostels with furniture. In one particular instance we even supplied the table napkins and the cutlery. It was a hostel for the employees, near Rockingham. There were a lot of unmarried people and they had to house them somewhere. They bought a huge old castle just outside Corby and one thing led to another. Our van was always seen in Corby – most days of the week, and in the end of course we used to get the directors' business as well. It led to an association that went on for a very long time.'

Fred decided to employ someone to manage the new High Street shop. Jack Thompson had been employed by Watts in Northampton for about 10 years. In his work he had displayed great initiative and drive, and this made him an obvious choice for the post of manager. Jack's early days with the firm were the beginning of a family link with Watts that was to last about 70 years.

Jack lived above the High Street premises with his family. His son, Norman, must have enjoyed playing in the orchard and stables behind the shop. He had to help his father sometimes and remembers

'dusting this and dusting that. And everyday for I don't know how many years I walked down from school with a basket with Dad's tea in – his chocolate eclair, every day.'

On a small scale the business was selling furniture and prams, and providing a cabinet-making and upholstery service. The pram manufacturers, Marmet, held a National Baby Carriages Display Competition in about 1932 and the window was then devoted to Marmet prams:

'Everybody had to dress the window. I went down one night and at about 11 o'clock when Dad was almost finished dressing, a photographer came along and took a photograph. We won 2nd prize.'

Kettering was fed with stock from the Northampton shop at this time. The newly acquired Northampton van had to have the sign with the Kettering address hooked on to the side when it delivered to the new branch twice a week. Fred, however, knew that he needed his own vehicle for deliveries to customers and as yet the business could not afford its own van. The problem was partly solved when they acquired a bicycle with a large basket on the front. Under the crossbar was hung an advertisement for A. Watts & Sons, and in the basket were transported any small items, usually relating to the pram side of the business. What to do about beds and chests of drawers?

Around the corner in Gas Street was a general grocer who was also a coal merchant. He owned a cart for delivering the coal. Despite the thick layer of dust which frequently covered the vehicle, Fred was not daunted, and arranged to hire the cart when needed. Norman can well remember the cleaning required before deliveries could take place!

Fred soon learnt that the character of the trade in Kettering was different from that in Northampton. The difference was in fact that Kettering was more up-market and customers wanted more expensive goods. This was not the experience in their shops in the larger, more industrial town of Northampton. There Watts occupied a niche in the more middle-of-the-road market. Caves (also of Kettering Road and still occupying their original site today) and Jeffreys of Gold Street catered for the upper end of the market. Fred was fortunate to have opened a branch in a town with so little competition.

Realising the difference in the two trades, Fred suggested setting up his own company. Francis recalls

'Some of the goods were not suitable for the trade we knew we could do in Kettering. So my father said to Uncle Ewart, in a very friendly way, "Look here, I would like to split this off and have Kettering and Wellingborough on my own." And that's how it was done. There were more wealthy people in Kettering, such as the numerous shoe manufacturers. The class of trade was streets ahead of that of Northampton. You see, it's not the same – having stuff sent over, as being in charge and buying it yourself. Jack Thompson and my father worked together and bought the stock.'

In 1928 the Kettering and Wellingborough branches separated from the Northampton firm. A new sign went up over the door – 'F.A. Watts & Co. Ltd.'

At about this time Fred was also ringing the changes in Wellingborough. Watts' first shop in the town was a small premises at no. 59 Oxford Street. The old stone house still stands, pleasantly set back from the road. It was soon obvious, however, that business might improve if premises were found that were nearer to the market square and the heart of the town.

In 1927 when Fred found that his friend Mr C.J. Mather of 39 Cambridge Street wanted to sell his private house, he was keen to purchase. He bought the property and divided it into two. He only considered it necessary to use half as a furniture shop – Wellingborough was, after all, quite a small town. The other half he sold to an ironmonger from Peterborough. He put in charge of the shop a man from Buckingham called Mr Holton. Much later when a new manager was in charge and also keen to purchase the business for himself and his son, Fred agreed to sell. This was during the Second World War, when business was of course difficult. No. 39a Cambridge Street then became Andrew Viccars & Son. (The building still stands and is now a betting shop.)

23. Francis Watts (1932).

In the promising early days of 1929, at the age of 17, Fred's eldest son, Francis, joined the firm. At first his jobs were any tasks that came along: cleaning windows and driving the new Chevrolet van. It was decided, however, that he would benefit from the experience of working for another firm for a few years, and so for two years Francis was employed by another furniture company – Hunters of Derby.

When Francis returned to work for his father in the High Street, Kettering, he could see what Fred had also realised by this time:

The shop had only a few years of the lease left to run. The property was in poor condition and very expensive to maintain. The 3-4,000 square feet was becoming inadequate for the business. The prime shopping street was not the High Street, but Gold Street.

Fred had just helped to arrange the removal of the Northampton shop to its prime position on Abington Street, with its new futuristic facade next to the Central Library, and he was very interested when the Old Post Office on 29 Gold Street, Kettering came up for sale. Francis has said that through the years Watts have experienced the truth of the old adage 'It isn't what you know, it's who you know', and the story of the purchase of the old post office is a good illustration:

'Out of the blue a Methodist friend of father called Charles Saunders (who was the chief architect of Gotch and Saunders and also a bible class reader in Kettering and a very strict Non-Conformist) – he said to father: "These premises in the Old Post Office can be bought for £6,000." My father said "Right. I'll raise the money somehow." So he agreed to buy it. This transaction was all done on a handshake in the street. Then, within about three weeks, this man, Charles Saunders – it just shows you how honest he was – he had a substantially higher offer, and he said "I promised these premises to Mr Fred, so I shan't break my word."

Now you don't often get that sort of thing in business, do you? So of course, when the premises were altered, Saunders became the architect to do the job. A Kettering builder named O.P. Drever & Son did the alterations, and of course this is where we got the nucleus of a lot of new customers from.

That's how it started in 1933 -- in Gold Street.'

The move from the High Street to Gold Street meant a move to the main thoroughfare and consequently increased trade. Although Gold Street was a few hundred yards from the market square and connected to it by the High Street, it was still an important shopping centre. Added to this was the huge increase in floor space from 3-4,000 square feet to 10,000.

The premises themselves were very impressive. They were part of a large Victorian building of red brick with a classical facade, known as the Old Post Office buildings and erected in 1887. Number 29 was to the left of the arcade.

Norman Thompson, who had by now officially joined his father in the firm, recalls the exciting change in the business.

'On Gold Street we had a prime position. It couldn't have been better. It was right in the middle of the street and went right back. There was an arcade which cut through as you look at the shop, on the right hand side, and the Odeon cinema was three doors below us. So when they had a very good film, you got a queue from the Odeon cinema right past our shop up the arcade.

The first floor was on two levels. It was a room that went right across the front and you had to go up three steps to it. For a long time we put that aside for prams and toys.

As far as the furniture goes, in the 1930s three piece suites always sold well. We had twelve one day. They sold at 19 guineas. We had a good cheap make of bedroom suite. You could buy a big wardrobe and a dressing table for £8 19s 6d. The bedstead, which included the spring, was £3 19s 6d.

The basement was for the mangles, wringers and linoleum. We supplied Stuart & Lloyds with plain brown linoleum. They put it down in every office. I suppose we used to supply miles of it. It came in different qualities. The A –quality was an absolute back-breaker. All you had was a knife and it was impossible to cut. It was terrible, especially in the winter when the lino was cold.

In the basement we used to have these rolls in – quite a few at a time. They weighed 4 ½ hundredweight. We used to slide them down the stairs. Every fortnight we had to put new rubber housing on the stairs, because it just got worn away. There was just no other way of getting the rolls down. The basement was a fairly big room, about 30ft by 12ft.

There was another room round the corner where we used to keep the bed springs. Every time we bought a bedstead, you see, it came complete with a spring, which is a very bulky object – about 6' by 4'6" or 3'.'

Fred was blessed with a good, loyal staff. Two names figure prominently in the business in these early days. They are Frank Solomon and Alfred Adams. Frank did all the upholstery, ran up curtains and helped with the linoleum flooring. Francis remembers him as 'an absolute artist'. He had grown up with Arthur in the early days of the business in Northampton and was put in charge of all the fitting. Alfred was employed as chief cashier and when they both retired in 1946 after some 40 years of loyal service, Watts held a special dinner in their honour, coinciding with their 50th anniversary celebration.

Jack Thompson and his son, Norman, were of course two other vital members of the Kettering staff. Norman remembers the first salesman being Brian Jackson.

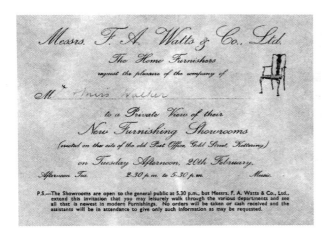

24. *Invitation to view the new shop (1934).*

In the office Daphne Porter began work in about 1934 and stayed for about 50 years. Vera Green joined soon after to help Mrs Porter. Norman recalls 'They worked together for years and years and years. Eventually Brian Jackson married Vera. They both live in Kettering today. . . . There wasn't much change in the offices at all. . . . I was a Jack-of-all-trades then. I took the blame for everything.'

The van driver/general mechanic was John Wood and he taught Norman to drive the small van which was used in the early 1930s. After Mr Wood came Walter Frost. Norman remembers that he was known to everyone as Gus.

'He was a little bit above the average lorry driver, and was quite capable of collecting the money from customers.'

Collecting money was an important job in running the shop and part of Norman's time was spent in carrying out the duties of a collector. He would have to get on his bicycle and cycle the 8-10 miles to Corby, collecting a shilling a week from a few dozen people, and at the same time delivering leaflets advertising the latest items in stock.

'It went on week after week. You enjoyed it, despite the fact that you got soaking wet some days when it was pouring with rain. You'd get to know the people. You'd know when you were going if you would get your money or if you'd got to wait another week.'

As a youngster Francis Watts also took his turn in delivering leaflets. One of his ideas on a windy day was to let the papers blow about so that potential customers would pick them up. This got him into trouble with the Reverend Greville Cooke, vicar of Cransley, who was trying to keep the village tidy. Francis, however, turned away wrath by complimenting him on his broadcast sermon – and the vicar bought a carpet!

With his usual business acumen Fred made sure that the opening of his new shop made quite a stir, just as the recent opening of the White House had done in Northampton. Personal invitations were sent out to previous customers for a private viewing of the new showrooms – on Tuesday afternoon, 20 February, 1934. Afternoon tea and music were also laid on. The invitation reveals that the general public would only be admitted at 5.30 pm and assistants would not be seeking to sell any items, rather they were there to give 'only such information as may be requested'.

25. The new Gold Street shop.

A clock had been fixed to the outside of the old post office. Fred soon saw the advertising potential it provided. He removed the figures from around the edge of the clock face and replaced them with the words 'Watts Time'. Everyone who walked along the street looked at the clock to see the time and immediately saw 'Watts Time'.

Even more expansion came quite rapidly when no. 46 Gold Street was purchased to provide an adequate display for all the prams and nursery equipment. The Northampton shop called 'Babydom' had already closed and become part of the White House, but the name was resurrected and used to highlight the new shop in Gold Street. A neon sign illuminating Fred's signature was chosen to call attention to the now thriving business.

A small workroom was leased in the post office arcade where curtains could be made and sold. It was conveniently situated opposite the back entrance to the shop. The arcade was about 90ft long and the van was stored in a garage at the far end. The arrangement may seem less than perfect when compared with the neat precision of purpose-built retail outlets of the 1990s, but it was an arrangement that worked, and worked well.

'We had wonderful loyalty from the staff. We've had as much happiness as any family firm can possibly have had.' (Francis (1976))

Some of the customers from the old days are still remembered with affection. Francis enjoys relating the story of the two brothers who must be almost the best customers any shopkeeper could wish for:

'They were two boot manufacturers. They came from London in about 1934 and eventually took over a local shoe manufacturer's. They were two right characters. The upshot of it was – once they got the money, they would come into our shop every few months, buy a lot of furniture, and then after another few months they would come back and say "Look, we're tired of this. We want a replacement." Towards the end of their lives these two brothers had got Rolls Royces and goodness knows what.

One of them would come into us and say "I don't like the colour of this carpet now. I want the house re-carpeting", or "I want some new furniture". Then a few months later the elder brother would come in and say "What's Bert been buying? He's just had a new three piece suite, hasn't he? I want

26. Calling Card (1927).

one." And they'd come in, order about £500 worth of furniture, pay £100 on account, and they were never really out of debt. We used to have to go to the factory to get the money – frequently. It went on for years.

It was absolutely fantastic – you couldn't go wrong. The furniture we took back from them was very saleable too. Of course the result was – when we tumbled to the fact that they would take a few months to pay, we stuck another 5% on to cover it, because if you've got money outstanding like that, you can't afford to give them discount. They always paid in the end. It went on for years and years this did.'

Not only are old customers from the pre-war days remembered with affection; Francis has happy memories of the travellers (as sales representatives were called in those days). In the thirties travellers did not cover miles of motorways in their visits to the various retailers. They arrived in a town by train and stayed in hotels for much of the week. Francis recalls how one traveller in carpets would walk up to the shop from the railway station pulling a cart full of samples. Sometimes Francis would even invite a traveller to stay in his own home overnight. The vast majority of these people were of course men, but there was one lady whom Francis remembers especially – a Miss Ashton who later became proprietor of the Osnath pram manufacturing company.

The outbreak of the Second World War in 1939 had of course serious consequences for furniture shops just as in every other trade. Any furniture made was called utility furniture and was only available to people who were getting married and who had the requisite number of dockets or coupons. Francis recalls the way in which the Kettering shop coped with the new situation.

'In the war you had to have utility furniture called the Cotswold range. You were quite free to go to an auction sale and buy second-hand furniture – well we had to to supplement our stock, because the amount of dockets a person could have wasn't enough to keep a business going. So we had to scratch around buying stuff up from houses and going to auction sales.

During the war the only people who could have utility furniture were people getting married – and then you had to have dockets for it. People only had a certain number and had to split them up – either in upholstery or cabinet-stuff or what have you.

But the furniture made under that scheme was very good. It was basic. It had a kitemark on. It was all stamped. There were penalties if you sold it except for the coupons. You had to send the coupons back to the suppliers to get more.

After the war there were a few manufacturers of doubtful reputation who produced a type of furniture which was terribly expensive and absolute rubbish, but we had to buy it to have something in the shop. It was terrible stuff – nowhere near as good as the utility was.'

Furniture shops may have suffered through their depleted stock, but the war opened up a new market for them – in black-out blinds. Curtain makers could quickly turn their hands to providing the enormous number of blinds which were now required by all the various institutions, as well as by individuals. It was such important business that it kept the young Norman Thompson out of the army for 9 months:

'We were making blinds for hospitals. We had a lath at the top and black Italian cloth and a roller. We gouged a groove out at each end so that the blind came down over this roller, and we pulled it down and it rolled itself up – a bit Heath Robinson, but they were cheap. People weren't prepared to pay alot. Most of them were sold to places like St Marys Hospital in Kettering, which had recently been the workhouse. I don't know how many windows there were – hundreds and hundreds, and no two alike. They were all stone and had to be drilled out.

We made these blinds down in the basement. We had this Italian cloth in – rolls and rolls and rolls of it. And we cut the poles down there. That kept me out of the army for nine months. I got so fed up with it, I said to my father "I'm going in the army". He wasn't very pleased.'

When Norman returned from the army, he was amazed at the way the shop had changed because it had not been possible to buy in new furniture.

'They had had to get what they could, so they'd bought all the second-hand furniture they could get their hands on. When I came back I thought it was junk. You couldn't see in the showroom from one end to the other. I came back to that and thought "Oh dear, oh dear, oh dear."'

With his forthright manner Norman decided to risk his father's wrath in order to smarten the shop up.

'My father went on holiday and I said to the staff, "We're going to shift some of this", and I had it all up the arcade outside. It was a job carting it out on the pavement. Knock-down prices – and we sold a good quantity. I got into trouble when my father came back from holiday, but that didn't matter really. At least we'd got a bit of room. When we got cleared out, we began to put on a reasonable show. Some of the stuff – you wouldn't give it house-room.'

After the war the furniture trade was not only slow to recover in terms of stock. New delivery vehicles were also hard to come by. However, a solution presented itself, for although the shop could no longer resort to hiring a dusty horse and cart, it could take advantage of the abundance of old ambulances now on the market. For several years a converted ambulance performed good service as the Watts furniture van.

In common with everyone else, F.A. Watts & Co. Ltd. had learnt 'to make do'.

Chapter IIII
A Political Interlude: the Year as Mayor, 1946

By the time the war was over, Fred was 61 and able to rely more and more on Francis to manage the shop. It is at this point that Fred's story branches out into the world of local politics. In 1945 he was elected Mayor of Northampton – a post he was soon to hold concurrently with the office of President of the Rotary Club (the first person ever to do so). In those stringent days of post-war hardship, the mayor had no grand official car. Fred had to make do with a small Ford Prefect.

His concerns and attitudes are of great general interest, for they reflect the issues which affected everyone after the Second World War – whether it be as world-wide as the threat of the new atomic age or as local as the question of playing games in the park and opening the cinemas on Sunday.

His duties as Mayor were in themselves of course a-political and in the months after the end of the war he was able to make some thoughtful speeches on the world which he observed around him:

'The world is on the march and has not yet made up its mind as to its destination. New ways, new habits, new philosophies, a different sense of our duty to our neighbour, the common suffering we have all endured in more or less degree, these are forming around us a new world our forebears would not recognise. (*N. I.* 16/11/45)'

The New Year of 1946 was rung in by peals of church bells from many churches, including St Giles and the Church of the Holy Sepulchre. In its coverage of the New Year celebrations the *Chronicle and Echo* reported the new mayor's New Year message in full. His message is founded on thankfulness and hope that the people of Northampton will not lose their sense of community spirit fostered and developed over the experience of the past six years:

'I would like to send to all the citizens of Northampton my sincere good wishes for the New Year.

We have celebrated the Christmas festival with, I have no doubt, peculiar thanksgiving, for even if the blight of austerity has fallen upon some of our material pleasures, the indescribable relief of a Christmas unshadowed by war and the thought of loved ones, though distant, in comparative safety, must have given wings to the season's enjoyment and happiness.

27. Fred as mayor (1946).

I have felt as I have moved about the community, the generosity, good will and graciousness of many folk. I should like to believe that though the season is fleeting its spirit might abide, for surely that would mean much to the life of the town.

Now we face the tasks and responsibilities of another year. There are, it seems to me, three things that might well be dominant in our minds as we voyage together into 1946.

The first is thanksgiving. Let us remember that there are few towns of comparable size that have so completely escaped the ravages of war as Northampton. Our Service folk are beginning to return – and how glad we are – to their homes and to a familiar and unmutilated borough. Surely because of this there should be the grace of gratitude in the hearts of all who live here.

I am not unmindful of the sorrow that casts a deep shadow on many a dwelling, and these should have their memorial in our abiding gratitude. Let us with pride and thanksgiving continually remember them in the coming year.

Further, I should like to express the wish that all worthy social and cultural activities amongst us should be fostered and extended in the days to come. We are justly proud of many things in our beloved community that have fed the recreative and social needs of our people. In particular, one is grateful for the noble and altruistic service that is freely offered by countless folk amongst us, whose desire is the strengthening of the best life of Northampton to a greater level of personal and social value.

Especially could I wish that 1945 would show an encouraging advance in the service of youth. The Northampton of the future depends very largely on the kind of ministry we are offering our young people today.

In the third place, may I express the wish that 1946 will bring, at any rate, the beginning of that prosperity which is the reward of vocational service to the community. I would like us all to believe that, necessary as our recreations may be, the most lasting happiness will only come in doing our job faithfully and well in the communal pattern, and that our pleasures are of little worth unless they have the background of honest and fruitful toil behind them.'

The months after the war were deeply affected by the public's knowledge of the destructiveness of the new atomic bomb. No-one in public office could fail to be aware of the shadow this cast over the world of 1945 and beyond.

In a lecture at College Street Baptist Church the subject of the promise of the new United Nations Organisation was debated. Fred presided over the meeting where Mr J.T. Catterall of Northampton spoke on the need for the UN not only to secure freedom from war, but reduce competition for trade and encourage economic co-operation. Fred concluded:

'We do not realise that these days are as pregnant with history as the days that have passed us.

We must approach present problems not with scepticism, but with hope.

Twenty-five years ago we did not realise how great our problems were, but now, with the coming of the atomic age, we realise that we must have peace – or the end of humanity.' (C & E 15/1/46)

A few days later Fred was to attend a meeting of the UN Association at the Albert Hall to welcome the UNO delegates. Speakers at the meeting included the Archbishop of Canterbury and Mrs. Eleanor Roosevelt. Mayors and Provosts from many parts of the country were invited in order to symbolise Britain's welcome to the delegates and good wishes for the United Nations. Fred's personal impressions of the meeting, recorded in an interview with a *Chronicle and Echo* reporter, reveal that he was a deeply thoughtful and perceptive man:

'My general impression was that throughout the whole assembly there was a will to peace, but apart from the Archbishop of Canterbury – who did strike a different note – any spiritual dynamic seemed in some measure absent.

In my opinion, in all these things there seems to be a glorification of the materialistic rather than an appeal to the spiritual dynamic. (C & E 18/1/46)

From the heights of such lofty debates as this to the more practical trivia of questions such as whether to allow cinemas to open on Sunday, Fred was deeply involved in the affairs of a world that had been devastated and transformed by six years of war.

Browsing through newspaper cuttings about his year as mayor gives a fascinating insight into what ordinary life was like for the people of Northampton. There is probably no better way of absorbing the anxieties and hopes of the period than by reading some of these stories – some that made the front page of the *Chronicle & Echo*, others that merited only a brief mention at the foot of a column.

Two debates stand out in the press coverage of council affairs of 1946. In view of the recent arguments of the 1990s concerning keeping Sunday special, they are of particular interest. The first is the debate on Sunday cinema. The second is the question of allowing games to be played in the parks on Sunday.

During the war the Town Council had granted cinemas a licence to open on Sunday afternoon and evening. In April 1946 the licence needed to be renewed, and so the Watch Committee met representatives of the cinema industry and the Church in order to make a decision. They decided that the matter should be referred to the Town Council and a stormy meeting was held, at which the strength of feeling is expressed by the following words of Councillor P.W.Adams:

'In Northampton we spend £250,000 yearly on education and in a few years it will be £500,000. What for? Merely to teach youngsters to go to the cinema? If we can't teach youngsters something better than that, then God help England!' (C & E 29/1/46)

Alderman Mrs. Nicholls announced

'I would prefer that young girls should go to the cinema and go home sober, rather than go to the public houses and go home drunk.'

Alderman A. Weston said

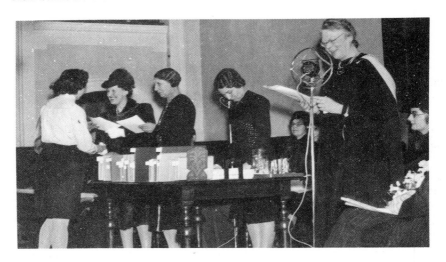

28. Hilda awarding prizes at the Speech Day of the School for Girls.

'The humbug which has been expressed on the Sunday cinemas of late has never been surpassed. People boast about democracy, which should mean to allow everyone to please himself, but to some people democracy starts on Monday and ends on Saturday night.'

During the war there were thousands of troops in the town and the opening of the cinemas was a measure devised to provide the soldiers with something to do on their day off, rather than have them 'aimlessly wander round the streets'. Children under 14 were never supposed to be admitted for several reasons. Firstly Sunday afternoon was a traditional time for Sunday School and the Council did not wish to provide any distraction from Sunday School attendance. Secondly, as today, Sunday was hailed as a family day, to be spent together. Thirdly, there were some people of the opinion that films were a harmful influence on the young. The Reverend Tyler Lane, representing the Northampton Free Church Council, declared:

'If we want to track down the causes of many things like the over-sophistication of our youth, it comes back to films.' (*C & E* 23/1/46)

Some Councillors were understandably angry that cinema owners had broken the agreement and admitted under-14 year olds in the afternoon. Young boys were being dressed in long trousers in order to gain entry. Canon Trevor Lewis, on behalf of the Church of England, did not believe that the majority of Northamptonians wanted Sunday cinema. He even offered that the Church would pay for a referendum on the issue.

'I firmly believe that so much do people resent the breaking up of family life by the eagerness of children to get away to queue for Sunday cinemas that the referendum would be on the side of the Church.'

The other side of the coin was presented by Mr H.D. Pascoe, Chairman of the local Entertainments Committee. He pointed out that as Sunday audiences averaged 10,000 people and as three quarters of these were civilians, there must be a large demand. He even argued that it was good for family life.

'Sometimes three families have to live in one house nowadays, and Sunday
cinemas give them an opportunity to get away from each other. There is
also the point of saving household fuel.'

It would seem that the police were also in favour of Sunday cinema, at least in
the evening, because it provided something for young people to do. The Chief
Constable, Mr John Williamson, had observed the increased number of young
people on the streets between 8 and 10 pm and would have preferred the 8.30
pm closing time to be made later in order to avoid the potential nuisance of
numbers of youngsters wandering around.

The Council meeting on the question of Sunday cinema divided the issue
into two motions – one on the renewal of the licence for Sunday opening and
the other on the specific question of hours. 28 voted in favour of the renewal of
the licence and 5 voted against. Regarding the hours question, a compromise
was suggested in order to please the Churches with their Sunday Schools. It was
noted that in Kettering, where no afternoon cinema was allowed, Sunday School
attendances had been maintained. The vote on opening from 5.30 – 10 pm was
halved and the Mayor warned the Council that if the second vote was also a tie,
he would use his casting vote, (being a Methodist there can be little doubt that
Fred would have wanted to restrict cinema opening to the evenings). As it turned
out, one Councillor had been out of the chamber when the vote was counted and
he swung the vote to 19 – 18 in favour of restricting the hours to the evening.

Two months later, how to keep Sunday was again in the headlines. The Estates
Committee of the Town Council recommended that the town parks should be
allowed to open up for more recreational purposes on Sundays, and a lengthy
heated debate was held on 1 April.

Prior to the debate there had been a weekend of intense activity in
Northampton by the National Executive of the Brotherhood Movement. Lord
Ammon, the National President of the movement, came to address Northampton
Men's Own, supported by the Mayor, Fred Watts. Lord Ammon stated that:

'While I was chairman of the L.C.C. I was able to keep London's parks
closed for games on Sundays. This was because I feel that Sunday should
be a different day from the rest of the week, and because it had been proved
that men and women who spent Sundays in strenuous games were not as fit
for work on Mondays as those who had spent a quiet restful day with a visit
to a place of worship.

As a trade unionist, I must point out that trade unions strive to obtain
double pay for Sunday work to make it too expensive for employers to ask
their work people to work on Sundays. '(*C & E* 1/4/46)

Fred clearly opposed the Town Council motion to allow games in the parks on
Sundays. His name heads the list of those who voted against. The voting was
very close – as in the debate on Sunday cinema, with 23 voting in favour and 21
against.

The arguments in favour were supported by both the religious and the non-
religious alike, and the central issue was one of human liberty to choose.
Councillor W. Lewis made the interesting point that Sunday restrictions were a
survival from the days when Sunday observance was obligatory by law. (The
1625 Sunday Observance Act prohibited people from meeting outside their own

parishes on Sundays 'for any sports and pastimes whatsoever'.) Also, games were needed to help people relax on Sundays, regardless of the anomaly that the tennis and golf clubs of the well-to-do were allowed to operate seven days a week.

Councillor A. Hope stressed the need to view the keeping of Sunday as a human problem and not a religious one:

'I would prefer people used Sunday intelligently by going to Church, if they so wish, or listening to lectures or reading – generally improving their minds. But it is their funeral whether they do or not.

The Churches are frightened they are losing their grip – because perhaps they think their case is weak. If their case is not weak, they have nothing to fear.

It is up to the Council to leave religion and secularisation out of the question and regard it as a human problem.' (*C & E* 2/4/46)

Councillor Mrs. Lee implicitly agreed that Sunday games would affect the religious keeping of Sunday, for she claimed that children should not be coerced into the Sunday Schools. 'Let them be free to develop as they wish.' She observed that attitudes had been altered by the experience of war. 'Six years of war have made a tremendous difference to our habits of living.' (*C & E* 2/4/46)

Perhaps she saw that people had had enough of rules and restrictions inevitable in war-time and wanted to enjoy greater freedom. Or maybe she was implying that people had learnt to live more for today and not pay so much attention to the spiritual dimension of life. Whatever lay behind her ideas, she firmly believed that the general public supported the Council's resolution.

It is interesting that those against the motion were not arguing from the point of view of religious dogmatism, determined to safeguard Church attendances. The familiar phrase of keeping Sunday as a special day occurred as frequently then as it has done in the 1990s in the debate on Sunday trading.

Councillor C. Chown questioned the idea that there was a large body of support for Sunday games:

'There were many people, believers in Sunday as a day of rest, who considered that the results of Sunday games would be far-reaching and disastrous. . . I believe that this question opens up a much wider issue than the opening of cinemas. If we pass this resolution we are making Sunday the great play-day of the week.'

Councillor J. Collier pointed to the resolution's far-reaching implications for society as a whole.

'Talk of the liberty of the individual was a two-edged sword. . . . The proposal affected the heart of everybody in the town. . . . While many members of the Council might deny the Divine inspiration of the Commandment relating to the keeping of the Sabbath, at any rate they would not deny its common sense.'

Letters were read from several local church leaders and the meeting was addressed by the Mayor's chaplain, the Rev. H. Tyler Lane, who declared to the Council that he was not only representing the Free Churches but also Canon Trevor Lewis of the Church of England:

'We do not approach the question from the puritanical or sabbatarian angle.

It has been said that the arguments against the proposal were 'old and familiar', but that does not necessarily mean they are out-moded.

The recreative value of Sunday lies in its being different from other days and the proposal tends to make the day the same as others.

The proposal offers severe competition to a vital work in the community, for it is not a proposal for social evolution but social deterioration.

There is owing to the war a decline in moral and spiritual values, and upon leaders of life rests a great responsibility.'

The more mundane and practical argument against Sunday games was from the employees' point of view. Working men would have to agree to work on Sunday, who would normally have been able to spend the day with their families.

Councillor P. Adams pointed out:

'If the Council decide to provide games on Sundays, they will be compelling groundsmen, caterers, and other workers to work, and deprive them of their Sunday liberty.

The issue is not Sunday games, but the entire secularisation of Sunday.

It will not stop at Sunday games, but if they give complete liberty, public houses and factories will open at all hours and every day.

If the secularisation of Sunday comes about, the Church and Sunday School will disappear.'

In a similar vein the Deputy Mayor, Councillor R. Smith, argued that the proposal would be

'harmful to the community as a whole. . . . Working-men do not want games at the expense of their fellow working-men who provide the facilities.'

The resolution was finally passed by two votes, with a ban still in operation on football because it was 'too noisy'. An amendment was then introduced to deal with the question of opening the children's playgrounds. The suggestion was made to open them at 3.45 pm as on weekdays, but it was defeated, again by a mere two votes. Perhaps the councillors were influenced by the (by present-day standards) extraordinary image presented by Councillor J. Ellis:

'Mothers of Northampton do not want them opened. I visualise – out of the clothing question – children being thrashed on arrival home for using the swings.'

A few items in the *Chronicle & Echo* in the ensuing weeks bring out some interesting points – firstly, the anomaly of the omission of football from the resolution:

'Yesterday morning I took a walk through Abington Park and to my great surprise saw a gang of youths playing football – not an organised game it is true, but they were playing with a football.

The policy, as I understand it, of the Estates Committee and the Town Council is to exclude football in the sports to be allowed. I should like a ruling on this point, as would many other people.' (*C & E* 8/4/46)

Secondly, it would seem surprising to people today how uncertain the councillors were about the level of support for Sunday games. Polls and televised interviews with the 'man on the street' would today claim to give a much clearer picture of the support for the new resolution. On the eve of the opening day for organised games in the parks this comment appeared in the *Chronicle & Echo* (30/4/46):

29. Fred and the March past on St Giles Street (8/6/46).

'For the first time in Northampton's history, tennis balls will be flying over the nets, and woods will be rolling up the bowling greens in the public parks and recreation grounds next Sunday (weather permitting).

Sunday is the day when the Town Council's much criticised decision to allow games on the Sabbath comes into operation.

It will be interesting to see whether the demand for Sunday games from the mysterious 'they' who were mentioned by the sponsors of the scheme is as great as was declared.'

Finally, the other anomaly – the ban on Sunday swings and slides – was tackled by the Town Council on the 3rd of June. A 2 o'clock opening time was defeated by 18 votes to 16 and once again a 3.30 start was also defeated, by 18 votes to 15. The Estates Committee realised that the situation was 'hopelessly inconsistent and exceedingly ridiculous'.

Some of the comments made by the councillors say a great deal about what life was like for children in the 1940s:

'There is no demand from the parents. Mothers know the children's Sunday clothes will be damaged. The matter ought to be deferred until more coupons are available. . .

The proposal would take children off the streets. . . .'

Councillor S. Betts, in favouring the 3.30 opening time, said

'I do not wish to compel children to go to Sunday School, but I do want to safeguard the children so far as Sunday schools are concerned.'

In 1950 the Council decided to restrict Sunday games to the summer because of fears of 'the Continental Sunday', and at about this time cinemas were permitted to open on Sunday afternoons following a public vote in favour. In due course during the 1950s the Council decided to lift restrictions on winter games and also on the playgrounds.

These then were the two debates that stood out in the Council's affairs during the time when Fred presided as Mayor.

As mentioned earlier, examples of the local newspaper stories of the year can serve to illustrate the kind of hopes and anxieties that were part of town life just after the Second World War. As Mayor, Fred was naturally involved in a vast array of events which were directly linked with the aftermath of war, from the question of how to remove air-raid shelters from the local streets to how to celebrate Victory Day on the 8 June, 1946.

Here is just a sample of the stories and events:

PARTY THAT NONE WILL FORGET
Mayor entertains War Orphans.
'You're going to raise the roof,' Councillor S.Kilsby told 200 Borough children whose fathers had been killed or died on war service, when community singing started at the Mayor's party at the Town Hall yesterday. The children needed no second invitation, and the roar which answered Mr Kilsby was deafening.

As they sang, Mr Kilsby and Mr Morley Parry kept the fun going by conducting and miming the words. When the Mayor's chaplain, the Rev. H. Tyler Lane, led in 'Molly Malone', the two trundled across the platform as a wheelbarrow. The children, enthralled by their antics, did not know that Mr Parry had volunteered to help with the party because his own child had recently died.

The party, which was arranged by the Mayor and Mayoress, Councillor and Mrs. Fred A. Watts, and a committee of friends of children, was for orphans from five to 14.

As the children arrived, and crowded to the tea tables, one small boy stood in a corner and wept. He was the only child who didn't want to go to a party.

During the tea, Mr Arthur Gilkes played the piano and after tea the fun began with community singing. This was followed by an entertainment by Mr Eric Lewis, magician; Mr Cecil Twistleton with his animal imitations, and Mr Walter Ashton, ventriloquist.

Then ice-cream was distributed, given by Mr J. Dean of Kettering Road, Northampton.

After games came the distribution of presents from beside the huge Christmas tree, decorated with little Chineses lanterns. Councillor Kilsby was Father Christmas. (*C & E* 5/1/46)

BOROUGH LEADS IN SHELTER 'BUSTING'
MAY BE FIRST TOWN OF ITS SIZE TO BE CLEAR
Northampton is the model town for technicians who wish to study the art of air-raid shelter 'busting'.

Mr H Ritson, Section Engineer, Ministry of Finance, Northern Ireland wanted to study methods of demolishing shelters, so Mr J Ruck, Regional Technical Coordinating Officer, Home Office, brought him to Northampton.

Why was Northampton chosen? 'Because', said Mr Ruck to a Chronicle and Echo reporter, 'the demolition in Northampton is being carried out by Mr R. A. Winfield, the Borough Engineer, with outstanding efficiency as to methods adopted, rate of progress and costs.'

And if the present rate of progress is maintained, said Mr Ruck, Northampton will be the first town of its size to be cleared of shelters.

NOISIEST METHOD

Miss P. Wiggins, who lives next door at no. 23 says she felt no disturbance when the shelter just outside the house collapsed under the 'basher's' punches.

'It's great', said Mr Ritson. 'That's a real job of work done.'

Cost when the 'basher' is used is 10s 6d per cubic yard.

Noisiest method of all was demonstrated in Great Russell Street, where the shelters are cut through the middle – roof and end walls alike – by pneumatic drills and then powerful jacks are placed under the walls and made to lift until the whole shelter is brought to the ground. The rubble is then broken up by the drills.

A variation of that method was demonstrated in Kingswell Street where the jack was placed horizontally between the wall.

By these methods it takes up to15s per cubic yard for shelters to be demolished. (*C & E* 18/1/46)

SHOE TRADE HOLIDAYS IN 1946

The 1946 holiday arrangements for the boot and shoe trade in Northampton, have been agreed upon by the local Board of Conciliation and Arbitration as follows:

Easter – Thursday, April 18 to Wednesday, April 24, or Friday, April 19 to Thursday, April 25.

July – Friday, July 5 to Tuesday, July 16.

September – Friday September 13 to Thursday, September 19.

Christmas – Monday, December 23 to Monday, December 30.

Whit Monday and August Bank Holiday Monday are regarded as normal working days.

Employers may open earlier than the stated opening dates, but may not extend the holiday beyond these dates without being liable to payment for the extension under the Essential Works Order.

The transferred-day provision will operate as in previous years where a day has been transposed for stock-taking.

The Easter and Christmas Holidays will be according to the usual custom.

The agreement is signed by Mr A. Hope (chairman), Mr P.C. Jones (vice-chairman) and Mr N. Barraclough (Secretary). (*C & E* 8/1/46)

WOMEN ASKED TO VOLUNTEER AS HOME HELPS

Fearing that present heavy maternity bookings at local hospitals may result in overcrowding, Northampton Council Maternity and Child Welfare committee want more women for 'home helps'.

In order to recruit sufficient numbers, they are revising their present scheme and increasing the weekly wage for helps from £3 to £3 10s.

Women who offer their services will have to do household duties in the homes of mothers-to-be before their confinement and for a short time afterwards.

Realising that most households will not be able to afford to pay the wages of the 'home help' the Maternity and Child Welfare Committee is heavily subsidising the scheme, and in most cases only a fraction of the £3 10s will be recovered from the family concerned. (*C & E* 20/2/46)

STEALING, LYING ARE 'NORMAL'
'Never enter a child's room at night without a light. Children are not afraid of the dark, but of things moving in it.'

'Stealing and lying are normal in a young child and should be treated calmly and not with drastic punishments.'

This was some of the advice given to mothers yesterday by Professor J.M. Mackintosh, former County Medical Officer, when he spoke at the annual meeting of Northampton Maternity and Infant Welfare Voluntary Association.

'The small one-child house is out of date,' he declared, 'And houses should be built for larger families. Rents for larger houses should be levelled to the rates of smaller ones.

'It would encourage people to have larger families if the dread of not being able to afford a larger house were taken away.'

Although infant mortality has decreased since 1911, the relative difference between classes had increased. While there were 33 deaths per 1,000 of children under one month in the upper class, there were 70 per 1,000 in the unskilled labourer class.

Presenting the honorary secretary's report, Mrs. S.H. Green said there were now 15 infant welfare centres in the town and more mothers were attending than in previous years.

The Mayor (Councillor Fred A. Watts) presided. Among officers present were the Mayoress Mrs. Watts (President), Mrs. J.T. Chamberlain (chairman) and Mrs. J. Woods (vice-chairman). Also present were Lord and Lady Henley, Mrs. R.M. Raynsford and Mrs. J.M. Mackintosh. (*C & E* 4/4/46)

FOOD GIFTS FOR THE AGED
The food parcels, promised for Christmas to the older citizens of Northampton from Australia and South Africa, have arrived, and are to be distributed tomorrow at the Town Hall.

Five hundred puddings and many tins of fruit, stewed meat, dripping and jam have been received, and each person over 70 who sent in an application will receive two pounds of food-stuffs. Old couples living alone will receive one pound each. The puddings are a present from the people of Cape Town and the other foodstuffs are from Melbourne.

All pensioners who sent in applications have been asked to attend at the Town Hall tomorrow.

The Mayor (Councillor Fred. A. Watts), Mr W.F. Floyd (Mayor's Sergeant), Mrs. Floyd and members of the Northampton W.V.S. will distribute the food. (*C & E* 30/1/46)

GRISEWOOD'S CALL TO BOROUGH GARDENERS

'It is not a case of digging for victory now but digging for dear life', said Mr F.H. Grisewood, the well-known broadcaster urging the need for greater production of fruit and vegetables, when he spoke at the inaugural meeting of Northampton's Food Production Week last night.

He was not sure the situation was not worse now than during the war. Then the food was in the world, but it was a question whether it could be brought to us. Now there was a definite world food shortage.

'It does behove everyone to take the situation very seriously,' he went on, 'and redouble his efforts.' (*C & E* 19/2/46)

MANY TASKS, FEW COMPLAINTS ABOUT POLICE
CHIEF PRAISES BOROUGH WAR RESERVE

'The Police Force is what the individual constable is. If he fails, the Force fails,' said the Chief Constable of Northampton, Mr John Williamson, speaking at a reunion dinner of the Auxiliary Police Association at Franklins Gardens Hotel, last night.

Responding to a toast to the Police Force, he said that considering the police were continually dealing with many matters, there could be no other body that had relatively so few complaints against it.

He paid high tribute to the work of the Reserve during the war years, saying he had never had any doubt about their value.

Referring to the fact that the Reserve had not had helmets like the Regulars, Mr Williamson said the uniform had been issued by a Government Department, and the Watch Committee had nothing to do with it. (*C & E* 19/2/46)

LEGION LASH C.O. CREDITS. PROTEST TO TOWN COUNCIL.
'MEN WHO HAVE FOUGHT WILL HAVE TO FIND MONEY'

'So far as we are concerned all conscientious objectors can go to Hades until every ex-Serviceman has been given his just dues,' says the Northampton Branch of the British Legion, who intend to contest vigorously the Town Council's decision to pay sixpence a day post-war credit to their conscientious objector employees.

A meeting of the British Legion Executive Committee hit out in the strongest terms at the C.O.'s right to have the credits, and called on all Servicemen and ex-Servicemen to protest against the Council's decision.

An official protest has been forwarded to the Town Clerk with the request that it be considered at the next Council meeting.

WILL GIVE IT TO CHARITY

Not all the C.O. employees of the Corporation are inclined to take the money.

Mr J.P. Wilson, senior dental officer at the school clinic, when informed of the protest, remarked: 'I do appreciate the point of view very deeply, and agree with a lot they say, but do they appreciate ours? On the general issue the C.O. who has Christian objections has served wherever he has been directed.

'The C.O.'s do appreciate that members of the Forces have served overseas, and have been wounded and killed.

'On their particular issue though my own personal view is quite clear. I am not going to accept the money if it is offered. I shall ask the Council to send it to any charity they like to nominate.'

Mr Wilson went on to say he had no malice against the British Legion. He had originally objected on Christian grounds, and had since worked for the Corporation on a soldier's pay and would continue to do so until his Army group – 35 – was reached.

'While working on this rate I have lost £400 a year for the last three years', he declared. 'If I had joined the Army in my own profession I should have got £550 a year more than I am getting'. (*C & E* 2/2/46)

DRUNKENNESS PROSECUTIONS LOWEST SINCE 1932

'Large numbers of young women have acquired the habit of regularly visiting licensed premises during the war years, which they might not have done in the ordinary way but for friendships and associations with members of the armed Forces,' stated Mr John Williamson, Chief Constable of Northampton, presenting his annual report to the Borough Licensing Justices at their annual meeting today.

Mr Williamson pointed out other various unusual matters that had arisen owing to the war – sections of the Armed Forces with plenty of money preferred to buy whisky at fantastic prices, and the presence in and around the town of large numbers of Canadian and Dominion troops, as well as Americans, Poles, Czechs and Free French, whose behaviour in view of the excitement and unnatural conditions had been exemplary in relation to the licensing laws.

33 PROSECUTED FOR DRUNKENNESS

During the year 33 persons (27 male, 6 females) were proceeded against for drunkenness, which was a decrease of one compared with the previous year, and the lowest number since 1932.

Of these, 21 were non-residents of the borough. . . .

The Chairman (Councillor Ralph A. Smith) said the further decrease in drunkenness was an indication of the increased sobriety of the people. There had been a steady decrease throughout the war which in itself was a remarkable thing when the added excitement of war was considered.

The Justices regretted though, that the cases against motorists had increased from two to four.

This was an offence which the Justices would have to deal with very severely. (*C & E* 14/2/46)

HOW RETURNED SERVICEMEN CAN BE HELPED

The young men who have grown up in the Forces and those who have been overseas a long time could be expected to have the greatest difficulties – physical, mental and emotional. Colonel Radcliffe suggested that schemes such as those used in helping prisoners-of-war to re-adjust themselves would prove as successful in such cases.

Returning men would have changed their views on many things on account of the different life they had lived and they should meet the returning people half-way and be ready to adjust their ideas. All resettlement schemes, he said, depended ultimately for their success on the existence of real goodwill between Service and non-Service employees.

In dealing with a returning ex-Serviceman an employer would have two problems to solve in order to get the best work from him. First, what was his technical or potential ability? Second, what incentive and environment would enable him to do best the particular job for which he was skilled?

PERSONAL TOUCH

Employers and officials should introduce the personal touch into the workings of their systems and get to know their men as individuals and friends. Other factors helping to good morale were team spirit and good comradeship, discipline, education, security of employment and sense of purpose and ideals.

'You have a dual task. First, to help these men and women to re-adjust themselves to civilian life and work. Second, to see that the fine qualities which they showed in war are given a proper opportunity to reveal themselves in peace-time,' he added.

'After that it is up to them – and I am confident they will not fail, and that the whole country will be richer for their contribution.'

The Mayor (Councillor Fred A. Watts) was chairman, supported by the Mayoress and representatives of regional and local offices of the Ministry of Labour. (*C & E* 21/6/46)

£140,000 WAR TIME BILL OF NORTHAMPTON Y.M.C.A.

. . . Finally, the Dover Hall was opened at a cost of about £3,000.

'We have,' said Alderman Glenn, 'been told many times that the accommodation offered there is as good as any in the country.

'We can surely claim that this last extension is a fitting and magnificent climax to our war effort.'

In conclusion, Alderman Glenn urged them to continue with their good work, for there were still thousands of serving men looking to the Y.M.C.A. 'Stay the course, even go the other mile, inspired by the same ideal of service that has won us victory.' The party, which was attended by over 600 voluntary Y.M.C.A. workers, was addressed by Lieut.-General Sir John Brown (chairman of the Council of Voluntary War Work), who stressed that the work of the Y.M.C.A. would be needed as long as we had the three armed Services.

'Wherever the British soldier has been, you will find evidence of the work of the Y.M.C.A.,' he said.

Giving general statistics of their work, he said that over 300,000 sheets of notepaper and over 150,000 envelopes had been issued to the men of the armed forces, and 268,000,000 hot meals had been served in London alone during the war.

Mr W. Cowper Barrons (managing editor, *Chronicle and Echo*) thanked the Y.M.C.A. workers on behalf of the many people who would like to have done the job, but were engaged in other work.

Lieut.-Colonel P.H. Cadoux Hudson, who attended in the place of Col. J.M. Slater (Commanding Officer North Central District) thanked the Y.M.C.A. on behalf of the fighting services. (*C & E* 28/2/46)

QUICK PRODUCTION – MR PAGET: 'MUST GET RID OF DOCTRINAIRE IDEA'

'This last war has thrown us back something like a hundred years in the economic sense', said Mr R.T. Paget, M P for Northampton, when responding to a toast of the 'Town and Trade of Northampton' at the annual dinner of the Insurance Institute of Northampton, held at the Masonic Hall, Northampton, last night.

We had to get back to full production at a time when our whole economy was thrown out of gear.

We had to get production going as quickly as possible. Some remarks had been made about private enterprise. In a job of quick production the best means must be sought. In some cases it was best for the Government to take over, in others to coordinate various manufacturers into a plan, and at other times for the Government to leave firms alone. All depended on the particular problem.

They must get rid of the doctrinaire idea, and get together in maintaining maximum production. No-one liked austerity, but sharing was the only way when there was not enough to go round.

There had been some gibing about working parties, but it was merely an effort to get all people in an industry together to decide on the methods to obtain maximum production. In Northampton he was sure all sides were going to do so, and he believed they would make a success of it. (*C & E* 2/3/46)

MEMORIAL SQUARE AS LARGE AS MARKET SQUARE FLANKED BY COMMUNITY BUILDINGS SCHEME

Northampton's War Memorial Square will be as large as the Market Square and will eventually be flanked by buildings of community interest, including a theatre and premises to house the headquarters of all the town's voluntary organisations.

Enlarging on the sketchy outline of the scheme given in the report of the Finance Committee, Councillor Frank Lee, at last night's meeting of Northampton Town Council, said the sub-committee which suggested the proposed war memorial on the site of St Katharine's Church*, was completely confident that when the scheme was fully understood it would meet with general approval and satisfaction.

It is not proposed merely to have an open space, although as an open space the site will be very attractive. It will be as big as the Market Square, and there will be no town in England with two such large open spaces in the centre of the town.

'It is intended to develop the area bounded by Katharine Street, Horsemarket, King Street and College Street, as a square and on three of four sides there will be facilities in the way of buildings for different sections of the community of Northampton.

PERSONAL MEMORIALS

'When we have the square, I think that people will look back and say we took a very good decision.

'There we visualise the commencement of a new part of the town's centre to be at the bottom of Horsemarket flanked by various buildings of community interest.

'In fact it may easily prove there are generous-minded citizens in our midst who may desire to present as their own personal memorial, a building of beauty and utility for incorporation in the general scheme, and this suggestion with many others will doubtless be considered as the full plans are worked out.'

The Mayor, moving the report of the sub-committee appointed to plan a war memorial, said: 'We had a number of meetings, and our first thoughts turned towards the provision of a public hall, which would be large enough for any likely purpose. No-one would dispute our need for such a hall. We very soon realised, however, that this would be impracticable for years to come. We know the paramount need is for houses.

CREATIVE AND FAR-SEEING

'We don't want war memorials to remind us of wars,' said Alderman J. Bugby, 'We want to forget wars, and I think those who have fallen would have preferred homes for old people.'

In reply to Councillor J. Ellis, the Mayor said the Ecclesiastical Commissioners had given the church and the site, and Councillor Lee added that the Commissioners would have to be satisfied that the consecrated ground was not used for purposes which would offend the feelings of the Christian community.

Councillor W. Lewis commended the scheme as creative and far-seeing, and said that when a long view was taken in connection with road planning and development during the next 25 years, as recently adopted by the Council, the scheme would present a very different picture from merely clearing the site.

The report was accepted, with Councillor Cogan and Alderman Bugby dissenting. (*C & E* 8/10/46)
*St Katharine's is now just a leafy oasis behind the Drapery and Gold Street – not the vibrant centre for this part of the town centre, as planned.

THE BOOK OF HONOUR

Today there have been several suggestions about the form the memorial might take – hospital extensions, a civic hall for communal gatherings, a first-rate club for ex-Servicemen and their families to meet and keep up the friendships made during the days of war.

There are many ideas, of course, and doubtless I shall receive many more. Should the present very uninspired plan go through – and one feels the planners jumped at the availability of an abandoned St Katharine's as an easy way out – I pass on one possibility.

Why not keep Northampton's roll of honour in book form and extend the practice of daily turning a page, with short, but impressive ceremony, and thus ever recalling the names of the men and women who gave their all? At least it would add a touch of imagination to a very colourless project. (*C & E* 7/10/46)

Some of the meetings which Fred had to attend as mayor are illuminating in what they reveal about the moral and spiritual concerns of the time. As far back as 1946 religious leaders were aware that Christianity in schools was in danger of being taught in an unconvincing manner. Fred himself made an impassioned plea for the Church to work to halt the deterioration in values.

Broken homes were acknowledged as the cause of much juvenile delinquency and one of the NSPCC organisers paints a gloomy picture of the growth of his charity's work. Although in several cases the effect of the War was recognised as beneficial in strengthening a common sense of responsibility, nevertheless there were fears that this attitude would not last, as material comforts were liable to increase people's selfishness.

Here are some of the stories:

THE MAYOR AND THE CHALLENGE

Reference to a 'deterioration in true values, varied and distressing in expression', was made by the Mayor (Councillor Fred A. Watts) at the Guildhall luncheon to which he welcomed both as 'Methodist and Mayor' the delegates to the Leicester and Northampton Methodist Synod now meeting at Northampton.

'It is the Church alone', said Councillor Watts, 'that can restore those values and renew in vital faith a shattered world. Potentially in this Synod, and in the many churches we represent, there is enough power if we are ready to seize it, not only to shatter complacency but bring to pass a revolution in many communities.

'To refuse it – as sons and daughters of John Wesley – is to be recreant in these sombre, yet hopeful, days.'

The Mayor went on to say that there came the clear call to the Church to restore the years that the locusts had eaten.

'It is the time for the Church to be the challenger rather than the challenged,' he emphasised. (*C & E* 15/5/46)

BOROUGH CRIMES RECORD BUT NO RISE IN GRAVER OFFENCES

Although Northampton Borough Police had to deal last year with the greatest number of crimes ever reported in the town, the Chief Constable, Mr John Williamson, is able in his report for 1945 to hand one bouquet to the population.

'In spite of the presence of large numbers of Dominion troops as well as Allied troops, together with all the other branches of our armed Forces trained and stationed in the town and district, the criminal statistics during the year show a state of things which is creditable not only to those temporarily among us, but to the citizens generally,' he states.

'There may have been an increase in the number of crimes as records show, but happily there has been no increase in the number of grave crimes of the type known generally as offences against the person.'

Similarly, in spite of the increase in the consumption of drink, there had been no increase in drunkenness during the year. (*C & E* 28/2/46)

HANDSOME APOLOGY

'The Mayor of Northampton Has instantly stamped on Attacks on Northampton's good name, Which give her the first place In records of crime and ill-fame.'

In verse the Daily Herald has made handsome apology to Northampton, victim of the label 'wickedest city' pasted up by the London daily the other week.

In 'Isn't it a shime', Scorpio, with mock humility, wipes the slate clean. I give two further verses:

'She's as clean as a whistle,

Compared, say, with Bristol,
As regards anti-social misdeeds,
And she reckons it's hard if
She stands worse than Cardiff,
Or Manchester, Reading and Leeds.

Northampton's committee
Thinks it more than a pity
That their town gets a kick in the . . . pants
She is shocked, shamed and stricken
When muckrakers pick on
Northampton, the pride of Northants.'
(*C & E* 26/3/46)

JUVENILE CRIME BEGINS AT HOME
HOW ST FAITH'S REFORMS GIRLS

'I take it that all of us here today would say that we are a respectable audience. We are not going out to buy clothes without coupons, to wander about, or to cause trouble in our own homes. Why are we like that?'

That was the question with which Miss D. Blizzard, speaker at the annual general meeting of St Faith's Home, Northampton, began her talk yesterday.

Miss Blizzard is organising secretary for moral welfare work in Birmingham.

She answered her question by saying that it was because of the homes they had when they were young. Over 60 % of juvenile delinquents came from unsatisfactory or broken homes.

'There is no good in thinking that education was going to take the place of the parent,' she said.

Pointing out that matrimonial disturbances were one of the causes of problem children, she asked her audience to consider the advisability of giving an opportunity for reconciliation, once divorce proceedings had been started, instead of as now, keeping husband and wife apart.

'FORCED MARRIAGES'

Half the broken marriages, she said, were 'forced marriages'. It made welfare workers stop to think about urging young people to marry to give a child a name.

'Every child should have the right to a happy home, and the right to both parents,' she declared.

In homes and institutions the first task was to overcome the resentment which the child felt at being ordered there. The real test of a home was how the girls behaved when they left.

Speaking of a recent visit to St Faith's, the Mayor (Councillor Fred A. Watts), who was in the chair, said that however much of a misfit a girl might be elsewhere, there was a place at St Faith's for her. This novel welfare work among girls up to 18 was extremely successful. Over 85 % of the girls leaving the home gave no more trouble.

The Superintendent, Miss E. Leyland Hodges, reported that during 1945 30 girls had been admitted, mostly through the juvenile court. (*C & E* 28/2/46)

MAYOR'S PRAISE OF LICENSEES:
RESPONSIBLE JOB WELL DONE DURING WAR
Tribute to the way the licensed traders of Northampton had conducted themselves during the six difficult years of the war was paid by the Mayor (Councillor Fred A. Watts), speaking at the annual banquet and ball of Northampton branch of the Northamptonshire Licensed Trades Association Ltd. at the Guildhall, Northampton, last night.

Responding to the toast 'Town and Trade of Northampton', the Mayor said licensees carried on their businesses with a sense of responsibility and were opposed to extravagance and excess as evils opposed to social well-being.

Theirs was a business that inevitably was exposed to criticism, but they met it by carefully safeguarding the welfare of the community and of upholding the ideals of sobriety.

They met it also as a prime charge upon a body of men and women who had more moral and physical responsibility than perhaps any other body of traders. (*C & E* 27/3/46)

As mayor, Fred also held the post of Chief Magistrate and several of the cases over which he presided and which were reported in the press, are interesting not only for the post-war crimes they deal with connected with rationing, but for the standards of behaviour which they reflect:

SISTER-BROTHER QUARREL
Elsie Livingstone (52), housewife, 32 Kingswell Street, Northampton, denied at Northampton Borough Magistrates' Court today using obscene language to her brother, to the annoyance of people in Broad Street on November 2nd.

'I admit I got a bit excited', she said, 'but I only called him a dirty blackmailing dog, which he is.'

Mr Bernard Tippleston (Messrs. Dennis, Faulkner, and Alsop), who prosecuted, said that the proceedings had been brought because the brother, Newton Pratt, 46 Lawrence Street, Northampton, was due for demobilisation from the army and wanted to resume his occupation as a horse dealer without interference from his sister.

She was fined £1 and ordered to pay costs.

Magistrates: The Mayor (Councillor Fred A. Watts), Miss M. Prentice, Councillor W.F. Belson, and Mr S. Strickland. (*C & E* 4/1/46)

SEARCH OF HOUSE REVEALED ARMY RATIONS NORTHAMPTON YOUNG MARRIED WOMAN FINED £15
A table at Northampton Borough Magistrates Court today was stocked with a variety of foodstuffs found in a house in South Street, Northampton, and subsequently identified as being Army property from the Military Dispersal Centre, Talavera Camp, Northampton.

In the dock was Doreen Kathleen Carr, a 24-year-old married woman of 5, South Street, Northampton, and she was charged with being in unlawful possession of 24 tins of marmalade pudding, 27 tins of meat and kidney pudding, six tins of vegetable macedoine, one tin of marmalade, 12 tins of jam, 10 tins of fruit, 9 tins of milk, a tin of syrup, 5 tins of sardines, 15 tins of cheese, 17 tins of pork luncheon, 4 tins of steak, 44 lbs of sugar, 6 lbs of tea, 21 lbs of lamb chops, 6 1/2 lbs of currants, 3 tins of pork loaf, 7 lbs of rice, 12 tins of beans and tomato sauce, 3 lbs of butter, 13 lbs of bacon, and 2 pickle jars.

Defendant pleaded guilty through Mr Bernard Tippleston (Messrs. Dennis, Faulkner and Alsop). She was fined £15 and ordered to pay 2 guineas costs.

GIVEN HER BY A CORPORAL

Mr T. Faulkner Gammage (Messrs. Becke, Green and Stops) who prosecuted, said that on January 1, Det.-Sergt. Watson and other civil and military police officers visited defendant's house and in answer to their questions, Carr admitted she had certain goods, which had been given to her by a corporal, and that the corporal was in the adjoining room.

In a subsequent search of the premises the goods were recovered. Carr made a statement in which she admitted that the goods had been given her by an army corporal, who was a cook at Talavera Camp, and that he had brought them to the house as rations, he being a frequent visitor to the premises.

The soldier, Mr Gammage said, had been dealt with by the military authorities. (C & E 21/1/46)

Finally there are miscellaneous, but no less important stories that describe what it was like just to live, find a home, find a job, and grow old in the town in 1946:

BOROUGH 'DARBY & JOANS' PROBLEM 'MORE URGENT WITH AGEING OF POPULATION' – Medical Officer

What is to happen to Northampton 'Darby and Joans', who, without anyone to look after them in their own homes, do not want to be inmates of St Edmunds Hospital?

Some provision for these old people is, says Dr. Stephen Rowland, Borough Medical Officer, in his annual report published today, 'one of the crying needs of the times.'

He says: 'I see no reason to think the want will decrease with the passing of years, but rather that the problem will become more urgent with the ageing of the population.'

The report, which is the last Dr. Rowland, shortly to retire, will publish, covers 82 pages of statistics which deal with health and social services in Northampton from the cradle to the grave.

SLUM CLEARANCE 'MORE URGENT'

Referring to slum clearance, Dr. Rowland says that owing to the great demand for, and slow production of, houses it does not appear possible to start work for some time to come, although the problem has become more urgent.

Inability to get repairs to property done during the last six years, means that houses scheduled for demolition in pre-war years must continue to be occupied. There were 13 cases of known overcrowding involving 102 people at the end of last year.

Turning to tuberculosis, the death-rate for which at 0.72 is 0.1 higher than for England and Wales, the Medical Officer says that 'there is not evidence of any undue incidence of tuberculosis associated with the boot and shoe industry.'

Dr. N.B. Laughton, the Clinical Tuberculosis Officer, in an appendix to the report, says that 'a matter that seems due for reconsideration is the official attitude which stresses the confidential aspect of notification of tuberculosis.

'In general it seems to have been emphasised more than ever in connection with mass radiography. It is difficult to see any real advantage in advocating this secrecy, and certainly it can produce difficulties and lead to evasion.

'To maintain the false stigma of tuberculosis by a hush-hush approach in these days is both unreasonable and unfair.

'It is misleading to imply that if trouble be found it should be kept as a skeleton in the cupboard. Surely the time has come to regard the disease in the same manner as one would any other infectious condition, such as diphtheria.' (*C & E* 23/9/46)

WIFE IN SANATORIUM PRAISES X-RAY SCHEME. CREATON DEVELOPMENTS PLANNED BUT STAFF SHORTAGE SERIOUS
Smiling happily as she sat up in her hospital bed in the corner of the white ward, gay with Christmas festoons, 24-year-old Mrs. Phyllis Titley of 1a Althorp Street, Northampton had a cheery 'Good Morning' for the Mayor and Mayoress of Northampton (Councillor and Mrs. Fred A. Watts) when they visited Creaton sanatorium yesterday.

She had too, a message for the people of Northampton.

For Mrs. Titley, a former Northampton shoe operative and wife of an airman serving in Burma, was found to be suffering from tuberculosis of the right lung when she was x-rayed under the radiography scheme for workpeople in the town a few weeks ago.

Now – less than a month after the examination – Mrs. Titley is responding well to treatment and as a result of the early detection of the disease, doctors are hoping that she will soon be completely fit again.

£3,000 NEW X-RAY EQUIPMENT
The new unit will be fitted with the tomographic apparatus that has recently been perfected, and to describe its effectiveness in detecting disease, Dr. Starkie drew a striking parallel.

Holding up a shilling piece, he said 'The new apparatus can photograph the lettering on a shilling – a great advance on the present equipment, which merely shows shadows on the plate. We must have it for our type of work.'

But there is an unfortunate aspect to the new advancement and improvements. Today, 50 beds in Creaton Sanatorium are empty – unable to be used because of the shortage of nursing staff.

In spite of a long waiting list of patients, and the prospect of more as the radiography scheme detects cases of tuberculosis that may otherwise have lain undiscovered for years, the hospital has been forced to cut down its full complement of 150 patients to about 100. (*C & E* 2/1/46)

(The husband of Fred Watts' niece, Kenneth Harland, who later became Managing Director of A.W. & Sons Ltd., himself suffered from tuberculosis and was treated at Creaton in the early 1970s.)

WIRE-PULLING WILL NOT GET YOU A HOUSE – URGENCY
DECIDES UNDER BOROUGH SCHEME
If you are one of the 4,000 people who are searching for a house in
Northampton, don't think that you can get one from the Town Council by
'wire-pulling'. You won't.

That was the satisfactory conclusion I reached (writes a *Chronicle and
Echo* reporter) last night after accepting an invitation to watch the Housing
Committee at work on one of the most crucial – and most painful aspects of
the great housing problem.

Their task was to select from 4,000 applications the names of tenants-
to-be of the few 'pre-fab' bungalows which will be available in the near
future. There were only 25 names required, and as I watched the six wise
men of Northampton's housing problem at work under the chairmanship of
Councillor S.H. Betts and the guidance of Mr H. Creegan, the housing
manager, I was glad the headache was not mine. (C & E 19/1/46)

AMBITIOUS DALLINGTON FIELDS * GARDEN CITY PLAN; UP TO
1,500 HOUSES, 50 SHOPS, SCHOOLS, CHURCH, INNS, SITES FOR
INDUSTRIES; COLOURED CONCRETE ROADS
Plans for the development of the Dallington Fields estate on Garden City
lines are to be presented to Northampton Town Council tonight.

The scheme provides for between 1,300 and 1,500 dwellings according
to the type adopted, industrial sites, some 50 shops, five schools (two nursery
schools, one infants, one junior and one modern), a church, a cinema, a
clinic, a community centre, a library, and two inns.

Allocation is made of two areas for car parks and a third for a group of
50 private garages.

Committee proposals are:

No road on the estate to have a gradient steeper than one in 20, and if
finished in concrete to be of different colours.

*now called King's Heath

BUS 'RING' ROAD
One main middle 'ring' road, which will be wider than the general housing
roads to permit a bus route, and so laid that all residents are within a short
walking distance of the buses.

Behind the general scheme is an underlying object – to avoid a one-
class community; otherwise a project of this nature could never become a
successful social structure.

It is suggested, therefore, that until building restrictions are relaxed
certain portions of the estate should be undeveloped to allow for the building
of larger types of houses.

COMMUNAL GARDENS
The greater proportion of the dwellings for the moment, it is proposed, will
be grouped in terraces, interspersed with semi-detached blocks of houses,
variety being secured by contrasting the treatment of the exterior of the
blocks and the introduction of different designs.

Each block will have grass garden frontages, common to all, unobstructed by any kind of fences, planted and maintained by the Estates Department, and each house will have its own private garden at the rear. (*C & E* 7/10/46)

MORE GIRLS TAKING UP SCIENCE – SPEECH-DAY COMMENT
The more science is studied by girls the better it will be for the world, argued Mrs Harold Jeffreys, lecturer in mathematics at Girton College, Cambridge, in an address at Northampton School for Girls' speech day yesterday.

An old girl of the school, Mrs Jeffreys recalled the days when she was a pupil there.

'Nowadays', she said, 'girls taking up arts subjects in the colleges of the country surpass the boys, but although the number of girls taking up scientific careers has increased tremendously in the past few years, the majority of those studying science are boys.

'However, I maintain that the greater interest women take in science in the future the more it will be used for the furtherance of useful rather than catastrophic influences.'

She was thanked by the Mayor (Councillor Fred A. Watts) and Councillor W.H. Percival.

TREASURED FLAG
Pointing to a flag over the centre door of the school hall, Miss Millburn, headmistress, in giving her report, said it was one of her most prized possessions. The flag, an old and battered red ensign, was one that the S.S. Sovac had flown throughout all its dangerous journeys during the war. It had been presented to the school in appreciation of all that had been done for the ship since its 'adoption' by the school in the early years of the war.

Mentioning school successes, Miss Millburn said two former pupils had gone to do scientific research work in London.

Miss Millburn welcomed Councillor P.W. Adams, new chairman of the governors, and also welcomed Miss Madge Prentice, an old girl of the school and the only qualified woman solicitor in Northampton, to the board of governors. (*C & E* 15/3/46)

When Fred came to the end of his year in office he cited as two of the most lasting impressions the Victory Day celebrations and the visit of Princess Elizabeth.

In particular he remembered the ceremony of granting the Freedom of the Borough to the Northamptonshire Regiment, which was part of the V-Day programme. The town seems to have been swept up in the excitement of the celebrations. Reading the newspaper articles on the way in which the people of Northampton would be affected by V-Day, there is an overall impression of a well-knit community whose lives relied on such things as public transport, supplies of fresh bread, and the facility of sharing a local butcher's refrigerator in the event of a very hot bank holiday.

There was clearly some who disagreed with celebrating victory, because the promised Peace, Prosperity and Plenty had not materialised. However, Canon Lewis reminded the town that they were still entitled to celebrate their 'resounding victory', for that was what the day was all about.

30. *Freedom of the Borough – The Parade in the Market Square, V-Day. 8/6/46*

V – DAY CAUSES NORTHAMPTON SHOPPING PROBLEM

Victory-Day, since it comes as an extra day's holiday at Whitsuntide, is creating a problem for Northampton housewives, shopkeepers, and other traders.

Bread is one of the greatest difficulties.

Owing to the variety of working hours of the different bakers in the town, the Master Bakers' Association have decided not to impose any special directions in the trade and to leave each baker to work out his own problems.

Mr T.R. Adams, one of the largest distributors in the town, told a Chronicle and Echo reporter that his firm were giving their staff a holiday both on V-Day and Whit-Monday. 'Our last deliveries will, therefore, be on Friday and we shall not deliver again until Tuesday. These arrangements have been carried out before on the occasion when Christmas Day fell on the Saturday.'

M.F.H. Underwood, secretary-manager of Northampton Co-operative Society, said there would be no deliveries either on Saturday or Whit-Monday. 'We have two groups of deliveries,' he added, 'And it will mean that those who receive bread on Thursday will have to take sufficient for their needs until Tuesday, and those who receive their bread on Friday to take in sufficient until Wednesday. If properly looked after by wrapping it up in a cloth, bread will keep moist.'

LONDON TRAINS

On Whit-Monday and Tuesday, with the factories working, the normal times will be observed.

The United Counties expect to run their Saturday services on V-Day with the exception of the workers' services.

'This means', Mr R.G. Howe, traffic manager, said, 'that buses will be leaving all termini just before 8 o'clock in the morning.'

No special trains will be run to London from Castle Station to see the Victory Parade. Ordinary service morning trains are: 4.23, 7.08, 8.00, 8.48, 10.01 and 11.46.

On the same day two special trains will run to Towcester at 11.50 am. and 12.22 pm.

DECORATED VEHICLES PARADE

A parade of decorated vehicles is part of Northampton's plans for V-Day celebrations, and the Chronicle and Echo has now been asked by the V-Day committee to receive entries.

Entries for all types of vehicles must be received at the Chronicle and Echo office before next Thursday morning.

The various classes will be judged by the Mayor and women members of the V-Day committee.

It is hoped that vehicles will be decorated during the week before the parade, to give the town a festive appearance. (*C & E* 30/5/46)

OPINION as my correspondence has demonstrated, remains divided on the subject of V-Day. To celebrate or not? What a vexed question it is. We have decided to celebrate, wisely I believe. We can, in these austere days, do with a day devoted to colour and pageantry and celebration.

And, as is pointed out by Canon J. Trevor Lewis (Vicar of All Saints):

'The people have won a Resounding Victory.

'It is much to be regretted,' goes on Canon Lewis, 'that there is no unanimity of public opinion on the subject. The cynics and pessimists have made free use of their opportunity. We were promised Peace, we were promised Prosperity, we were promised Plenty, and where are these things, say they, what is there to rejoice at, what calls for hilarity and jubilation?

'Well, here are one or two things not to be forgotten:

'The people have won a Resounding Victory.' (*C & E* 4/6/46)

RAIN DID NOT BAFFLE VICTORY CROWDS

NORTHAMPTON CELEBRATIONS TOOK PLACE INDOORS

Rain, rain, rain. After the ceremony on the Market Square on Saturday when the Freedom of the Borough was presented to the Northamptonshire Regiment, it must have seemed to the visitor to Northampton that V-Day had 'had it'.

But in celebration of V-Day, Northampton scored a victory in its own right – a victory over weather that was even more gloomy than the forebodings of the most pessimistic.

Alternative arrangements were the key to Northampton's victory on V-Day. Although the promised fine weather did not materialise, the dampness outside did not penetrate into various halls in the town, where people gathered and enjoyed themselves.

GLUM FACES SOON SMILED

Gladstone Terrace was the, proud winners of the street decorating competition. Arrangements had been made for a street tea party, but when Mr J. Cooper, transport manager, appeared to take the winners on a tour of other decorated streets, he was met with glum faces.

Residents took him into the back room of a little shop at the end of the street and showed him all the food that had been collected for the tea party that was not going to take place because no inside accommodation could be found. This was one round to the weather.

'Don't worry,' said Mr Cooper, who at once sent down to the transport depot for buses.

And the end of the round meant a complete k.o. for the weather. The whole party was moved lock, stock and barrel to the recreation-room of the transport depot.

The Mayoral party heard of this, and promptly went to the transport depot. But when they got there the children had just left for a tour. . . .

CROWD ENJOYS FIREWORKS
Then when darkness had come, there were fireworks – such a display as Northampton had not seen for years and a bonfire was lighted in Towcester Road.

During one and three quarter hours, Northampton Borough lost £200 while some 500 fireworks were exploded, and the drifting smoke rendered the work of the police more difficult in stopping the small boys who insisted in swooping from beneath barriers to carry off the 'empties' in triumph.

As the display began, the crowds grew in size. By 10.30 the area round the firing base was surrounded by a dense mass of people.

Roads round the park were crowded with cars and bicycles.

With showers of 'golden rain' spraying on to the river, large rockets and 'phantoms and shrapnels' soared into the sky, scattering red, white and green stars.

It was nearly midnight when the display ended with six victory flares lighting the sky. (*C & E* 10/6/46)

The visit of Princess Elizabeth was made at the end of July and it centred on the General Hospital where the new Barratt Maternity Home had been recently opened and where tribute was to be paid to all the towns and villages of the area who had contributed to the War Memorial Appeal for £250,000. (This was a fund set up nearly 2 years previously to increase the number of hospital beds, and update the hospital services.) The visit concluded with the Princess opening Grendon Hall as a county youth centre.

CHEERING WELCOME FOR THE PRINCESS
NORMAL TALKS WITH CHILDREN AND MOTHERS AT HOSPITAL
Northampton fell in love today with Princess Elizabeth. Paying her first official visit to the town, the Princess, with graciousness, charm of manner, and lively interest in the programme arranged for her gave to what might have been a formal occasion a happy informality.

That was the characteristic note of the whole visit – and that which Northampton will remember most of all.

There was a smile and an interested word for everyone who was presented to her or to whom she chatted while making her tour of inspection.

Northampton showed its warm affection for the Princess with the enthusiastic welcome it gave to her.

From the borough boundary to the General Hospital, the way of her car was flanked with cheering citizens and children waving flags, and at the main gates of the hospital thousands of people were waiting for the arrival of the Royal visitor.

When the Princess entered the forecourt of the hospital the large crowds surged across Cheyne Walk and Billing Road, swarming around the main gates to try and get another glimpse of the Princess before she went into the hospital, where she presented souvenir cards to commemorate meeting the target figure for the Hospital War Memorial Appeal Fund.

CROWD SURGES ACROSS ROAD

It was five minutes past the half-hour when the Royal car, pennant waving in the strong breeze and with headlamps full on, had come into view.

The Chief Constable's car which had been parked higher up the road, beyond the Hardingstone turn, slowly moved off, with police motor-cycle escort ahead, and preceded the Royal car over the Borough boundary for the first official visit of Princess Elizabeth to Northampton.

Little could be seen of Princess Elizabeth, but nevertheless the crowd went wild, and surged across the road to leave a barely sufficient channel for the vehicles.

Flags waved, women blew kisses, and the men raised their hats as the cars continued down the London Road, picking up to 30 mph where the crowds had thinned out.

At Bridge Street level crossing the crowds in their hundreds started cheering.

When the Princess' car swung into Victoria Promenade, spectators lined the road in depth, but here and into Cheyne Walk up to the Hospital the cars had a clear run, as the pavements had been roped off to prevent expected wild surges in an endeavour to obtain an even better close-up of the Royal visitor.

PRINCESS AMONG THE CHILDREN

The walk from the nurses' home towards the children's ward and Barratt Maternity Home was in contrast to the distinguished gathering in the festooned hall where the Royal visitor had shaken hands over 100 times.

It was in miniature a perfect cameo of the general welcome Northamptonshire had given her today. From the Billing Road cheers arose as the crowd glimpsed the Princess returning again amid the avenue of nurses, with the background of geraniums and dahlias. Behind the nurses, stood under a tree a group of dungareed workmen, as enthusiastic as watchers from the roadside, roof, and bedecked balcony of the Crocket Ward.

And it was in the children's ward and the Maternity Home, surely, that the day's happiest scenes were enacted. There were still the lines of visitors, but there were also the children whose ages ranged from five days to eight and nine years.

Outside the children's ward in a lovely retreat made lovelier by warm

31. Fred and Princess Elizabeth (1946).

sunshine, lay 14 children with their favourite story books, their dolls and teddy bears. Some were very wide-awake as they opened big eyes to gaze at the 'beautiful Princess Charming in blue', as one nurse described her later. But there will be some disappointments for, unaware of their visitor, one or two children slept happily in the warm sun.

One tiny tot, answering to the name of George, did his best to smile when the Princess leaned over the cot and asked him about the toy he hugged so tightly, but shyness and sickness were too strong.

Charming everyone with her radiant smile as she entered the Maternity wards, the Princess showed at once that this was no formal visit. She was very interested; and she showed it in her demeanour as she leaned over cots in which reposed babies born only a few days ago and spoke to their mothers. (*C & E* 30/7/46)

The final days of Fred's time as mayor were marked by several speeches given at various occasions – at Northampton's Men's Own, the name-day celebration at All Saints Church, the planting of a tree in Abington Park, and the very last engagement for Fred and his wife – the Autumn Fair at Holy Trinity Church.

MAYOR TURNS BACK THE PAGES
MAN WHOSE DOG LICENCE HE PAID
As fascinating as flicking back the pages of a snapshot album was a talk given to Northampton Men's Own, at the Central Hall, Abington Square, by the Mayor (Councillor Fred A. Watts) yesterday afternoon.

Accompanied by the Mayoress (Mrs Watts), the Mayor spoke of his year of office, and at the end he envisaged that we were becoming so used to wearing the shackles of controls that the freedom of spirit would become endangered too.

Chief impressions of the Mayor's year of office, rapidly drawing to a close, were the ceremonial of the Freedom to the Northamptonshire Regiment, his visit to Plymouth to welcome back Northampton's adopted ship the Loch Insh, after two and a half years' away from home waters, Princess Elizabeth's visit in the summer, and a service for deaf and dumb people which he attended.

BROKEN IN SPIRIT
He was deeply impressed with the welcome home to prisoners-of-war, 'men broken in spirit and bruised in body, and still not used to the new-old life',

as well as the entertaining of 400 children, 'whose mothers came to fetch them home, but their fathers alas, were absent.'

But among the grave there was a leavening of the gay. Even though his term as chief magistrate was often unpleasant, there were bright interludes, and the Mayor told on one occasion when a man, summoned for not having a dog licence, said that he could not afford it.

'If you will pay the fine, I will buy the licence,' the Mayor told him. The delinquent promised to pay the fine of 7s 6d in a few days.

He did, and the Mayor kept his side of the bargain, but on the next Court day he was handed a message from the dog owner, thanking him for his action and saying: 'If the Mayor likes to come down --- Street any night after dark he can always have a rabbit.'

PRINCESS' VISIT

'I have had an easy time,' he said referring to his chairmanship in the Council Chamber. Occasionally one or two councillors had to be kept in order, but otherwise it had been a single task. His function had been to conduct the business without bias or prejudice.

To be the Mayor was almost a full-time job. There were many traditional engagements to be carried out, such as the welcoming of the Judge at the Assizes and the Recorder at the Quarter Sessions. Incidentally the Recorder was the only person who preceded the Mayor into Court.

After referring to the granting of the Freedom of the Borough to the Northamptonshire Regiment on Victory Day, the Mayor spoke of Princess Elizabeth's visit as an 'unofficial one' but one 'in which everybody seemed to take part'.

He said that the Princess was 'one of the most gracious personalities of her age that one could possibly meet'.

Of the well-known celebrities he had met, the Mayor singled Dr. Joad and Freddie Grisewood, the broadcaster, and he mentioned that he had welcomed to the town Dutch children, Swedish delegates and Welsh girls in industry.

RIVAL CREEDS

On the subject of the two ideologies – or creeds, as he preferred to call them – which elevated man, or regarded the individual as a worm and of no account Canon Lewis preached with all his accustomed cogency and vigour. As he knew England and the people of this country, they would never be a party to the dethronement of God, which meant the dethronement and debasement of man.

And so to an expression of the 'grace of gratitude' to the Mayor, the officials who so rarely got their proper credit and reward, and all concerned with the good government of Northampton. As for the Mayor – 'If what Northampton wanted in its Mayor was a man of character and personality, prepared to spend and be spent for a period of twelve months for the benefit of the town and its citizens, then the town had had this in Councillor Frederick Watts.' He knew the Mayor would hate him to say it, but in his view the Mayor followed in the train of the saints who gave their name to the church.

The Vicar spoke his final sentences direct to the Mayor. It was an impressive tribute from the pulpit, well-deserved, fitted to the occasion, perhaps unique, and notable too in that it came from an Anglican vicar to a Nonconformist layman.

A double-flowering pink cherry tree – the first to be planted by a Mayoress in Abington Park – was 'dug in' by Mrs Fred A. Watts yesterday afternoon to commemorate her year of office.

It was the 27th tree to be planted in a Northampton park by a retiring Mayoress. But yesterday's was almost a co-operative effort. Mrs. Watts had the help, in her horticultural task, of five other holders of her office, the Mayor, two ex-Mayors and members of the Council. The Mayor's Chaplain (the Rev. H. Tyler Lane) and the Mayor's Sergeant (Mr W. F. Floyd) were also present.

The Mayor paid tribute to his wife for her 'self-sacrificing year of office', and Councillor Cyril Chown, congratulating both the Mayor and Mayoress, spoke of their 'strenuous and very fine year'. . . .

The Parks Superintendent (Mr J.J. McIntosh) tells me, incidentally, that the 27 trees planted have been nine beech trees, two oak, one acacia, one Indian bean, two mountain ash, two silver birch, one tulip tree, two witch hazel, one magnolia, one Judas tree, two maple, one bird cherry, one mulberry, and yesterday's double-flowering pink cherry tree.

Councillor Fred A. Watts, Northampton's retiring Mayor, told an audience at the Holy Trinity Church Autumn Fair yesterday: 'This is positively my last engagement, and I feel as though I am a condemned man awaiting execution.'

Councillor Watts said that the happiest moments of his Mayoralty had been spent among people of the churches.

'I have not had one unhappy day as Mayor of this town,' he said, 'and looking back I must admit that a great deal of my success has been due to the fine partner that my wife has been to me.'

As parting gifts from the organisers of the fair the Mayor was presented with a large tin of tobacco by Mr W. Butcher, a sidesman, and the Mayoress received a bouquet from three year old David Hollowell. (*C & E* 10/46)

The pleasure with which Fred looked back on the year 1946 must have been matched by his happiness at seeing the firm of A. Watts & Sons Ltd. celebrate its jubilee in the same year – 50 years of continued success in business.

The jubilee dinner coincided with the retirement of two employees who between them had been with the firm for a total of 88 years – Mr A. F. Adams, the chief cashier, and Mr F.G. Soloman, under-manager. The two men were honoured at the dinner by a presentation from the Watts family and from the staff.

One of the speeches was given by the President of the Chamber of Trade, Mr W. Cowper Barrons, who of course congratulated the firm on the attainment of its jubilee. The rising tide of socialism that was sweeping the country provided the background for the theme of his speech:

'There have been remarks made at the present time about the merits or otherwise of private enterprise. Opponents of private enterprise can see in the Watts firm that there is something warm, real, vivid and human in that

32. Fred planting a tree in Abington Park (Nov. 1946).

enterprise.

'There is, however, no such thing as private enterprise. It is 'individual enterprise', and in the Watts firm it is not individual but 'mutual enterprise'. Fred also seemed haunted by the spectre of socialism with its opposition to private enterprise, and by memories of the restrictions endured by everyone during the War. In replying to Mr Barrons' toast he remarked that

The success which has come to the firm since its early days is due to the work of my father and the staff he gathered round him.

The new generation growing up is accustomed to shackles and controls, and there is a danger that it might look upon controls as part of its normal life because it has known nothing different.

There is only one logical conclusion to the ending of a certain pathway set out before us, and we shall have to fight again for the freedom which we had once. (*C & E* 5/11/46)

So by the end of 1946 Fred's 'political interlude' as Mayor of Northampton was over. He had made his mark as a caring and religious man. Throughout his year as mayor he had kept an album of cuttings depicting the various local events and debates in which he had been involved. Fifty years on, these cuttings present more than mementos of one individual's experiences; they can conjure up for people in the 1990s a vivid picture of what life was like in Northampton just after the end of the Second World War.

From local politics Fred could now turn his attention to the future of his business in Kettering, and later of his church at Queens Road , Northampton.

Chapter V
Francis Watts and Kettering in the
Post-War Years

Even though Fred had set up his own company in Kettering and Wellingborough, he still remained a co-director with his brother of A. Watts & Sons Ltd. of Northampton. By the end of the 1940s he was only going into the Kettering shop twice a week, leaving it largely in the capable hands of his son Francis and his manager, Norman Thompson. His involvement with the White House must have seemed less relevant as the years went by, and in the late forties Fred made several important decisions affecting his life.

Firstly he made a complete break with Northampton in 1948, leaving Ewart in sole charge of the White House. A year later he stepped out of local politics when he finished his service as a councillor and as a Justice of the Peace. He had been elected in 1940 as the Liberal representative of Kingsley ward and after his year as Mayor, had served as Deputy Mayor in 1947. Then in the same year – 1948 – he moved out of Epworth, the home he had had built back in 1923 in the buoyant days of the firm's expansion. With his wife and youngest daughter, he moved to a house in Greenfield Avenue, not far away, off the Kettering Road.

As in the case of his brother, his energies for work in local affairs, whether political or otherwise, seem boundless. The *Northampton Independent* ran a series on prominent local citizens entitled 'They Confess'. The magazine chose to interview Fred for the series as a way of expressing Northampton's gratitude for his services to the borough. Four years later Fred was to receive another honour: largely for his work in the National Savings movement he was awarded an MBE in the New Year Honours list in 1959.

In the *Independent* article the list of Fred's offices and activities is a long one. The twenty questions posed provide a more amusing insight into his life:

FRIENDSHIP IS HIS MAIN CONCERN
 He was president of the Northampton Rotary Club and Mayor of the Borough at the same time, the only instance of such a duality on local record.
 His other offices and activities include past president of the Y.M.C.A., and Northampton Chamber of Trade and the County Ground Bowling Club; past chairman, Youth Employment Committee; many years member of now

defunct Public Assistance Committee; life-long Methodist and local preacher for over 30 years. He is now chairman of Northampton Savings Committee. President of Good Samaritan Society and for the past nine years, chairman of Governors, Northampton School for Girls. He is also vice-chairman of the Local Valuation Court; vice-chairman of Northampton Municipal Charities, vice-president of the Men's Own and vice-president of the Northampton County Cricket Club.

With an expression of Northampton's gratitude for his services to the borough, we present the answers to our 20 questions of
MR FRED A. WATTS.

1. What is your earliest memory?
Being dressed in a bluey-green velvet suit with a lace collar and with thick pants that were much too tight.

2. What was your best subject at school?
Mathematics.

3. What was your worst?
Chemistry.

4. If you had not undertaken your present career what would you have chosen and why?
The Law! Its interests are so varied and advocacy is fascinating.

5. What is your favourite dish?
Duck and green peas, followed by apple pie, like my mother used to make, and plenty of clotted cream.

6. What is your favourite drink, alcoholic or otherwise?
Tea, hot, sweet and strong enough to allow the spoon to stand upright.

7. If you smoke, which do you prefer, cigarettes or pipe, and why?
A pipe – it's a SMOKE.

8. What is your favourite colour?
Maroon.

9. What form of holiday do you enjoy most and why?
Motoring to the French or Cornish coast – with time to stop and stare.

10. What is your favourite recreation?
Motoring, bowls , billiards.

11. What are your pet aversions?
Meanness in thought and deed. Intolerance. Crooning.

12. What is your special hobby, if any?
Collecting Wesleyana.

13. Have you a secret ambition?
Yes! To be known as a friend.

14. What and when was your most anxious moment?
In 1911. Being helpless to assist my bride of three days when in a perilous position on the Cornish rocks and knowing that a false step might mean death.

15. What single thing would you most like to own?
A quiet mind.

16. What type of reading do you most enjoy?
Autobiography, philosophy.

17. What single human quality do you most admire?
Loyalty to friends and ideals.

18. **By what animal or bird are you most attracted and why?**
The dog. He knows more than he can express.
19. **What experience would you most dread?**
A friendless and unloved old age.
20. **What question in this list did you find most difficult to answer?**
Number 4. (*N.I.* 17/6/55)

Fred's son, Francis, shouldered most of the responsibility for F.A. Watts & Co. Ltd. in Gold Street. In the promising days of the 1950s he could not foresee the battles that lay ahead or the turbulent changes and developments that would sweep the quiet country town of Kettering.

Hard work lay behind the success of Watts in Kettering. In the evenings at home Francis would read the local paper and note down engagements, births, planning applications. . . . The people involved would then receive a Watts leaflet or a call with the offer of any help they might need in furnishing their new house, nursery, or extension.

Every year, about three months before Christmas, Francis would create a gift section in the shop. In the furniture trade it was difficult to benefit from the Christmas rush to buy presents, but small items such as glasses, ash trays, tea-trolleys, nests of tables – these sold well, and so they were included in the annual gift section.

The window was treated as 'the eyes of the shop'. Window-dressing was quite an art in those days and one which Francis feels has sadly declined now:
'In Kettering, if we didn't sell something out of the window, we thought there was something wrong! . . . People would take a whole dining suite setting out of the window and say "Yes, we'll have that. Would you deliver it on Saturday?" Or a bedroom suite – anything like that. We had a Mr Pitt working for us then. He was wonderful at dressing the window.'

Above all the human touch was the aspect of the business in which Francis had greatest faith.
'If you've got a nice pleasing manner, you'll sell anything. If you're really nice to a customer, no matter what it is – if you're friendly, people will react, won't they?'

Even the van drivers were seen as important. When delivering goods a customer might say:
'"I'm thinking about a corner cabinet to go here," or something like that, and the van driver would say "We've just the very thing." I always say the van driver's just as important as the salesman. They are the last people who see the customer.'

When Fred visited the shop, Francis as well as the staff might find themselves subject to his critical eye.
'If there was one thing my father couldn't abide it was dirty vans. If he came over to Kettering and saw a dirty van, he'd comment, and we'd say "We've been so busy, we haven't time to clean them." My father always said "A van is a shop's advertising. The success of Adnitts in Northampton was their clean vans. You never saw their vans dirty."'

Norman Thompson remembers Fred's visits:

'We didn't see much of Fred. He was very much "the old head of the household". He used to come in at 11 o'clock in the morning, go and sit down in his office, walk round the shop. You'd got to call him "Sir."'

Prams as well as furniture were still a major item of stock. When one of the reporters from the *Northants Evening Telegraph* had the novel idea of writing a feature on the history of the pram, F.A.Watts & Co. Ltd. were approached, and from the depths of the shop Francis wheeled out what was thought to be the oldest pram in the town, dating from about 1810.

The feature article itself is worth including here as it provides a little known history to this most common and popular of family items – the baby carriage:

FASHIONS HAVE CHANGED SINCE THE WOODEN WHEELED PERAMBULATORS

Of every 100 babies born, fifty will want a brand-new pram or push-chair. The other fifty will make do with one handed down from an elder brother, sister, or cousin, or will ride round in a second-hand baby carriage.

This is one trade estimate, and be the numbers high or low, the pram business is a sizeable one, as can be seen from the figures for births in these counties during the December quarter.

There were 1,217 new babies in Northamptonshire, 2,371 in Leicestershire, and 1,094 in Bedfordshire.

Altogether there are 3,000,000 prams and push-chairs in use in Britain, some of them 40 years old and still going strong.

1910 MODEL

In country districts an old pram is a proud possession. Within the last few weeks a 1910 pram was sent in from Rutland to Kettering – to be upholstered ready for a new baby.

The Royal Family has set a fashion for using handed-down prams.

Princes Charles and Princess Anne have both been wheeled out in the pram used for Princess Elizabeth and Princess Margaret when they were babies.

First recorded prams in Britain were built for Lady Georgina Cavendish in 1780. A coachbuilder made them on the lines of miniature horse carriages.

Preserved at Chatsworth, they have ironshod wooden wheels, fine linen upholstery, and leather canopies. One has a body like a bronze scalloped shell, and uses the snakes of the Cavendish crest to attach the springs.

It was so heavy that it had to be drawn by a pony.

LIKE CARTS

Most people began buying prams about 1840. They were built like carts and rumbled over the bumpy pavements, pulled by mother or nurse.

Carts which could be pushed, developed because it was easy for the baby to fall out of the earlier type unobserved, or for thieves to steal its blankets.

These cumbersome vehicles were three-wheelers with wooden wheels, flat rims and no springs. Even in 1850 there were only four pram-making firms in the whole country.

The big advance came exactly 100 years ago, when prams were shown at the Great Exhibition, and at once became popular. By 1856 there were more than 20 pram manufacturers in London alone.

ITS NAME

Springs were fitted in 1873, when prams still had three wheels. Then came cycle-type wheels, increased use of steel, rubber tyres, the folding pram and the introduction of light alloys.

The perambulator has stolen its title from something that had nothing to do with babies. In the Peninsular War, British Army surveyors pushed along wheels mounted at the end of handles.

Connected to geared counters, the wheels measured how far the troops marched, and were called perambulators.

It was because of their resemblance to these instruments and lack of a better name that early baby-carts were christened perambulators too.

Pram fashions vary. In Bedford, say stockists, folding prams are very much more popular than coachbuilt models because they take up less room and are handier for travel.

In Northamptonshire relative popularity is estimated at 50-50. And in Scotland, Wales and Cornwall women still carry their babies in shawls.

(*N. E. T.* 27/7/51)

As always the routine of shop life was enlivened by the characters who became customers:

'We had a farmer who lived outside of Kettering and we'd supplied him – £800 it was, which was a lot of money in those days. He rang me up and said "If you'll meet me in a certain cafe in the town, I'll pay you in notes." So we duly turned up at this cafe and he paid £800 in notes. It had a funny smell. It was wrapped in the dirtiest newspaper you ever saw. He'd got it out of his attic – it was chicken money – cash he'd made from selling chickens and eggs on the side.'

Another unusual customer was a man from Corby who became extremely enthusiastic about Ercol furniture. Ercol is a firm that began in High Wycombe, Buckinghamshire, as William Skull & Sons. They made their furniture out of temperate climate woods – elm, beech and ash, and had only a limited number of outlets. Francis was also very enthusiastic about the exclusive quality of the Ercol name and tried to persuade A. Watts & Sons Ltd. in Northampton to open up an account as well.

It is Norman who remembers in particular the man from Corby:

'He got the Ercol bug. You had to wait 10-12 months for a piece, but a lot of the furniture was like that. Eventually we thought we'd really go for it and have a show – if you stocked a fair bit, you had preferential deliveries.

This man bought one or two bits and he kept coming in all the time. I think his house was full of Ercol – so much so that he wanted a new corner piece making.

Now Ercol don't make things for anybody, but I said I'd see what I could do. He gave me all the dimensions. After badgering Ercol for a couple of months they agreed to make it – he was tickled pink. Of course every time he came in he had his 10% discount. We knew he'd always come back.

33. Francis Watts (1951).

In the end there were many people in Ercol who knew this customer.

By the time we'd got a show of it, we could get most things within 6-8 weeks – we were able to shift it, you see. That was brought about because Ercol started pruning their outlets. We had it in Kettering and that was it.'

Francis remembers that reproduction furniture in general was making a comeback in those early days after the war. Veneers in mahogany, yew and walnut were popular. Although teak is a finish which is now very familiar, he recalls that it was only in 1947 that this particular wood became popular. The heavy oak furniture of the 1930s was no longer in fashion.

Francis worked hard building up the Kettering shop into a thriving business. He must have inherited his family's boundless energy for serving their local community, for he was not only a Borough Councillor from 1952-1964, he was a member of the Kettering Divisional Education Executive Committee and a governor of Kettering Grammar and High Schools. He founded the Kettering Round Table and belonged to the Kettering Chamber of Trade and Commerce. While a borough councillor he served on the Town Development, the Library and Arts, and the Plans and Licences and Buildings Committees. It is not surprising that in 1961 he was elected to serve the town as Mayor – a year of which he and his wife have many happy memories.

In 1962 when he returned to the politics of the Council meetings, he realised that his position was becoming awkward and unsatisfactory. It was at about this time that plans were being discussed for the development of Kettering town centre. As a local shop keeper directly affected by these plans, he was not able to join in the debate or vote, and so he decided to resign.

Within a few years he was again standing for election, but this time for Northamptonshire County Council.

'At that time the County Council was pretty non-political, which I liked. The Borough had been quite involved in party politics, which I wasn't so keen on because if you want to represent a ward, you want to represent the interests of Kettering. Political activity doesn't help the affairs of local people very much.'

For twelve years Francis served on the County Council and became involved in the Planning and Library Committees.

34. Gold Street looking West (1950s).

What were these plans which led to Francis resigning from the Borough Council? What events led up to the day in 1975 when Francis would stand on his shop doorstep and see bulldozers razing the next door properties to the ground?

The story of the development of Kettering's town centre is a story of angry debate, dramatic pleas and equally dramatic destruction. What happened in Kettering mirrors what has happened in hundreds of towns all over the country, including Northampton. What happened to F.A. Watts & Co. reflects what has happened to too many independent traders. It is a story worth remembering, and one which is remarkably captured in Tony Ireson's book 'Old Kettering and Its Defenders', to which I am indebted for much of what follows:

In the late Victorian era the architectural firm of Gotch & Saunders designed what became known as the Old Post Office building on Gold Street. It was of a red terracotta colour with stone pilasters, ornamented with large oriel windows on the first floor. The frontage was gently curved, highly decorated, and included some exotic gable ends.

The building consisted of the post office and several other shops. An archway led through an arcade to the small lanes of Richards Leys, Tanners Lane, Bakehouse Lane and Northall Street. The shopkeepers lived over their shops in ample accommodation designed for large families and their servants.

At the western end of the building stood another of Gotch & Saunders' designs – the Victoria Hall, which was opened in 1888. In 1907 the hall became a full-time professional theatre and by 1920 it had been transformed into the latest kind of entertainment – a cinema. The Odeon chain soon acquired the

35. Gold Street looking West (1970s).

property and covered the Victorian stonework with green and black tiles. Right up until the 1950s the cinema queues would stretch up Gold Street, but with the coming of television the cinema was turned into a bingo hall, and was eventually closed. The hall's use promised to turn full circle when there was a move to re-open it as a town theatre. Other plans, however, forced the idea to be abandoned.

The dozen acres or so behind this northern side of Gold Street consisted of a higgledy-piggledy pattern of small roads and alleys that followed the lines of ancient paths and cart-ways. It had once been densely populated and had seen the start of much of Kettering's early industrial development.

In the 1920s and 1930s the top of Gold Street (the eastern end) was the busiest spot in Kettering, being the junction with Silver Street, Montagu Street and Newland Street. The route from this junction down Gold Street and along the High Street to the Northampton Road became known as 'the bunny run', for it was here that courting couples would parade up and down. Police even found it necessary to move on any young couples who stopped to talk in shop doorways.

Kettering's main streets were full of shops run by family firms and its back streets were well served with general shops owned by local people. Gold Street was once described as 'a throbbing artery of town life' frequented even in the evenings by lively sociable crowds. Even up to the early 1960s Kettering town centre looked much as it had done fifty years earlier. It had been a market town for 700 years and had grown with the development of its shoe-making industry. However, the 1960s and 1970s brought an upheaval that affected town centres all over Britain. The new fashion was for shopping malls, tower blocks, pedestrian precincts, multi-storey car-parks and ring-roads.

36. Francis as mayor of Kettering with his wife Jean (1961).

In 1960 proposals were revealed for the redevelopment of the centre of Kettering — based on the rectangle formed by Gold Street, Newland Street, Lower Street and Northall. Proponents of the scheme said that trade in the town had tended to run down because of the lack of any development. Shoppers would be encouraged to return to Kettering if redevelopment took place. There was even a scheme to alter the market square, although this was finally abandoned.

Objectors to the proposals said that Kettering could not support the amount of shops involved in the development. Success relied on out-of-town shoppers who would no longer come once neighbouring towns had their own shopping centres. Kettering already had 276 existing shops.

It was not long before people everywhere were having second thoughts about comprehensive development. Ted Rowlands M.P. wrote an important letter to the Times on the 23 August, 1969 which conjures up a striking vision of what town centres should become:

Certainly in many town centre schemes there has been no attempt to measure the real need for more shops. The result has been social chaos. The important fact is that town centre land is precious to the community — by definition it is strictly limited. Empty or under-used supermarkets waste land really needed for centrally situated homes, schools, colleges, art centres, youth organisations, community centres, churches, chapels and theatres. There is something wrong with a society that squeezes out these social amenities to make way for empty or unnecessary shops.

Over the last 5 years a glorious opportunity has presented itself to realise a vision of the new town centre as a hub of the community's total activities — alive after 6pm, providing a complete range of activities desirable in modern social living. Instead, what have we been given? A concrete wasteland of unwanted shops and offices.

How angry we should be with a society that has fouled up the opportunity of creating a worthwhile urban environment.

The Old Post Office was earmarked for demolition. It was held in affection by

37. Pram display in the Gold Street shop (1953).

shopkeepers as well as the public. Francis quite naturally felt deeply concerned. He also felt ignored, accusing the Council of overlooking the local firms whose members had devoted their time and interest to town affairs. The Council was seen as going out of its way to assist the multiples. One of the biggest criticisms was that the Council had in fact kept the local shopkeepers in the dark, and that improvements could not now be made to local businesses because of the threat of demolition.

Since 1902 one of the old shops next to F.A. Watts & Co. Ltd. had been J. Stanley & Sons, a leather goods shop now owned by Mr W.J. Cavell. He remarked

'It will be such a pity if we have to leave – this shop has atmosphere. The question is – do Kettering people want small shops giving personal service, or multiple firms? Small traders will find it difficult to carry on if they have to move and pay high rents.'

The debate became so intense that a public inquiry was held in 1972. The local traders pointed out that the shops in the Old Post Office building were not obsolete – they were solidly built and well suited to modern trading if rear access was provided. They had good basement storage and a generous ceiling height. The proponents of the redevelopment scheme suggested that the building had been spoilt in its central section because the terracotta had been covered in white paint. Francis Watts was quick to promise to remove the paint if the building was retained, explaining that the paint had been put on to mark the coronation.

1975 was to be European Architectural Heritage Year and the Kettering Civic Society emphasised this point when trying to muster support from the government. They claimed that the enclave of buildings north of Gold Street and including Beech House, Mission House and all the old gardens, was worth preserving, restoring and landscaping as a fitting contribution to European Architectural Heritage Year. A letter was written to the Prime Minister Edward Heath, with copies to Harold Wilson and local M.P.'s, but the appeal failed. The historic heart of Kettering seemed doomed.

In contrast to the lack of political support – when the Civic Society wrote to Sir John Betjeman about the proposals in 1972, he gave as much support as he could:

"It is hard to believe after all the warnings we have had against shoddy, greedy development that anything as reactionary and unimaginative as the development plan you have sent me could have been proposed. I am an admirer of the works of Gotch and of the remaining old buildings of Kettering, which give the town a distinction which Northampton itself is losing. Fight on, and good luck with your campaign."

In 1974 the bulldozers moved in. The public inquiry and the various appeals had failed to change the Council's plans for redevelopment.

One of the Watts salesmen, Gordon Hardy, remembers the frustration and disbelief at what was going on around Gold Street:

'They knocked down the original old Grammar School property which was near the corner of Bakehouse Hill and Gold Street – it was a beautiful old ivory coloured stone building. It was there on Saturday night and gone by Monday morning. No-one publicised that it was going to be demolished. It was knocked down while people were at church.'

The old stone building of Beech House was another of the first to be destroyed, in the initial phase of the scheme. The Old Post Office buildings were next, but demolition was postponed until finance for Phase 2 had been arranged. Most of the businesses in the Old Post Office building had moved out by September of that year, but F.A. Watts & Co. Ltd. were still holding out . Francis was quoted as saying:

'Customers are appalled by the inconvenience we are experiencing, and the disruption of our business, but we are going to carry on as long as we can.'

That month the old Odeon cinema was demolished and three months later work was started on gutting the empty shops alongside Watts. Francis had been warned that the Council meant to start building the new shopping centre on 1 March, but he obstinately continued to carry on trading. It was only the threat of legal proceedings to evict him that led him to yield in 1975.

'We moved out and the next day the padlocks were put on. I was just making it difficult for them. We were the largest freeholder. We hadn't got a leg to stand on, but I didn't feel adequately compensated. We'd had a public inquiry lasting a week and I made my feelings very well known, but they'd made their mind up that they were going to develop it, so it made no difference.'

Forty eight hours after Watts' moving out, demolition began.

This was not before the Council had two surprises – the first being the listing of the building at 43 Gold Street (Perkins former garden shop); the second – the resignation of Councillor Ray Dainty as a protest against the secrecy of the Council. He declared that the scheme would cost far more than the Council admitted.

Another surprise awaited the Council in the matter of the public right of way across the land to be developed. The Post Office arcade and Richard Leys were to be replaced by lockable shopping malls. The idea was not allowed to go ahead and the Council had to create a new right of way called Crofts Way. (In fact even in 1982 the Council attempted to close this route, but the Crown Court refused permission.)

Over the next few years official attitudes towards redevelopment began perceptibly to change. Before continuing the story of what happened to F.A. Watts & Co. Ltd. in the difficult days of the early 1970s, it is worth following the events that took place in Kettering in general. They provide a picture which can illustrate the major changes in the history of shopping which we can see today, in the 1990s.

The Newborough Centre, as the new shopping centre was called, attracted interest and brought more shoppers to the town, but its finances were not healthy. In fact when they were examined in 1980 by the Industrial Ratepayers Action Group (an organisation founded to keep council expenditure under scrutiny), it was revealed that the Newborough Centre was losing money heavily.

In 1981 market traders protested at how the Centre adversely affected market trade. The High Street (which links Gold Street with the Market Square) was said to be shrinking and Sheep Street (the continuation of High Street beyond the market) was dying.

Richard Tallbut of the Market Traders Association said:

'The town is too drawn-out and straggled. This end is now a third rate shopping area. Traders feel that pedestrianisation and parking charges add to their difficulties, and we were considering at one time paying for a bus to take shoppers from the Centre to the market.'

The general feeling was that the Newborough Centre was nothing like it was promised – an asset that would bring life to the town centre, attract shoppers from elsewhere, and pay for itself.

By 1977 the Council announced restrictions on development of existing businesses: It would resist much expansion of existing shops and major additions to retail floor space in the town centre.

Francis along with many other people considered this decision to be harmful to local shops:

'The Council thinks that nothing must conflict with the Newborough Centre. This is a rigid line to take. They might exclude some firms which we need in the town. It may harm present traders who want to expand. We should be thinking instead of revitalising the town centre and attracting firms.'

On 6 August, 1977 the *Northants Evening Telegraph* published a stirring letter from Francis:

THE BULLDOZER BLITZ

Following the space you gave on shopping restrictions, I cannot allow some of the remarks of Kettering's chief executive to go unchallenged.

He says, for example – and I quote from your article 'There is a danger there may be over-provision of shops and we want to protect existing shops.

What hypocrisy. But who has caused this great concern that people have about this situation? Not the existing traders in the town. The responsibility should rest fairly and squarely on the policy of the former Borough Council, and which the present administration appear to be prepared to follow.

In the late sixties there were many people who voiced the fear of the danger of too many shops, and I rather felt that their views were treated with derision. The very fact that the planning restrictions have already split Council officials is not without some significance.

If only to reinforce my point of view, I understand that a Building Society which has its roots and origins deep in our County may have been dissuaded from extending its present premises to the adjacent property. The present office is literally bursting at the seams and additional space is urgently needed, and I would have thought that this type of planning application was a matter of urgency.

The greatest destroyer of small businesses since the war has not been competition, it has been the large scale redevelopment in towns and cities. Local Authorities in all our older cities must consider changing their attitude towards the smaller enterprises.

I think it is now generally conceded that the bulldozers have destroyed more houses, more communities and more small businesses than did the blitz, and this remark applies just as much to other expanding towns in the county.

No doubt the Kettering Chamber of Trade is fully alive to the position. FRANCIS WATTS, 29 Gold Street, Kettering.' (*N. E. T.* 6/8/77)

The Council seemed to be learning from the problems that were growing in Northampton, where the new Grosvenor Centre had led to many established shops in the town centre standing empty. There had been an over-provision of new stores.

As the 1970s drew to a close there were signs of a new development in shopping: out-of-town stores. In 1977 the DIY store, B & Q, applied to build on land on the outskirts of Kettering. The Council rejected their application. Five years later, in 1982, the Co-op submitted a similar plan for an out-of-town store. This also was rejected. In the light of the experience of the 1980s and 90s, this attitude would seem to many to have been a wise one.

Kettering Council went on the defensive over the still burning issue of the loss-making Newborough Centre. In 1978 they blamed traders and the Civic Society for adding a million pounds to the cost of the centre by delaying the scheme for a year.

Francis was incensed and his views were reported in the *Northants Evening Telegraph* (28/3/78):

It is just a red herring. They are trying to cover up the fact the scheme was grossly undercosted in the first place – something which local businessmen have maintained right from the start.

I did not believe the Council would stoop so low as to blame freeholders for their objections. They complain they had to pay dear for our freeholds – but they tried to buy us out cheap.

All we asked for was fair compensation and we had to get legal representation to fight for it.

38. 15 Dalkeith Place, vacated by Watts in 1985, still empty in 1994.

He conceded that the Centre had generated interest in the Gold Street area, but said the new parking and access restrictions had hit traders hard in the adjacent areas. Trade has dropped since the restrictions were brought in. People are being put off because of them. But the Council doesn't care what happens to businesses outside the area around the Centre.

Redevelopment, however, had not been abandoned by the Council despite its restrictions on existing shops. A third phase was planned to rebuild the area to the north-east of Gold Street – Newland Street. By 1981 it was already being recognized by Council and traders alike that the poor trade in Kettering town centre must be linked to the recession, if not as well as to the new shopping centre.

Francis' views were again published on the issue of the third phase.

It is a foolhardy idea. If they put shops there, there is no chance they will be occupied in the present economic climate.

I disagree with wholesale demolition in the way they propose, because I don't think the town can stand it.

In 1982 the Civic Society made a similar plea to scrap phase 3. It claimed that over 8% of town centre properties were empty and 29% were under-used (with empty or little-used upper floors).

The list of old shops closing down was growing: In 1979 Pipedream, the tobacco shop in Gold Street run by Colin Page and dating from 1918, closed. In 1984 on Newland Street Ernest Lewin's 60 year old butcher's shop closed, along with Clive Chester's 18 year old second-hand goods business.

Another extraordinary event occurred in this year which rendered the whole situation almost farcical. Sainsburys decided to move out of the Newborough Centre, hoping to build a bigger out-of-town store. The people of Kettering realised with disbelief that the site of Sainsburys old store, now standing empty, was none other than the old Grammar School which had been demolished to make way for Sainsburys.

By the mid-1980s attitudes were changing in favour of the new trend for out-of-town stores.

In 1985 not only Sainsburys but also Tescos and the Co-op expressed their hopes of opening 'superstores' outside Kettering, quoting the town centre parking charges and lack of parking space as reasons. The Kettering Civic Society appealed for a refusal of Sainsburys' application for the very reason that it was out-of-town.

By 1986 the Council had allowed several out-of-town stores to go ahead: B & Q and Comet were among the first. Then the Co-op won its appeal for a major food retail outlet on the edge of town. Cramphorn Garden Centre was opened next-door. Do-It-All arrived that year. Two years later MFI were interested in a site.

The Council saw that something needed to be done to revive the town centre and plans were discussed to 're-centre' the town near the market and redevelop the Dryland Street area (Dryland Street being a side street leading off the High Street and Market Square). They also resisted Sainsburys' appeal to build out-of-town, and finally in 1987 Sainsburys were persuaded to build a new town centre store. The Council had realised that a large food retail outlet must be kept in the town centre as a prerequisite for preserving trade in the heart of the town.

In 1987, only 12 years after the Newborough Centre had opened, the Council found it necessary to sell it. Shopping habits had changed so quickly in the space of a decade. The Centre was redecorated and re-named 'Newlands'.

Two interesting events took place that indicate the gradual reversal in attitude towards redevelopment. As the 1990s approached, it became more acceptable to emphasise heritage and to value smaller premises: In 1989 one single shop in Market Street was converted into five specialist shops and christened the Market Street Mews. It was a 'tasteful' development that received much praise in the press. In the same year while the Newborough Centre was being altered, it was suggested that a new shopping mall be called 'Post Office Arcade'. . . .

However, the boom of the 1980s had brought with it consequences which could not so easily be reversed or softened : Firstly the M1 / A1 link was built close to the west of Kettering. Secondly, the road led to Kettering becoming more attractive as a business centre and market forces made rents rise astronomically. The average rise was 36% in 1988. The President of the Chamber of Trade, Paul Richards, complained that rents had gone up so fast that small independent traders could not continue. He himself had to close his premises on Gold Street.

It is worth remembering how Tony Ireson viewed the changed scene in 1984 in his book *Old Kettering and Its Defenders*:

> Now, to stand on the corner of Silver Street and glance down the north side of Gold Street is to receive an object lesson in missed opportunities. The top corner with Newland Street is occupied by a dominant block, designed by Kettering architect, J.T. Blackwell, at the turn of the century and built by Chris Lewin before he was 21. It is harmonious, dignified, and to me heart-warming and friendly. The next building, dating from about 1930, carries on this feeling to the classical facade of Fuller Church.
>
> Then there is a sad change. First comes the intrusive, windowless and prison-like first floor of the new Boots, then the huge glass and artificial stone cube of the Newborough Centre office and restaurant block, and finally another projecting jail-type wall as a prelude to the row of smaller shops in

toothpaste architecture – 'squeeze out as much as you want until it fills the space'.

What had happened to F.A. Watts & Co. Ltd. in the meantime? It may be that more tasteful, sensitive development was making its mark in the centre of Kettering by the late 1980s, but this might be too late for many local independent traders.

Francis moved his shop to 15 Dalkeith Place, on the corner of Silver Street and Carrington Street. From owning a freehold property he was in the unfortunate position of having to take on a lease, from the Nationwide Building Society. There was no alternative. They were in fact lucky to have obtained the lease at all. Twelve other firms were interested in the shop and it was only through the help of a friend of a friend that Watts were successful in obtaining the lease. Every five years the cost of the lease went up until ten years later it was five times what it was originally.

No-one expected the move to be easy. As Gordon Hardy put it – 'It was like putting a gallon into a pint pot.' Gold Street had of course had its problems – in the last few years the shop had begun to suffer badly from dry rot and the ground floor had been replaced. Nevertheless the shop had always benefited from passing trade. Dalkeith Place was very much a secondary shopping street, where there was no easy way of attracting custom.

The premises had been the offices of a leather merchant, W.H. Staynes & Smith, in the early part of the century. By 1925 the building was being used as the Dalkeith Billiards Hall and was also occupied on the ground floor by a dentist, Chas. W. Pears. By the time Watts bought the lease it was owned by the Nationwide Building Society, who kept the use of half of the property.

Gordon Hardy remembers the difficulties incurred by having to move the shop from 12,000 sq. ft. to 7,000:

'All the displays were shrunk. We carried the same range, but showed much less of each – the Ercol range was much the same, but not in room settings as before. Carpets used to be in a stack of squares – all sizes from a 2 x 1 rug, up to as big as you wanted to go – they had to go. The display became sample books instead. The curtains became a few samples and books instead of rolls of fabric. Everything had to be reduced.

Our curtain-making ladies had to move from Brown's warehouse in the Post Office arcade to a building next to Boston's hairdressers, and our warehouse moved to the top floor of the old Munn & Felton factory.'

The carpet workrooms had to close because there was no room in Dalkeith Place, and so carpet-fitting had to be contracted out. Work was not therefore completely under Watts' control and the situation was consequently unsatisfactory for a firm with the high standards of personal service such as F.A. Watts & Co. Ltd.

Watts moved into the new shop in 1974, fearful for the future, but putting on a brave face to the press and to the public. It was especially important to do so, for in two years time Watts was going to be celebrating its 80th anniversary. It had been decided to make the 80th a special landmark so that the celebration could be attended by the many older members of staff and family who might not live to see the centenary.

The dinner was held at the Cornhill Manor Hotel on the 23 March, 1976. The speeches were full of optimism and faith in a firm founded on the traditional values of personal service and staff loyalty.

Francis made one of the speeches:

'When family firms are taken over by big companies, the latter are only too glad to keep the family name over the facia and keep the staff on for as long as it suits their purposes.

A balance sheet is a cold thing. It doesn't really tell you about the involvement of the firm at all – about the people who come in the shop, or the man who delivers the goods, or the caring and dedication that goes on all year.

In spite of the fact that old family firms are not as they used to be, I think the old-fashioned courtesy and the opening of a door for a lady customer, whether in or out, and just little courtesies like offering a customer a cup of tea, are still the stalwart and the strength of any family firm that is prepared to put themselves out and look after the wants of their customers.'

The manager of the Kettering shop, Norman Thompson, made a speech in a slightly more cautious vein:

'The whole country needs men and women who are above all loyal, enthusiastic, and who take a pride in a job well done. We are fortunate that we have around us men and women who have and who have had those very qualities. (Having said that, may I quickly add that applications for wage increases tomorrow will not be entertained!)

Their length of service speaks well of the understanding between staff and management.

Gone are the days when customers came in their droves to buy. In the present time we need to use all our powers of salesmanship, to give our customers and ourselves a bit of a push. I think we have the staff capable of rising to the occasion, and that being the case, I think we need not fear for the future.'

However, much as Francis and his loyal staff tried, business deteriorated in Dalkeith Place. Two members of the family rallied round to join the workforce and try to help save the shop – Graham Watts and Alan Harland, both grandsons of Ewart, but it was all to no avail.

By 1984, just before Kettering Council bowed to pressure to develop out-of-town stores, Francis took the decision to retire, at the age of 72.

The Northampton Independent realised the significance of the event when they published an article about Francis by Charles Henry. The article opened with the dramatic words

Kettering is coming to the end of an era. 'Mr Furniture', Mr A. Francis J. Watts, is retiring this year, after 55 years in the furnishing trade.

The furniture business did in fact soldier on for a few months under the ownership of A. Watts & Sons Ltd. who supplied it from the Northampton shop, but there was no hope. The *Northants. Evening Telegraph* reported on the closure with the bold headline:

SHOP TO END 60-YEAR LINK WITH TOWN
A long established Kettering firm has bowed to economic pressure and is

pulling out of the town.

F.A. Watts, the furnishers, will close its doors later this year after being associated with Kettering since 1923. The three members of staff will be offered jobs at the Northampton store.

Managing director Roy Harland said it was decided to close the shop because of the economic situation and the retirement of Mr Francis Watts.

'There is no immediate family successor and as the shop is far less profitable than the Northampton store we have decided to close it.

'But this does not mean that in the future we will not open another shop in the town.'

Mr Harland said the problems started seven years ago when the company's shop in Gold Street was compulsorily purchased by the council and demolished to make way for the Newborough Centre.

'We left a freehold shop in a prime position to take over a leasehold in Dalkeith Place. But it has simply not proved to be the right position for us.

'I am very sad that we are leaving Kettering, but we will still offer the same service from our Northampton store,' he said.

(*N. E. T.* 10/3/84)

What had happened to the founder of F.A. Watts & Co.? It is perhaps fortunate for Fred that he did not live to see the demise of his company and the return of his shop to the control of the Northampton firm, A. Watts & Sons Ltd. He died in February 1968, having suffered a stroke seven months previously which deprived him of his eyesight. Fred had always been a studious man and was an avid reader. His sudden blindness was devastating. It is said that he was never the same person afterwards and felt bitter, with all his interests gone.

His wife Hilda survived him by another twenty years and lived to the remarkable age of 98. She died in 1988, having lived through and witnessed great changes in the fortunes of Watts the Furnishers and in shopping trends in general. She had seen her husband plan for the opening of a new branch of A. Watts & Sons Ltd. in Kettering, and she had seen her son stand on the threshold of his Gold Street shop, threatened with eviction by the Council and deafened by the roar of the bulldozers razing to the ground the shops next door.

The story of Fred's life, however, cannot yet be closed. He is of course an interesting figure in the history of local business and was Mayor at an important time in Northampton's social and political life, but there is yet one more chapter which must be devoted to this man.

It has already been mentioned that he was a deeply religious Methodist. His influential position in local Methodist circles helped him to play another important role in the life of the town, back in 1959.

Chapter VI
Healing the Divisions –
Fred's involvement with 'Queens Road'

In these days of unity when the old dissenting sects of the Congregationalists and Presbyterians are now joined in the United Reform Church, and when the Church of England is discussing union with the Methodist church, it is hard to imagine a time when divisions were deeply felt within the Methodist church itself – so much so, that only 45 years ago two Methodist churches stood on either side of Grove Road (on the Kettering Road) and a proposed unification of the two congregations was inconceivable. This was the opinion of no less an influential figure than Fred Watts himself.

In 1959 he was quoted by the *Methodist Recorder*:

I have sat in the same pew at Queens Road for seventy years. If anyone had suggested closing the church at Union (i.e. 1932) or even ten years ago, I should have replied 'Only over my dead body.'

1959 was the year in which the two Methodist groups – the Primitives and the Wesleyans – amalgamated in Northampton. It is remarkable that although the two groups had united nationally in 1932, the divisions in Northampton were so strong that they remained for almost another thirty years.

In the end events led Fred and other leading Methodist figures to realise that the two groups of Methodist churches must unite. The decision was seen as 'the Northampton miracle' by the *Methodist Recorder*. The story that lies behind this event is an interesting one, for Methodists and non-Methodists alike, for it is a story that reflects the development of one of the major non-Conformist faiths in Northampton.

In order to explain the divisions, it is necessary to go back to the early years of the eighteenth century – to the time of John Wesley himself, the founder of Methodism. For much of what follows I am indebted to the work of Mr David Walmsley, a former Mayor of the town and son of Arthur, who worked closely with Fred in healing the Methodist divisions in Northampton.

In 1714 the accession of the Hanoverians to the throne of Britain ushered in a time of some religious apathy in the Church of England. This was understandable when viewed in the light of the previous two centuries of religious controversy and upheaval.

Bishops were sometimes appointed for political reasons and they often did not reside in their diocese. The apathy of those in high office affected the lower clergy. The clergyman's religious duties usually consisted of nothing more than reading the services and preaching on Sundays, and services were often mere duets between parson and parish clerk. Communion was usually only celebrated three times a year, at Christmas, Easter and Whitsuntide. Sermons were more likely to be concerned with problems of ethics than with the teaching of Christian doctrine.

Basically the Church lacked enthusiasm, and it was this that distinguished the spirit behind the Methodist movement. Another spiritual movement of the time was the Evangelical revival. Evangelicals lacked the organisation of the Methodists and preferred to work within their own parishes. Also they tended to follow the ideas of the Swiss religious reformer, Calvin, one of whose main doctrines was the theory of pre-destination. This theory states that our individual fates are determined before we are born.

One of the rectors in Northampton (of Weston Favell and Collingtree) could be described as an Evangelical – James Hervey. He came under the influence of Wesley in Oxford and became a member of Wesley's 'Holy Club', but he disapproved of the Methodists' itinerant preaching and was a decided Calvinist.

John Wesley was born at Epworth in Lincolnshire, where his father was rector. He was ordained in 1725 and in 1729 returned to Oxford as a Fellow of Lincoln College, where he became the leader of a small band of men known as 'the Holy Club'. These men tried to live their lives under rule and method – hence their nickname of 'Methodists'. They were strict as regards their observance of fast days and their communions, and they devoted much time to active works of mercy and charity.

In 1739 John and brother Charles (the hymn-writer) decided to form a 'Methodist Society' in London. It is important to remember that at this point and throughout his life, John wanted to work within the framework of the Church of England. With his gift for teaching, John was encouraged to go out and preach in the open air to great crowds of people, and during the rest of his life he covered 250,000 miles, preaching 40,000 sermons all over the country, both in churches and outside.

Unfortunately the Bishops of the Church of England distrusted John Wesley on account of his message and his methods. He was after all implicitly criticizing the established church. Finally, his action in ordaining his preachers to administer Holy Communion in America (in 1784) and in Scotland (in 1785) and thereby perform a function only previously performed by priests, meant that the division between the Methodists and Anglicans was irreconcilable.

Wesley set up a tiered structure within his organisation which made it very easy for Methodism to endure as a separate entity, and which continues today. At the bottom of the pyramid are Societies (the equivalent to a church). Societies include classes – small groups which meet for instruction in the faith. Societies combine to form Circuits – a local group of churches. Circuits are headed by Circuit Stewards. Nowadays these people are changed every 3 to 4 years and report to a circuit meeting which is held three times a year. Their two main jobs are to engage new clergy and raise money from the various Societies to finance the clergy and their houses. The actual Ministers are invited to a post for only five years, but may stay for ten years. Circuits are united in Districts, and the whole national organisation is sometimes referred to as 'the Connection' and meets together in a Conference.

Northampton has a strong tradition of dissent. The town was a Puritan stronghold in the Civil War and by the eighteenth century there was a strong following for Congregational and Baptist causes. Wesley became a close friend of Dr. Philip Doddridge, the well-known Congregational Minister of Castle Hill chapel, and during his life visited Northampton 24 times. On his second visit in 1745 there were no Methodists in the town, but by the 1760s the situation had changed.

The Royal Horse Guards were being quartered in Northampton during the 1760s and used some large stables in the centre of town as the Regimental Riding School. This was situated on the Ridings (the road joining St Giles Terrace and Fish Street), the actual site being approximately the area bordering on St Giles Street from the property opposite Castilian Street to the Ridings arcade. (It is interesting to note that on part of this site the Watts family have now established another showroom for their town centre store. The Methodist connection continues.) One of their captains, a Captain Scott, was a devout Methodist. He soon arranged for worship according to the Methodist forms to be conducted in the Riding School, for the building had two galleries and seated almost 2,000 people. Wesley himself sometimes preached there, and by 1765 it is recorded that there were 217 Methodists in the town.

When Captain Scott was posted to Leicester, a new meeting place had to be found. By this time the Methodists were in the charge of the Reverend Richard Blackwell, and the Society was moved to a building at the bottom of Bridge Street, just south of, and opposite the Plough Hotel, above premises known as Dickens Forge. These premises provided a very long room stretching from Cattle Market Road to Bridge Street. As their numbers grew, the Methodists had to move in 1770 to a chapel on The Green, just south of Marefair near St Peter's Church. It had been vacated by a strict Baptist sect.

By 1793 an even bigger premises was required and this time a new chapel was built. It was situated on Kings Head Lane, now called King Street and just off College Street. The building no longer stands. Further premises were acquired for Sunday School work, but already within 22 years the decision was taken to build a new chapel, this time in Gold Street. It is an interesting reflection on the importance of this area west of All Saints Church and the Market Square. Originally this area was the hub of the town and the natural place to build the town's Methodist chapel.

When the new chapel was opened in 1815, the Sunday School transferred to the Old Chapel on Kings Head Lane. It was not just a school for one day of the week. On Sundays instruction was given on the Catechism, but on weekdays and evenings other subjects were also taught. A portion of the floor was covered with a layer of sand, and this provided endless opportunities for practising writing and arithmetic. The school was known as the Methodist Day School. Old Northamptonians who remember Adnitts (the department store on the Drapery that was bought by Debenhams) will be interested to know that two of the pupils at the Methodist Day School belonged to the Adnitt family. (It is perhaps noteworthy that many local shopkeepers in the town, whose businesses date back to Victorian times, belonged to the Methodist church.)

Meanwhile in 1791 John Wesley died. He had remained a member of the Church of England until the end, and constantly urged his followers to remain within the established Church. Nevertheless, in 1795 the Methodists separated from the Church of England. The Evangelicals stayed within the Church, the leaders all remaining beneficed clergy. Both of these reforming groups, however, had a great influence on life in the country as a whole. David Walmsley suggests

> They not only restored Christianity to its place as a living force in the life of men, but they were also pioneers in the field of social reform, and to John Wesley, perhaps more than to any other man, is due the increased kindliness which was exhibited in the latter part of the 18th century.

The reforms of William Wilberforce and in the nineteenth century, of Lord Shaftesbury are but two examples.

As with any breakaway group, once the precedent of breaking away has been set, further fragmentation is bound to occur. The precedent is set for an individual rather than an organisation to have the right to determine what is correct and true. The original Wesleyan Methodist church remained the largest body, but there soon appeared no less than four other branches. The Primitive Methodists were the largest breakaway group and established a strong following in Northampton. They were numerically stronger than the Wesleyans – which fits with the strong non-Conformist tradition in the town. Nationally Wesleyans were in the majority. Eventually the Primitives had eleven churches in the county run by three ministers, while the Wesleyans had thirty, run by two or three.

The Wesleyan Methodists believed that the greatest authority in local church affairs should be in the hands of the minister. The division between them and the Primitives grew up because the latter wanted to return to Wesley's original vision of open-air preaching and prayer groups, and wanted their churches to be run by laymen and to have a less sacramental tradition in their worship. The most important gift for a Primitive Methodist Minister was the gift of preaching. The Wesleyan Minister must be a good preacher, but had also to organise the worship. The non-sacramental tradition of the Primitives is exemplified by the lack of formal prayers to celebrate the Lord's Supper.

It is this division that became so deep-rooted in Northampton that the situation arose where two Methodist churches could exist within 30 yards of each other on the Kettering Road, each run as an entirely separate entity from the other, and each maintaining allegiance to the cause founded by John Wesley. It is to the Wesleyan tradition that the Watts family belonged.

Although Northampton became one of the strongest Primitive Circuits in the country, the first Primitive Methodist Missioners who arrived here in 1834 met with considerable opposition. The town was already a stronghold of established Dissent (i.e. the Baptists and Congregationalists), and local people called the Primitive Methodists 'Prims' and 'Ranters'. In fact the Baptists are still an important non-Conformist church in the town. Nevertheless, slow progress

39. Queens Road Church (c. 1950).

was made and in 1840 the first Primitive Methodist chapel was opened – on the Horsemarket. (It was rebuilt in 1872, but finally closed in 1942.) The mid-nineteenth century saw a period of religious revival nationally and after an uncertain start the Horsemarket chapel increased its numbers to such an extent that a second Society was established in the town, in Henley Street. (This moved to Towcester Road in Far Cotton in 1924).

By about the 1870s the town was growing eastwards and the Abington Square Mission Hall was built. This Victorian red-brick chapel still stands, nearly opposite the statue of Charles Bradlaugh, with the inscription on the foundation stone still visible. It is no longer a place of worship. A galvanised building on Overstone Road (near the Mounts) provided a make-shift building for worship for the people living in the area north of the Kettering Road. This was the chapel that was eventually replaced by the grand building of the Kettering Road Society which still stands today and is now called Queensgrove. It was founded by the efforts of the Reverend Jesse Ashworth and Joseph Gibbs, a prominent boot and shoe manufacturer of the day. The founding of this church was marked by a service in the Abington Square Mission Hall, followed by a procession which marched down Wellingborough Road and Cleveland Road to the new site on the corner of Kettering Road and Grove Road.

The spirit of religious revival at that time can be seen in the speed with which new churches grew up. Of course the town population was expanding at the same time, but the growth is still remarkable. In 1886 the Primitive Methodists divided their Circuit in the county into two. The First Circuit included the churches in Horsemarket, Henley Street, St James, Kingsthorpe, New Duston, Greens Norton, Astcote, Heyford, Paulerspury, Abthorpe and Hannington. The Second Circuit consisted of the churches at Kettering Road, Milton and Moulton. A Third Northampton Circuit eventually became established – at its head the new Harlestone Road Church built in 1899.

Regarding the Wesleyan Methodists, their numbers were also on the increase.

Already by the 1830s the Gold Street congregation had grown to such an extent that a second chapel was opened in Todds Lane at the top of Grafton Street. (The lane is no longer in existence.) Once again it is interesting to note that the main part of the residential area of the town in the early nineteenth century was on the western side, towards one of the tributaries of the River Nene. Todds Lane chapel was transferred to Regent Square in 1876. Country chapels were opened at Little Houghton and Roade, and Mission Halls were erected in Scarletwell Street and in 1888 in Hester Street (off the Barrack Road). The Methodists were clearly very active, as Scarletwell Street and Hester Street are quite close to Todds Lane. In fact the Mission Hall at Scarletwell Street built up what was at the time one of the largest Sunday Schools in Northampton.

In the latter part of the century as the town expanded eastwards the Wesleyans looked for a site to build a church to rival the Primitive Methodists' new building on the Kettering Road. In the 1870s there lived on Ethel Street a man called Elijah Irons. (Ethel Street is situated near St Edmunds Hospital between the Wellingborough and Billing Roads.) His house was used as a 'house-church' where Wesleyan Methodists met for praise and prayer. This small group of people helped to raise enough money to buy a site at the foot of Queens Road, which was at the time a sand-pit. Eventually in 1887 the imposing building known as Queens Road was built. (1887 was the very year in which Arthur Watts moved to Northampton.) Queens Road soon grew to have the largest congregation of Wesleyan Methodists in the town. Thus, within 30 yards of one another, there stood two impressive Methodist churches, each with thriving congregations.

'Queens Road' was the church attended by Arthur Watts and his family. His son, Fred, sat in the same pew for 70 years, and it is not really surprising that he should have been so troubled by the prospect of the church's closing.

Back in the halcyon days of the late nineteenth century the Wesleyans continued to build new churches. Nowadays some of their locations seem to us remarkable for their proximity to one another – Osborne Road, near Kingsthorpe Park, (1895), Kingsley Park, opposite St Matthews Church (1898), and Stimpson Avenue, later called Trinity (1900).

In 1888 the Wesleyans decided to divide their Societies into two Circuits, headed by Gold Street and Regent Square, but unlike the Primitives, they could not continue in this way for long, and by 1904 returned to having just the one Gold Street Circuit, with the Gold Street chapel at its head.

In the early years of the twentieth century people with an entrepreneurial spirit were interested in the selling off of the Wantage estate in the north-east of town. This was the former land of Abington manor, the most notable portion of which became Abington Park. With great foresight the officials of the Primitive Kettering Road Church bought a plot of land that was to be at the corner of Park Avenue North and Abington Avenue. About 20 years later a 'Forward Movement' was started and by September 1925 the new Park Avenue church was opened. Eighty members of the Kettering Road church were 'transferred' to this new venture in order to give it strong support and it was not long before Park Avenue became the leading Primitive society in the town with the largest number of members and benefiting from the comparative wealth of its congregation of leading town businessmen.

It was in 1932 that the Methodist Church at last chose to heal its divisions and unite the Primitive and Wesleyan branches, but what could be achieved nationally under Methodist Union could not be so easily put into practice in a town having two such strong opposing traditions as Northampton.

In 1940 the three Primitive Circuits amalgamated to form the Northampton (Kettering Road) Circuit. This had to co-exist with the well-established Wesleyan Gold Street Circuit. These two Circuits had now to be referred to as ex-Primitive or ex-Wesleyan, but their separateness was still very obvious. The division was, however, a friendly one, with preachers from the one circuit speaking in churches of the other. The ex-Wesleyans in fact needed the support of ex-Primitive preachers because they had many small country chapels. The ex-Primitives had three ministers for their eleven churches and the ex-Wesleyans, two or three for their thirty.

The anomaly of two co-existing Circuits was brought into sharp relief by the fact that Kettering Road and Queens Road churches were within thirty yards of one another. Moreover, youth work was being carried out by both churches, proving an undoubted waste of resources.

In the post-war years Methodist youth work was very successful, as can be seen in the account of the Misses Riches mentioned earlier in chapter two, who remember the flourishing Guild of Friendship at Queens Road. In 1952, however, the problem of the two circuits' duplication of effort was addressed by two important ministers – the Rev. George Gregory of the Kettering Road church and the Rev. John Ashplant of Gold Street. They held talks, but came to the conclusion that amalgamation was at present impossible and a decision would have to be postponed for a few years. Resistance to the idea of unity was still strong in 1956 when further talks had to be abandoned. The lack of enthusiasm on both sides made unification seem totally impractical.

Individual friendships between ex-Primitives and ex-Wesleyans were important in keeping the idea of unification alive. Arthur Walmsley, who was the Kettering Road Circuit Steward for nine years, was a good friend of Fred Watts, a leading layman at Queens Road. As the 1950s progressed, they could both see 'the writing on the wall'. The town was expanding again and resources were limited. A fusion of the two circuits would release a minister to work on the outskirts of town and would make funds available for improving buildings there, in particular at Harlestone Road which could serve the housing development at Duston.

Arthur's son, David, has an interesting recollection of one of Fred's ideas for the future of Methodism in the town, which he discussed with Arthur. His scheme reminds us of the entrepreneurial spirit that had fired his enthusiasm for his new company at Kettering, F.A. Watts & Co. Ltd. He had a vision of a Northampton Central Methodist Hall, heading a Northampton circuit. Where better to build it than on a central site, selling Gold Street, Regent Square, Queens Road *and* Kettering Road? There was the possibility of buying the Arcade on the Market Square and it was this site which inspired Fred's dream – a Central Hall overlooking the great expanse of this square right in the heart of town.

This particular vision may not have materialised, but another more practical venture was embarked on – one which bore lasting fruit. One of the obstacles to amalgamation was not always a lack of will, but just a lack of any mechanism whereby the two groups of Methodists could work together. With his usual genial friendliness Fred decided to set up a 'Northampton Methodist Luncheon Club', 'to foster and encourage the spirit of goodwill and fellowship among Methodists'.

In the summer of 1958 he sent out an invitation to fifty laymen in the two circuits to meet him and the ministers for lunch with a view to forming such a club. 42 enrolments were made at the very first meeting and officers, elected.

Arthur Brown, who used to be Circuit Steward at Gold Street and was a good friend of Kenneth Harland and Fred, recalls the importance of the club in bringing Methodists together:

> 'It was from that luncheon club that the men started talking together and got to know each other. And the amalgamation then became a smoother operation.'

The club continued for a good number of years, meeting monthly at the Wedgwood Restaurant in Abington Street (opposite St Giles Terrace). It only came to an end when the Restaurant was sold by its owners, the Adams family, and became unacceptably expensive.

Unfortunately, due to their belief in temperance, the Methodists could not meet in a pub and could find no other suitable venue at which to continue their meetings.

By 1958 the spirit among Northampton Methodists was being transformed. Not only were the ex-Primitives and ex-Wesleyans meeting together; now talks were proving to be more promising than ever before. Whereas two years previously talks on union were abandoned, in 1958 at a joint meeting of representatives from all the churches of the two Circuits, there was a great deal of enthusiasm for the idea of amalgamation. The meeting was called by the superintendents of both Circuits – the Rev. Henry Wigley of Kettering Road and the Rev. Joseph Dowell of Gold Street. One of the representatives instrumental in amalgamating the two circuits was another member of the Watts family – Kenneth Harland who had married Ewart's daughter, Joyce, and was by now in charge of the Northampton firm of A. Watts & Sons Ltd. He was also the Gold Street Circuit Steward, although still attending Queens Road. The two circuit stewards – Kenneth Harland and Bernard Pearce of Kettering Road – submitted the plans to their Circuit meetings and were delighted that not a single vote was cast against them. A united Northampton Circuit could now be formed. The superintendent would be the Rev. Henry Wigley, who would now be based at Park Avenue as this society had the largest membership (364). Both he and Joseph Dowell were interviewed by the *Methodist Recorder* and described the decisive vote as 'astounding' in the light of all that had gone before. The article about the amalgamation and its history was called 'Northamptonshire Miracle'.

The way was now clear for the two churches on the Kettering Road to unite. Sadly one of them had to be made redundant. The end of this story of Methodist union is told in the *Methodist Recorder*:

> Last July the Kettering Road leaders, led by the Rev. Norman C. Panton, proposed to those of Queens Road that a new, united society should be formed, occupying the Kettering Road premises but in a re-named church with officials elected by the new leaders' meeting and representatives of

40. Interior of Queens Road Church at Freda Watts marriage to Dudley Pearson (1944).

both uniting societies; that a new trust should be formed, eventually, of continuing trustees from both old trusts plus others willing to serve; that the two present ministers, the Rev. N.C. Panton and F.A. White, should be joint ministers of the united society until the end of the connexional year; and that the actual union should take place, possibly on the second Sunday in January, 1960, with the Chairman of the District (the Rev. Wilfred Shepherd) as the preacher.

This generous gesture by the Kettering Road leaders' meeting has been cordially received and accepted by the Queens Road leaders' meeting. The Queens Road trustees have already applied for permission to cease services. It is, therefore, virtually certain that the two societies will come together on these terms. Thus a problem which has sorely troubled and perplexed many Methodists in Northampton for years, and for so long seemed incapable of solution, has now been happily solved. (*Methodist Recorder* 1/10/59)

The new church was re-named 'Queensgrove'. It still stands today, presenting its distinguished Victorian facade to the shoppers and residents in this now minor commercial area of town, and hiding behind this facade its history of division and non-conformity.

The old church of Queens Road is partially still intact. Considering the efforts of Fred Watts and Kenneth Harland, it was a cruel twist of fate that the church's trustees sold the site to a firm in competition with A. Watts & Sons Ltd.– Jones the Furnishers. The simple fact was that Jones put in the best offer, and neither Fred nor Kenneth could honourably refuse to accept it.

Now in the quiet basement showroom of Jones, amid the beds and the three piece suites, there is no trace of the lively youth groups and the Guild of Friendship whose activities once resounded within these walls, beneath the noble edifice of Queens Road church.(It is ironic that in 1996 now that Ken and Peter Jones are ready to retire, the business and building at Queens Road could be re-purchased by A. Watts & Sons.)

Fred may not have been in the forefront of the efforts to unite Northampton Methodists across the Primitive / Wesleyan divide, but he was a very influential figure in his local church and in his own way helped to encourage his fellow-Methodists and lead them forward into union. His leadership in the local Methodist church has been carried on by his great-nephew, Roy, and Roy's father before him.

It seems fitting to conclude this chapter on the development of Methodism in the town with a brief summary of the present situation.

At the formation of the Northampton Circuit there were ten churches in the town and nineteen in the surrounding villages. These were served by six ministers, a lay pastor and about fifty local preachers. Membership totalled over 1800.

Today there are seven churches in the town – Park Avenue, Queensgrove, Kingsley Park, Kingsthorpe, Towcester Road and St Andrews on Harlestone Road and Emmanuel shared church at Weston Favell Centre, where Methodists, Baptists and Anglicans worship together.

(The other churches in the Northampton circuit are at Astcote/Eastcote, Great Billing, Harpole, Hartwell, Holcot, Roade and Wootton.)

So in the last thirty years or so the town has lost no fewer than four Methodist churches, the first of which was of course Queens Road. The Regent Square site has been sold, making way for the present casino. Osborne Road and Gold Street have closed; the former now a Gospel Hall. Trinity church was sold to be converted into shops centred round Classix Interiors. The ex-Primitive church on Harlestone Road has been closed – founded in 1899 by the fiery preacher, the Rev. Jabez Bell, it was replaced by the new St Andrews Church built further out on the Harlestone Road in the New Duston area.

On a more promising note, the 1990s have seen the development of many of the remaining Methodist chapels in the Northampton circuit as well as the closure of others less well supported, such as the chapels at Quinton, Moulton, Shutlanger, Maidford, Stoke Bruerne, Hester Street, Trinity and Osborne Road. However, this reduction in numbers has enabled modernisation and growth at Astcote, Roade, Hartwell, Harpole and now the launching of a new church to be built in the new area of Wootton Fields in co-operation with the United Reformed Church. It is money gained from selling Trinity that has made it possible to finance the Wootton Fields scheme, just as it was the money from Regent Square that led to the founding of the large Kingsthorpe chapel.

Fred's great-nephew, Alan Harland, has been very active in advising and supporting this cause. Alan's brother, Roy, the present Managing Director of Watts, acts as treasurer of Northampton Shared Churches Ltd. which oversees the joint ecumenical church at Emmanuel at which Roy is a lay preacher. It is one of the only meetings of senior denominational clergy and lay people in the Northampton area, encompassing as it does Anglican, Methodist and Baptist church representatives with town and county responsibilities. The divisions in the Christian faith witnessed by Fred Watts seem long gone, when different denominations can work together so successfully.

Emmanuel, 'the Shared Church', is thriving and needing more space. It has in fact planted two daughter churches to serve the Eastern district, one of which is an ecumenical group using a school hall. This kind of ministry may well be an important feature of the development the Methodist church will see in the more stringent and ecumenical times of the late twentieth century and beyond. At all events the days of erecting glorious Victorian chapels are over. Today as living examples of this period of great religious fervour within the Methodist church there only remain Queensgrove and Kingsley Park.

Chapter VII
Kenneth Harland through the 50s and 60s

The story of the Watts family must now take an abrupt turn and move back to Ewart's branch of the family and events at the White House on Abington Street.

In 1954 Kenneth Harland became managing director of A. Watts & Sons Ltd. Married to Ewart's daughter, Joyce, and manager of the shop since 1946, he was the obvious choice, although Ewart delayed his appointment as long as possible. He was of the same generation as Fred's son, Francis, and had gained considerable experience in the furniture trade, but Ewart must have envied the natural transfer of power from father to son in Fred's firm. Kenneth was only given a small number of shares in the company, his wife Joyce having the larger portion, and their joint share together being equal to Joyce's brother and sister's.

Kenneth now had responsibility for running one of the largest furniture stores in town. What was the situation like for a shopkeeper in Northampton in those post-war years? In a similar way to Francis in Kettering, Kenneth continued to build up and improve the trade. In the 1950s, however, businesses still faced many limitations as a consequence of the Second World War, such as Higher Purchase restrictions, price controls, the rationing of furniture and of the floorspace in new houses.

At the time when Kenneth became manager in 1946, one of the most immediate problems was the lack of rear access to the White House. Kenneth encouraged Ewart to broach the subject with S. & W. Motors, the firm directly behind them on the Ridings. As mentioned before in chapter 2, Watts' approach to this firm seeking an arrangement to share the latter's yard for the purposes of rear access to the shop, met with a haughty refusal. Nowadays it seems amazing that Watts could have built a shop in 1931 without rear access or without addressing the problem. A furniture shop has such bulky items to be delivered that such access would seem to be of great importance. It is a problem that besets the business even today. The story of the development of the rear of the shop serves to explain the awkward situation that continues to exist.

There are still members of staff who remember the premises as they were just after the war. Vernon Nicholls, the present manager, began work in 1950 when the shop finished where the lift shaft is today.

'We relied to quite a large extent during the summer on using the light from the roof, because we had huge holes in the floor where the light filtered down. That's why the glass roof was on the top floor – because that was the means of light. Although they had electric lighting, whenever you could, you economised in those days by using natural light.

At the back there were some steps down into the place where the horse and cart would have been kept. Mr Harland's office was up a flight of rickety old steps, above the stable. This part was the old building on to which the White House had been built in 1931. S. & W. Motors occupied the site to the rear as far as the back of the houses on St. Giles Street. The Ridings was not a thoroughfare and a gate closed it off near St. Giles Terrace. Watts had to garage their own vans at a warehouse in Albert Street (now under the Grosvenor Centre).'

In 1951 minor improvements were made to the rear part of the building, but it was not until 1958 that Kenneth decided on a more major extension to the rear of the shop. He listed the advantages to be obtained and soon convinced the other directors that the outlay would be warranted. One of the reasons demonstrates the success of the shop in the late 50s:

'On Saturday afternoons in the pre-Christmas period, we cannot accommodate our customers. Their numbers could be increased by as much as 50% and Watts could have the largest toy display in town.'

The building recession was cited as another reason to extend as soon as possible. Building costs would be £2,000 cheaper than previously. Furthermore Watts should seize the opportunity while they could of using the next door shop's rear entrance to bring in building materials. The shop next door at no. 82 was in fact Johnsons sports shop. The agreement for Watts to make use of their rear entrance was a verbal one. If only Kenneth had been able to foresee future developments, he would have tried to obtain the agreement in writing. The White House even today has no guaranteed rear access, and this must of necessity reduce its value on the property market. Present day customers might wonder at this when they see the small private car-park by the back door of the shop, but appearances deceive. The rear of the shop today is in fact leased from the Council.

In 1961 S.& W. Motors moved out and Watts were able to lease the vast area down to the back of the St. Giles Street houses. The Borough Council soon decided that they needed the greater portion of this land for the present Ridings car-park. The Ridings was made a thoroughfare, and this left a sizeable area to the rear of the White House. Unfortunately for Watts, the Council would not sell them the land in case it was ever wanted for an extension to the Central Library. All Watts could do was accept the offer of a renewable short lease. A major extension was planned and in fact opened in 1963, but the building was only an unheated, 'temporary' structure, still standing today. Much attention was drawn to the new carpet and hard-flooring showroom housed here, but Kenneth (and later his son, Roy) felt aggrieved that the new extension could never be more than temporary, determined by the three or five year lease granted them by the Council. Even as late as 1970 the cost of rebuilding no. 80 with a permanent extension would have been a financial possibility. Then it would have cost a quarter of a million pounds and finance could have been obtained.

However, the prospect is now beyond the reach of a family firm such as Watts, even if the Council were to sell the land. Roy still feels aggrieved:

'The Councils don't support us in the way that we've supported the town – like letting us buy these premises.'

He sees a change in the kind of people who now serve in local government. Before the Second World War there was a significant number of business people who were politically active.

'Now in my generation there's very few principle business people involved in local politics. Now we have to fight the Council. . . . Watts' major problem is that it doesn't own all its property. They lease more than they own. In the old days businesses did own their properties.'

So the physical and financial restrictions that are imposed on A. Watts & Sons Ltd. remain, even though Kenneth's bold programme of extension was carried out in 1963. As mentioned in the beginning of this chapter, there were several other restrictions on the life of a shopkeeper in the 1950s – the practical restrictions resulting from government interference in an economy damaged by war.

For several years after the Second World War furniture was included in the government's schedule of controlled prices. In these days of shopping around for the best price, of customers' even bargaining with retailers over the phone, it is hard to imagine the atmosphere of a world in which a potential customer knew that wherever he went, a particular item of furniture was very likely to cost the same – a maximum price being established by law. Although times were hard, shopkeepers such as Watts must have felt very secure, not fearing the cut-price competition from the shop up the road, let alone the stores out of town.

In a yellowing copy of *Furniture Control and Maximum Prices* published by the British Furniture Trade Confederation in 1946 there are many pages of lists giving the precise maximum prices of all kinds of items. Retail pricing seems to us now to be amazing in its bureaucratic precision. A wardrobe built of class A wood, between 3'3" and 4'3" wide and 9" deep, not fitted and with 2 doors, was £13. If the front was bow, hollow or serpentine, the price went up 25%.

[A chair] with back wholly or partly comprising sticks, rails, slats, spindles or wood panel (excluding chairs with upholstered seat having an overall seat width of 18" or over for chairs without arms, and 22" or over for chairs with arms) could cost no more than 15s if its seat was of cane or wood, but £2 if made of oak or mahogany. [This last group excluded] chairs, the exterior of the front of which was made of class C wood, or of class B wood other than oak and mahogany.

[Pricing must have been a painstaking task of bureaucracy.]

Of course the maximum pricing only applied to 'scheduled' furniture. In the case of a wardrobe, it was classed as 'unscheduled' if it was 'fully fitted', (i.e. with more than 7 sliding trays, drawers, trouser racks and /or compartments with glass fronts'), if it was over 4'3" wide, or had 3 or more doors.

Separate lists of maximum prices applied to Utility furniture. This was the special brand of war-time furniture manufactured according to precise instructions, and which has already been mentioned in chapter 5. Second-hand items, both scheduled and Utility, had their own tables of maximum prices, involving all manner of complications as to the definition of 'cost of repair', the

Home at last....

Account No. ....

Name ....

Address ....

....

....

Minimum $\frac{\text{Weekly}}{\text{Monthly}}$ Savings of £   : : _____

In .... Months this secures

£   : :   of

GOOD QUALITY
FURNISHINGS

If you could look through a mirror and see **YOUR** future home ! The way to make your vision reality is to **SAVE** and **PLAN**.

SAVE . . . by joining our Furnishing Savings Plan.

PLAN . . . by using our Free Advisory Service.

Details of all the most up-to-date Furniture and Furnishings are yours for the asking.

A. Watts & Sons Limited
Furnishers as Modern as Tomorrow

41. A Watts saving book from the 1950s.

date of manufacture and the reasonable price when it might have been sold if new on the 17 August, 1942.

Added to these controls was the shopkeeper's duty only to sell to customers with buying permits and units (coupons). In other words, furniture along with everything else was subject to rationing. A 4' wardrobe required 12 coupons in 1946, a dining table, 6, a dining chair, 1.

If a shopkeeper was selling second-hand furniture or new non-Utility furniture, he was obliged to inspect the buyer's identity document, which normally meant the National Registration Identity Card. The details about the buyer, including their identity number, had to be entered on the stock record. Similarly, if a trader was buying second-hand furniture, he had to inspect the seller's identity document. Detailed provision was made to cover the eventuality of a purchase by post, so that a buyer would be instructed how to have their identity document certified by a W.V.S. official, even if, as in outlying districts in Scotland, the certification itself would have to be done by post. Shopkeepers today who complain of the amount of paperwork might like to reflect on the bureaucracy of this post-war period.

The last restriction which must be mentioned regarding the post-war retail trade was that on Hire Purchase. All furniture was subject to Hire Purchase restriction on the minimum deposit payable and maximum period of credit. By 1958 the minimum deposit was still 20%. The furniture trade had been agitating since 1955 for a relaxation of the restrictions, and in 1958 they were partially lifted. There was, however, still a long list of goods now subject to a statutory minimum deposit of one third and a maximum period of credit of 24 months. These included radio and television sets, gramophones, domestic appliances and vehicles.

The younger generation at the end of the twentieth century is brought up with the idea of credit cards, so they may well be surprised to learn that in the decades after the Second World War, borrowing to buy 'on HP' was very much discouraged by law. The economic reasoning behind the restrictions was complicated, but basically designed to ensure a sound recovery for an economy damaged by war.

Once HP restrictions were lifted, sales increased. It is interesting to note the swift dramatic changes in the history of hire purchase: Ron Harrison began work at Watts in 1947, and in those early years of his employment he remembers how one of his duties was helping out to collect bad debts.

'If I was out and about, at Kettering say, measuring up, they'd say "Oh would you call in and get this money. You might as well call in and not make a special trip." That's how you were expected to work.'

Watts still employed a collector-salesman, Mr Wallington, to act as debt collector. He used to ride an old Norton motor bike. He was helped by Mr Fitzhugh, and Ron remembers that the very last collector was in fact Mrs. Fitzhugh, who carried on after her husband's death.

The vast number of sales on HP in the 1960s and 70s led to volumes of ledgers being kept by shopkeepers such as Watts. Roy Harland, the present managing director, took over in 1978 and recalls the situation:

'The shop at Kettering Road had been down-market. Everyone bought on HP and weekly payments. They were going up-market by moving to Abington Street. In the early years there, most items were still bought by weekly payments. Even in my day I remember inheriting massive HP ledgers. It's only the advent of the finance companies that saw the end of that.'

So the existence of credit cards today is only a continuation of the HP system on a more sophisticated level. All the shopkeepers' work entailed in maintaining huge volumes of HP agreements is now carried out by the finance or credit card companies. The customer has only to hand over to the retailer his credit card and the shop will be paid by the finance company. Credit cards are essentially no different from the little booklets kept by a customer to be filled in and signed every week by the collector-salesman, calling at the door on his bicycle.

Kenneth was a dynamic man. He saw the need to move forward in order to survive even as early as 1947, when it might be thought that shops could be forgiven for just being glad to have made it through the war. Some reminiscences of Brian Coles are particularly evocative of the atmosphere in the late 40s, both in the shop and in more personal affairs. He was employed by Watts from 1946 to 1949 and was only 15 when he began.

'I used to go round the factories with him (Kenneth). Furniture was in short supply in those days and he was trying to buy what he could.

I got on very well with him. He taught me to drive. He gave me just six lessons – in three different vehicles before I took my test. I'd been three times in the car (the Austin 10), twice in the Morris Commercial, and once in the Jowett Javelin van. He was a very good teacher. I passed. Of course there wasn't any traffic in those days. On the other hand, the day I took the test we were around the Stimpson Avenue area, which was all shoe factories in those days, and there were hoards of workers coming out on bikes. I was with them all the way down the Wellingborough Road to the town centre.

I left in 1949 to go into National Service and when I came out I went back. I'd only been there six weeks and I had to go into hospital with a spinal complaint. I was in hospital for just over two years. Kenneth was instrumental in my getting a war-disability pension. He visited regularly while I was there.

When I came out it was the intention right up to the week before I started work that I was going back. Then it transpired the shop hours had changed to 6 o'clock most evenings and I was still living at Olney. I had no transport in those days, so I was relying on the bus. There was no bus home between quarter to six and half past eight and we both thought that as I'd just finished convalescing it wouldn't really be suitable. (Before I was ill, I used to cycle to Yardley Hastings from Olney because there were more buses.) That was the only reason that I didn't go back – the transport.'

Some of the early innovations in the shop are recalled by Brian – the new book-keeping, the cash-tube, the switchboard.

'One thing about Mr Ewart – he wasn't keen on Kenneth introducing new book-keeping methods. So when Mr Harland went on holiday, I was told to keep books 'as they should be kept'! I kept two lots for that week! Kenneth knew when he got back. It was quite a joke.

The general office and what used to be Kenneth's office used to be at the bottom of the main stairs. I was employed as an accounts clerk and was sent to do shorthand and typing lessons two afternoons and one evening a week, in Wood Street. I never did take to shorthand. Kenneth installed a cash-tube down from the pram department, so all cash came into the cash-desk. There was also the new switchboard – dictograph it was called.'

It was a great new gadget designed to make the running of a large shop so much easier.

The last of Brian's memories reflects again on the scarcity of goods to sell. 'Bill Wallington used to go around on a motorcycle without a headlamp – he never had a headlamp. He used to go round the auctions and outside sales, buying second-hand furniture. As I say, furniture was hard to get in those days. One of the biggest auction rooms was Beattie, Son & Leslies, which was situated where Peacock Place is now. There was the Peacock Hotel and the auction room was in the hotel yard in the back of it, between there and Church's China.'

Apart from furniture items there were other goods in short supply which we take for granted nowadays, such as carpets and blankets. Vernon Nicholls is now manager of the furniture department, but his longstanding service to the shop goes back as far as 1950, a period of which he too has many evocative memories.

'I started work in 1950. In those days it was Utility and Non-Utility. Utility was supposed to be the basic standard which you could get. Non-Utility you could say was your luxury. Most of the things that were sold were Utility in those days. And of course you couldn't buy things like carpets without waiting years sometimes to get them.'

Blankets were in short supply. In those early days I used to go up to

42. Mrs Wallington's 100th Birthday.

Yorkshire with Mr Kenneth. We used to buy the blankets from the mill, fill the car up absolutely – you couldn't see out of it – blankets on your knee, blankets on the back seat, blankets in the boot – drive back down, put them in the window and they'd all be gone in a few days. They were just basic woollen blankets. There was no choice. It was just you got what you could get.

And with carpets we used to go up to Birmingham and twist arms to buy as many as we could. They'd say 'I can only let you have three' or something like that, and we'd usually finish up getting a couple of dozen by devious means – you know, a bit of arm-twisting. The carpets were very often sold before we even got them there. We had a waiting list – 'If you can get me a carpet size 3 by 4 . . . I don't mind about the pattern.' It was wonderful really because you'd got a captive market for it.

We had three floors and a basement. Where the lift shaft was there was a packing room where we used to keep springs and things like that. Bedsprings were awful things. They used to get pushed together and one day I always remember, Miss Margetts was sitting in her office, which was a sort of recess that went by the side of the packing room and there was only a glass partition. I was separating some springs and suddenly this one shot apart, broke the glass and it all showered down on her. Miss Margetts was a very prim and proper lady and I always remember she was horrified. I don't think she forgave me for some time.

Bob Barnatt was another character. He was a wonderful person. He used to take all the young people under his wing and help them. You know those days were very strict and severe and I'd only been working here for about six months. You used to wear a shirt with a separate collar, you see, and I always used to wear a silk front to my shirt and a Van Heusen collar. One morning in a hurry, I don't know why, I came down here and got off my bike and went inside. Mr Harland was due in and Bob took me to one side and said "Have you looked in the mirror this morning?" So I said "Yes, I looked in the mirror when I shaved" So he said "You've forgotten something rather important. I think you'd better go with me." So I didn't know what was wrong. He took me up to St. Giles Terrace where he lived, (he was the caretaker as well, you see), and he said to his wife "Beatt, I've got a bit of a problem this morning. Young Vernon's come without his collar and tucker on!" So he went through his drawers to find the collar that would be a reasonable fit and lent me a tie, so I wouldn't be in disgrace with the bosses. You see it was very strict in those days. It was a very worrying thing. Thanks to Bob he saved my bacon that day. That's the sort of thing he would do. He was like that.

Bob Barnatt was another long-serving member of staff at Watts, who started in about 1928 at the age of 16 and continued until 1968. He did deliveries for a few years (and in those days had not had to pass a driving test) and then went on to floor-laying. Tiles had just arrived on the market at the time and were very expensive. Unfortunately, the fumes given off by the adhesive gave Bob asthma, so that he again changed his job. There was no question of him leaving the firm – Ewart valued his employees and gave Bob the job of salesman, where he could drive out in the clean country air to collect orders. After Bob's war service Ewart helped him and his wife to buy a house on St. Giles Terrace. In fact Ewart bid for them at the auction. The close proximity of St. Giles Terrace to Watts was an advantage because Bob could then act as a caretaker – and as Vernon Nicholls remembers, Bob took care of more than just the building, but the younger members of staff as well.

The Barnatts had much for which to thank the Watts family regarding their help in purchasing the house on St. Giles Terrace. This generosity was experienced by many other members of staff. Bill Wallington has already been mentioned in connection with his motorbike sorties. He had in fact worked for the firm since about 1902 when he made the deliveries by horse and cart. He finished work in 1947 and he and his wife were still looked after by the Watts family. The couple had always gone on their annual holiday to Wells-next-the-Sea, travelling on Bill's motorbike and sending their luggage by train. Now that they were growing old, Kenneth would instruct one of his employees, George Worth, to take the couple in Lily Watts' car for their holiday. Kenneth himself would fetch them back. When Mrs. Wallington reached her 100th birthday, Watts gave a party in her honour – a tea-dance at Turners Merry-Go-Round.

In the mid-Fifties there was another figure in the shop who is remembered with great affection as one of the 'old era' when the atmosphere was more relaxed and easy-going. Edgar Lewis was appointed general manager in about 1957 and worked there until his death in 1971. His sudden death came as a great shock to the firm. The shop closed so that staff could attend his funeral and Kenneth gave a warm tribute to Mr Lewis' friendly and co-operative disposition. 'He will be affectionately remembered by hundreds of customers who appreciated his constant desire to be as helpful as possible to each and every individual.'

Edgar's widow remembers that in those days it was a very happy shop. Her opinion is echoed by many members of staff who can recall that period in the Fifties and Sixties. Vernon Nicholls comments:

'I think the happiest times were in the more relaxed days of the 1950s and 60s. You know the sort of thing that would happen then: Mr Lewis would say to me "I just want to slip down to Swanns. I'll be back in about an hour."

And one year on the day of the boat race, it was a dreadful day – snowing, and there wasn't a customer in the shop. Mr Kenneth drove his car round to the front and "I wonder if you'd like to listen to the boat race?" And we sat in his car listening to the radio. Now that couldn't happen today. That's why when we think back, the pressures today are so much greater than they were in those days. You seemed to get to half past five and switch off, but nowadays there's pressure all the time. There's always something on the go. You're always trying to beat the competitor. You're always looking over your shoulder.

Mr Ewart used to believe that if you had a happy staff, then you got the best from them. Mr Kenneth carried that tradition on. I think you can make people happy within their own little team, within their own little domain, but it's something you have to work at. It needs to come from the top.'

Kenneth introduced staff outings after the war and took great pride in their meticulous organisation, having trial runs and booking the morning coffee, lunches, teas and dinners.

Ron Harrison remembers the outings.

'Usually we had two buses from Yorks. We went on a Thursday and closed the shop completely – all the families piled in. They were very good trips – to Bourton-on-the-Water, Cheddar Gorge, the Wye Valley, the Thames. We'd stop for coffee, then at a hotel for lunch. Then we'd have afternoon tea and then an evening meal, maybe at Banbury on the way back. Pretty nice hotels, not a cheap outing – decent well-planned – we appreciated it. Eighty odd people used to go on the outings – wives and children too.'

Alongside this relaxed atmosphere was the strict observance of high standards of courtesy and tidiness which were enforced by 'Mr Kenneth'. In this connection the figure of Miss Margetts stands out in many reminiscences as a kind of Victorian mainstay of the whole shop. She worked in the office many years.

'She knew everything about that shop. (Mrs. Barnatt) She was one of the old type of person. She had values and she stuck by them – very precise. She'd take a tremendous amount of trouble over what she wanted to do. . . She was very prim and religious. You'd never swear in front of her.'

Kenneth mentions her at some length in his speech at his retirement party:

'Naturally I have been recalling the year I started work with this company, 1931. I must take care what I tell you because we have with us tonight Miss Dorothy Margetts, a real stickler for accuracy, who by that time had completed a few years with the firm. It's a good thing we did not have to write Job Descriptions in those days; Dorothy's would have had to read something like Junior Clerk, Senior Clerk, Office Manager, Cashier, Shorthand Typist, private secretary to two Directors, with particular responsibility for drafting minutes of all Church Meetings, obtaining season tickets for Cobblers, County Cricket matches etc. as well as booking coffee dates with any

43. Kenneth Harland with Edgar Lewis.

prospective customers or likely clients, at the same time keeping up to date
    Customers' accounts and later most of the Company's Books and Ledgers.'
The strict observance of courtesy has always been a feature of Watts' service.
Pauline Swan started work in the shop in 1962 and she sees no change in the
attitude towards customers that was always fostered by Kenneth.

    'We've always felt that manners were our plus point. I still 'Sir' and 'Madam'
    people absolutely automatically. You can't drop it really. And people must
    be spoken to and not allowed to wander round without being spoken to or
    greeted. I think that's absolutely essential because it's where you can score.'
In connection with these strict rules on the treatment of customers there are two
amusing anecdotes of Vernon Nicholls (the present manager). They speak for
themselves on the possible difficulties involved in staff/customer relations:

    'One morning quite early – in about 1952 – a man walked in and he looked
    incredibly scruffy. He looked more like a tramp to us. I went up to him and
    said "Good morning" to him, as we were trained to do, and he said "I want
    to buy some furniture". I got my notebook out and said "Where would you
    like to start? Is there any particular item you're looking for? I always
    remember he said "Well yes. I'll have this dining room suite here, this
    sideboard and table and chairs". I didn't take a lot of notice. I didn't use my
    notebook. I left my pen in my pocket. And he went off and looked at a
    lounge suite and said "I'll have that". I said "Do you not think you should
    sit in it to try it?" "No, no, no. I haven't got much time. I want that lounge
    suite. Now I want some bedroom furniture". I went downstairs. He said
    "I'll have that wardrobe and that one and I'll have the dressing table and
    chest of drawers. Oh and I want a bed". He kept on like this and he was
    buying no end of stuff, and I wasn't taking any notice really. I was being

polite, but suddenly he said to me "I'll come back and pay for it later." And with that off he went. I never gave it another thought really. Anyway at about half past four in the afternoon, this gentleman came back in carrying what looked like a shoebag. It was calico, very dirty – filthy actually and it had got a string top. He walked up to me and said "I'm in a hurry. Take your money out of that and I'll collect the change in a little while." So anyway I hadn't got any of this detail, so I handled the bag and I could see it was full of money. So I said "Right, to be perfectly honest with you, I'd just like to recap on what it is you want. I haven't got your name and address." He seemed a bit annoyed that I couldn't remember. He went off and I summoned another member of staff and we both went into the office and emptied all this money out and started counting out the bills, which by then I'd written up, and there was quite a lot of money left. He came back and picked it up and he turned out to be a very genuine customer. He was a farmer and he'd been down at the cattle market selling sheep. Hence the clothing. He turned out to be quite a wealthy man actually. I nearly blew that one!

I thought I must never allow that to happen again. A few years after that I had this charming lady in and she said "I want to furnish a vicarage". She told me who she was – the Reverend somebody's wife. It was a few miles away, at Hemel Hempstead. So this time the notebook was out, you see. Anyway, she bought a 3-piece suite, dining furniture – no end of things – absolutely enormous inventory. So at the end of it I said "I'll make a bill out". She sat down with me and she gave me the full address that it had to be delivered to, but she said "You'll have to contact my husband for payment. I have the authority to buy the stuff, but I'm not sure how he'll want to pay for it." She gave me this phone number. As soon as she'd gone, I thought "That's a nice order. We must get the money as quickly as possible." So I phoned this man and he said "Good afternoon. Reverend So-and-So". I said "Watts of Northampton. Your wife has been in and selected furniture which she wants us to deliver, but she's asked me to telephone you for payment." So he said "Oh dear, oh dear, oh dear. Not another houseful of furniture." So I said "Pardon?" He said "My wife is a patient at St Andrews Hospital, and this is a thing with her. She goes into furniture shops and chooses a selection of furniture for the house. I can only apologize to you. I'm awfully sorry." But you would have thought that she was absolutely normal!

Shopkeeping was a difficult life in the years after the Second World War when the economy was beset by shortages and restrictions, and the relaxed atmosphere remembered under Kenneth is perhaps, therefore, all the more remarkable. Kenneth could certainly not relax, however, in his position as managing director and was always planning ahead to keep the business profitable. Although there were no huge multiples in those post-war days providing stiff competition for a family firm like Watts, business was still difficult enough in the furniture trade for Watts to be strained in their relations with other local rivals. Vernon Nicholls recalls the problems:

'In those days it was dog-eat-dog. You would not offer any crumbs to any competitor and you wouldn't mention a competitor's name. If you did, you were likely either to get severely reprimanded or if you made a habit of it, you'd be looking for a job.'

By the late sixties the carpet trade was a very profitable part of the business, but competition was becoming fierce in this field as well, as carpet shops began to offer free fitting and a free underlay. The growing development of the town meant that new council tenants were becoming a profitable source of customer – wanting to furnish and carpet their new homes virtually overnight. Watts realized that although they might not want to get involved with the high street battle of 'free fitting and free underlays' they could compete on the speed of service by holding in stock a range of the most popular carpets.

Apart from competition Kenneth saw another major threat to the business in the form of inflation – as early as 1958. However low the rate was in the late fifties, Kenneth realized the need to increase turnover in order to maintain profits.

'If only approximately the same amount of profit is to be produced each year, the turnover must rise at the rate of 5 to 6 times the rate that expenses increase. Therefore, if expenses rise £500 p.a., the turnover of the business must rise by about £2,750 p.a.'

This statement was found in a letter dated 14 January, 1958 among the dusty files of correspondence that have recently been examined. It is a letter from Kenneth to his fellow directors and it reveals the opposition which he frequently met from other members of the Watts family, who often wanted to carry on 'just as they had done in the past'.

During the Fifties Kenneth had introduced several changes to the shop in order to achieve this increase in turnover. He had enlarged the repair workshops, begun a Contracts Department, a Fabric Department and a Floor Tiles Department. The Toy department had been substantially enlarged and fireworks were now stocked. Equipment had been bought to make it possible to undertake more removal work, and finally several furniture items were now manufactured by Watts themselves.

In the Fifties and Sixties the vans were blue. The converted ambulance had only lasted till 1949 when Watts bought a bull-nosed Morris commercial van with an open back. In 1947 they had bought a Jowett Javelin with the body cut down to reduce the height to make it more suitable for fitting. Vehicles were in such short supply that firms were not particular about what kind of van they could acquire. Any van would do. Before Watts bought the workshops and garage on Albert Street (now under the Grosvenor Centre) they had to keep their vans in Groses garage on Mayorhold – a considerable distance away from the shop.

In 1958 Kenneth's latest idea was for a Decorating Department. His letter shows that he knew the idea would cause consternation among his fellow directors. He wrote: 'Under the present difficult trading circumstances we must go forward in business, or get out of it quick . . . which?'

The circumstance which had prompted Kenneth to plan a decorating department were related to the Cosford building and decorating firm, which had the property next door to Watts warehouse in Connaught Street (behind Campbell Square). Mr Cosford senior was Watts' landlord and Mr Cosford junior, the adjoining tenant. Only a year previously, in 1957, Watts had moved from their warehouse premises in Albert Street to Connaught Street. It was agreed by Kenneth and Mr Cosford junior that a partnership in a new decorating firm would be mutually beneficial. Kenneth's wish to have a wallpaper department would be fulfilled, and it was hoped that customers would be attracted by the convenience of buying the wallpaper and the services of a decorating firm all in one transaction.

(The firm of Cosford was much older even than A. Watts & Sons Ltd. It had been founded in 1832 by Mr Cosford junior's great-grandfather. Their extensive works in Connaught Street were surrounded by streets some of which had been laid out and named after ancestors of the family. They had done a great deal of major construction work in the town, ranging from the building of Teeton Reservoir to Nazareth House on the Barrack Road and St Mary's Church, Far Cotton. Cosfords were in fact chiefly noted in connection with churches, having also erected Holy Trinity at Kingsthorpe, the first portion of Christ Church, and Queens Road Chapel.)

Kenneth succeeded in persuading the other directors to allow him to pursue this venture, the new firm being called Watts and Cosfords. The business would be run from one of the top floors in the Abington Street shop and the staff of the two companies had to be advised of the importance of fully cooperating with one another. 'We can therefore offer our customers a complete service for all household repairs and re-decoration and re-furnishing schemes.' The aim sounded worthwhile and promising, but unfortunately the business did not last for more than about ten years, closing in about 1969.

The flooring department, on the other hand, experienced no such difficulties. For many years the manager of the carpet department had been Frank Solomon. He had served Watts for about 40 years and retired in 1946. His place was taken by a man whose name will be familiar to many of Watts customers – Ron Harrison. He continued in his position until he retired in 1991 – another example of the long-standing service with which Watts has been rewarded by its staff.

In those early days there were three teams of fitters for resilient flooring and three for carpets. Ron Harrison managed the carpeting side and Bob Barnatt, the hard flooring. One employee, George Worth, has been able to recall his memories of that time concerning the fitting of resilient flooring, and another long-standing member of staff, Ted Williams, also has many anecdotes that have brought recent history to life. (Ted still works for Watts and has been fitting carpets there for nearly 40 years.)

Right up until the 1980s Watts did a great deal of contract work for the County Council and to a lesser extent for the Borough. Schools required not only flooring but curtains for stage, showers and cubicles, and venetian blinds. Hospitals too all over the county ordered their vinyl floors, carpets, blinds, cubicle rails and curtains from Watts. There were strong links with local firms such as Plessey and British Timken. Watts could also supply loose covers and Ron Harrison remembers working on a contract for the County Council to make up two sets of loose covers for about twelve suites in a retiring room of County Hall. Watts enjoyed an important position that enabled it to win these kinds of contracts, but gradually the department had to reduce its staff. Although it did not close, as the decorating department had done at the end of the sixties, the six teams of fitters were reduced to four in 1972 and Ron Harrison was managing

44. One of the staff outings.

both the hard flooring and the carpets.

Ron remembers how Watts used to take on young men as apprentices and train them up.

'But when they got to 18, 19, 20, they'd want to branch out and earn big money. They'd either go on their own or work for another firm where they could get better money because we'd trained them! Eventually we decided it wasn't worth having lads because we didn't get the benefit of it.'

It was a difficult problem for which there seems no easy solution in a firm that is no longer expanding.

George Worth was by then quite a senior member of staff, but he had started as a novice in the field.

'I went to Watts in the first place to work under Mr Barnatt. He was the floor-laying expert there. I learnt a fair lot from him – all this new flooring that came out, the vinyl tiles, the sheet vinyls, which we did at all the hospitals – St Crispins, St Edmunds, and also at the schools.

I used to do all the sanding of floors in these gymnasiums. It was a dirty job. I used to come home like a sawdust man. I was sent down to the Boys Brigade place down near the Mayorhold. It was a big job down there – a job right out of the book. It was a bit of a tricky number, that one was, because they wanted grey tiles and black tiles. You went in the door and it was about five tiles wide, (which was five of the 9" tiles). In the centre they wanted this black one with a line leading into it, and they'd got two doors, so they wanted two black lines leading in from each side. Then you went into a very awkward sloped foyer and they wanted this black line to follow straight across at an angle to the bottom of the stairs. And they wanted a cross doing in one place, and up the centre of these stairs to the upstairs where it was like a church assembly room with very narrow windows each side. They wanted this black line going straight up the centre. Then they wanted a black line of tiles leading straight to the centre of these windows. It was terrible working out how to hit the windows right! I had to lay them all out before I could find out which way I was going to turn them for the lines.'

Ted Williams remembers that as a carpet fitter he was required to do the kind of work which today would not be in demand:

'I think we used to do a lot more servicing then. People used to have carpets up in the Spring for spring-cleaning. I can remember we used to do a lady at the end of the Billing Road. I took carpet squares up there in the Spring and put them on the line. She used to give us the beaters.

We used to do more repair work. People had more repairs done: "Can you come and move the stair carpet to even-wear them?" whereas you don't these days. People had a lot more squares and you'd turn the squares round for them. You'd put fireplace cuts in them and turn the carpet. Instead of cutting the piece out, you'd turn it under. You'd bind the edges and you see, another time you could pick that carpet up and turn it round and open it up, so they'd wear – all the four corners, and things like that. Well, we don't do that sort of thing any more.

You went into customers' houses and did a lot more repair work – as I said – taking curtains down so they could clean. Spring-cleaning was a bigger thing then. The company would do anything required.'

Watts used to advertise its spring-cleaning service in about the middle of March and it was surprising how much response there was. Jobs included curtain-cleaning, re-making curtains, as well as cleaning carpets. They sometimes took carpets to a firm called Northampton Beating and Cleaning Company. Vernon Nicholls remembers

'It was quite a useful additional source of business. You see those were the days when work was so hard to come by that we used to have to lay off people in the workshop. Spring-cleaning was an opportunity to get work during what was otherwise a slack time. It worked for many years up to about the late 70s, although on a reducing scale.'

Repair work was also done on furniture and prams. The workshops at Connaught Street were useful as a base for this kind of work. Ted recalls the old premises there:

'It was a yard with garages and the workshops were all upstairs. So everything had to be carried upstairs, either from the front or the stairs at the back.

All our warehouses then were upstairs – on St Michaels Road, Artizan Road, Roe Road. They were cheaper because they involved more hard work. In Connaught Street it used to be an outside stairs that came up on to a small balcony and then into the workshops. At that time we used to make bench-seating for clubs. It was a real difficulty getting it out of the door and dropping it over the side. We might moan about lifting today, but we did an awful lot years ago. Everything seemed to be bigger years ago.

At that time we had a cabinet-maker, Fred Bloodsworth. He had an apprentice, Harry Howard, and then there was an upholsterer, Les Stevenson. Fred did a lot of repair work and re-polishing. We used to do a re-polishing service, but obviously we don't now.

Also he'd repair the prams. He'd re-tyre wheels, re-spoke them. We also used to renew hoods and aprons. I used to do a bit of everything. We'd probably go into the workshops for the first hour and a half doing upholstery. Then Ron Harrison would pick us up to fit a carpet. So it was all working together. When Ron wanted help, he'd call on anybody. You did anything.'

Both Ted and George remember turning their hand to anything during their time at Watts. Not many people would imagine that this flexibility could encompass chauffeuring older members of the Watts family or doing their gardening. It was a flexibility that tied in with the happy relaxed atmosphere of this family firm in the 50s and 60s.

'I used to do a lot of work with George Worth when I first started, [Ted recalls]. At that stage he used to run Mrs Lily Watts around. She used to visit her sister, Mrs Dixon, in the Mumbles in Wales. Then when he stopped doing that, I used to run other members of the family about. Mrs Harland used to have her own car, a Humber Hawk. I used to run her down on Christmas Eve to her brother, Dr Watts. . . . It was all something different.

We're a happy firm now, but when I started it was happier – more content. We had a lot of fun in our work. Pressures alter that now.'

George remembers

'I used to do different jobs for Mrs Harland and also for Mrs Lily Watts. I used to drive her to her son's and her sister's. She used to bring a flask of tea and a sandwich. I did that besides doing my normal job. I was a floor-layer, but they used me for everything. I've done floor-laying, removals, alterations in the shop, serving – you name it, I've done it for them.'

The carpet and hard-flooring teams worked in the same premises as the machinists who made the loose covers and curtains. Glenys Farey can recall the earlier days at Albert Street as she worked there between 1950 and 1957. Unlike at Connaught Street, where there were sometimes as many as five ladies employed, Glenys remembers working in a small team of only three.

'It was good fun. We all got on well together and a laugh. . . Albert Street workshops were a bit of a dump really. It was a big place. There was a big garage for the vans underneath and at one end you went up some stairs and you'd come to the cabinet room. Just inside the door, just a little way along you'd turn left and you went up two flights of stairs and you'd come up to our room. It was a big room. It was cold in the winter, because there was only one gas fire in those days. There were windows all along one side, so there was plenty of lighting. You looked out all over the roofs.'

Before the days of heat-seaming to join up carpet widths, Glenys recalls the hard work when they had to help out with the carpet-fitting.

'We did all the back-strapping in the carpets. We used sometimes to do them in the workrooms if we could. First of all they used to only come in widths, so you had to machine them all up, press the seams out. (The men used to do that.) Then I'd go off with them and we'd backstrap all round in the doorways. It was quite hard work at times – some of those carpets.

In the workshops we made loose covers, curtains, bedspreads, anything in the soft-furnishing line. Sometimes we used to make pram-hoods – it was horrible – and the pram aprons. You know – people had bought prams and wanted them repaired. We always put corner-shields on the hoods of the prams. Some of these were quite difficult to put on as well.

We used to machine aprons, but actually to recover hoods, you more or less had to sew it on a kind of ribbon round the edge, and the corner-shields – we had to hand-sew those on. They were quite tough. You didn't know any different in those days. It just came in what you were doing. In fact I still make loose covers. I've been in that trade all my life. I went to Jeffreys till they closed down. And I've been at Caves for 15 years.'

Sometimes Watts did soft-furnishing work at Althorp for Earl Spencer, the grandfather of Princess Diana. The Earl always supplied his own special materials whether for drapes or curtains or upholstery. Contracts were also won to do major work at various other country estates, including the Duke of Gloucester's at Barnwell Castle. So from sewing on pram hoods to making the drapes for Althorp House, the workshops were able and willing to turn their hand to any task.

Glenys is another who remembers the happy atmosphere and how they decided one year to enter a float in the Carnival Parade. The main feature on the float was a chair 'before and after'– one before it had been upholstered and one after. Alongside the van they pushed a pram with an L-plate on it – one of the first prams ever sold by Watts.

Prams were of course an important part of the Abington Street shop and in those days Watts' Nursery and Toy department was a popular attraction for young families. Nowadays with the advent of the baby buggy and the two-car family prams are out of fashion, but right up until the 80s prams were a major selling item at Watts. Kenneth had built up the toy and nursery side of the business since the war and it became a flourishing department.

In 1962 he appointed a new manager for the toys and nursery goods. Pauline Swan had just arrived in England from South Africa. Her experience in the toy trade enabled her to take on this new job, but she admits that as prams were still the main item stocked, she had a lot to learn.

'In those days a baby carriage – the top whack – was about £20, which was a lot of money. And if you sold a coach-built hand-built Osnath pram, it was getting on for £25. The day that they came in at £35, we said "Well, we'll never sell any of these" and it was one of our best sellers. It was the most beautiful brown and cream coach-built pram. We sold quite a number and were thrilled to bits.

Osnath came from the name Ashton. It was a Miss Ashton who did those Osnath prams. She used to come and see us once a year to make sure we were worthy of her prams.

I couldn't tell you exactly when the sale of coach-built prams started to go down. Then the buggies started to enter. The first year that Andrew McClaren designed this buggy, it was so different from anything else. It folded up like an umbrella, whereas before they'd always folded flat. This was light! A child could sleep in most of the pushchairs and in the first buggy they had to sit upright. This lady brought us six and said we could send them back if we didn't sell them. I think it took us twelve months to sell those six. Of course now you don't sell much else. And of course they've been copied right, left and centre, and McClaren make prams and lay-back buggies and all sorts, as well as those folding-up umbrella-type ones.

Then soft-bodied prams became the major seller – things that would fold down and go in the car. People didn't walk into town. Then Miss Ashton died and Osnath went. The London Baby Carriage company went, and other manufacturers went to the wall. That left Lawrence Wilson who makes Silver Cross and Marmet as the main pram people. They still make hard-bodied prams, at about £300 now. They have metal bodies now. We always used to think of coach-built as wooden – all hand-finished and sprayed and really beautiful, upholstered with horsehair inside, a hood and apron – the works.

ESTABLISHED 1896   **PHONE. 4545 (2 LINES)**

A. Watts & Sons ltd

T H E   F U R N I S H E R S

THE WHITE HOUSE · 80 ABINGTON STREET
NORTHAMPTON

G1/KGH/TNG   21st July 1962.

The Rt.Hon.The Earl Spencer,
Althorp,
Northants.

My Lord,

We write in connection with the 5 pelmets and 4 curtains which have been cleaned and re-lined and are now ready to receive their trimmings.

We require 14½ yards of fringe and have received from you only 8 yards of the heavy gold fringe.

We require 72 yards of braid and have pleasure in submitting herewith 2 patterns for your consideration.

We shall look forward to receiving your further kind instructions in this matter which will be given our immediate and careful attention.

We have the pleasure to be,My Lord,your Lordship's obedient servants.

Enclosures.

p.p.

K.G. HARLAND
MANAGING DIRECTOR

96 yds @ 3/3.

45. Letter to Earl Spencer.

Leather straps of course. They were beautifully sprung and wonderful to push. There's just one or two on the market now.'

Eventually under Kenneth's son, Roy Harland, it was decided that prams were just not profitable with all the cut-price competition. They took up a lot of space which could be used more profitably by toys. The decision to move the nursery goods off the ground floor to the back of the basement did not meet with success. Retailing is such a delicate business that the trade once lost could not be re-gained. 'Although we brought them back upstairs at the beginning of the year, we'd lost it.' (Pauline Swan)

Regarding toys, Miss Swan used to accompany Kenneth Harland to the toy fairs. In the early 60s they would go to one in Harrogate as well as Brighton. (A few years later the toy fair moved to alternate venues from Brighton at Earls Court and the NEC, Birmingham.) Unlike in these purpose-built exhibition halls Miss Swan remembers the awkwardness of the displays in Brighton and Harrogate, each firm having the use of a bedroom in a hotel, with several hotels being used.

'It was unbelievably tiring, trailing round. They were in the bedrooms of these hotels, and if there wasn't anyone in there, you didn't like to go in because you didn't know if you'd get out. The salesman would pounce on you and you'd be there having to go through all this stock even when you didn't feel it was your particular item.'

One of the most revolutionary developments in the toy trade was the advent of television advertising in the early 60s. Miss Swan recalls the difficulties it produced in the early days before retailers had grown used to its effect, and also even today when the extent of new fashion has to be predicted.

'Soon after I started, television advertising started in the toy trade. The first Christmas of television advertising we hadn't been prepared at all and we were asked for all these things which we hadn't got. And so after Christmas

Mr Harland suggested that we bought them, but after Christmas of course they didn't sell. It was the TV advertising that was selling them and they weren't a particularly good choice.

Fashionable toys (as opposed to traditional) all began with TV advertising. We still major in on farmyards and doll's houses and nice doll's and doll's prams, but you've got to have the whole range if you're going to be a decent toyshop, which we like to think we are – keeping the full range all year, for birthdays as well as Christmas. There used to be so little TV advertising, it wasn't too difficult to stock everything that was on TV, whereas now there's such a huge range you pick and choose. You don't always pick the winners, but you do your best. Just because they're on TV doesn't make them a really good toy.

The fashionable figures – character merchandise it's called – like the Turtles and Gladiators – they have such a short life. We got caught out several times. To pick and choose and to know which is going to be a winner, whether it's Captain Scarlett or Thunderbirds or what – you've got a job to know. Jurassic Park was great, but for a very short time. Turtles lasted longer, but then you couldn't get them easily. They're so crafty; they will put out a selection of twelve and one or two of the most popular ones will be in that twelve. To get some more you've got to buy another twelve and so you've got ten that don't sell and two that do. People can't understand why you've got hooks and hooks of turtles and not the one you want. It's so annoying. When the toys are no longer popular, you're left with all these things which you've got to job out at below cost. Also character merchandise is high-priced to start with, because the manufacturers have to pay a certain royalty. They're not good value. You need a crystal ball to know which one's going to be the popular one.'

Despite the difficulties posed to the retailer by television advertising of toys, this new development was a great bonus. The takings increased quite dramatically. The major difficulty for Watts was how best to use the space available in their Abington Street store. At that time they were still confined to the premises at no. 80. Miss Swan remembers how awkward it was to display their vast range of toys:

'We were on the first floor. We had a centre platform in a zig-zag shape and above it to the ceiling we had pegboards. So we had samples on display on all this pegboard and then all the stock above or on a shelf and then bikes underneath, and pushchairs and doll's prams and that sort of thing. The actual baby prams were arranged against the wall and cots and so on. It wasn't a good lay-out, but we did very well. On a Saturday in the Christmas period you could not move. I've known people come to the top of the stairs and look at the melee and say "Oh no. We'll come another time or go somewhere else." In those days Saturday was by far the busiest day. Through the year now we don't find Saturday as busy as it used to be. We find other days busy. I think the shopping is more spread.

One year we had some toys up on the very top floor. We did expand to two floors. We had all the bigger toys upstairs – the wheeled toys. (We were still selling cycles in those days.) It meant another member of staff had to be upstairs all the time. We had to use a manual lift to get everything upstairs.

46. *A Christmas toy advertisement (1960).*

When it was very cold I used to heave on it just to warm up. It warmed you up a treat. It was always cold upstairs.'

At this time Watts were renting the property across the Ridings and using it for storage space. It was the old tramshed belonging to the Borough and dating from the pre-war days when trams were used for the town's transport system. (The property was next to the old stables used when the trams had been pulled by horses.)

Miss Swan along with all the other members of staff found the situation quite awkward, involving as it did a long walk to find an item in store.

'Inside this enormous tramshed were three floors. (There was also an old cottage. I don't know who had lived in it. The tramshed had been built round it.) We stored our big toys on two of the floors. The legwork we did at Christmas if you had to fetch a doll's pram! We had to run downstairs, then down again, then through, and then upstairs sometimes to fetch a doll's pram or whatever it was! You can't visualise it now, but it was quite something, and of course very cold.'

Despite the various inconveniences of the lay-out of the shop, business boomed in the toy department. Fashionable toys advertised on television may have been a major contributing factor, but Watts have always realized the value of what might be called 'traditional toys', such as farmyard animals, toy soldiers, dolls and of course marbles.

It is thought that Watts is the only shop in town that displays marbles in gondolas – huge numbers can be sifted through by interested children and a selection made of various sizes and colours. However, first of all Watts sold them in little bags. Called cat's eye marbles, they were sold in bags because they were transported as ballast in the ships coming from Hong Kong. It was only in 1988 that Watts had the idea of selling them individually. Miss Swan recalls seeing them at the House of Marbles stall during a toy fair.

'I remember thinking that would be a good idea, and by golly it certainly was, because there's good margins on those and we sell such a lot.'

Watts' toy department is still valued by customers as one of the few well-stocked high-street toy shops. In the 1970s the firm took the important step of leasing the ground floor of no. 82, the adjacent property to the White House. The toy shop could now expand and be properly housed with its own front entrance, rather than upstairs. The department still enjoys a position of popularity which has never faltered. As far back as the early days in the 1950s the *Northampton Independent* published articles on the shop, emphasising its prestige locally and even internationally.

A decorating department, flooring department, fabric department, an enlarged toy department – Kenneth achieved a great deal for his business in the twenty odd years when he was managing director. The White House, built with such hopes and promise in 1931 just before the hard years of the Depression and the Second World War, was at last coming into its own, alive and buzzing – at times even bursting at the seams.

As always Christmas was the time when shops were at their busiest. Kenneth was one of the ten original sponsors of Christmas lights along Abington Street. The cost of the electricity was to be met by the Abington Street (incorporating Abington Square) Traders' Association. The *Chronicle & Echo* article on the event in 1960 suggests a picture of a vibrant shopping area that is popular far and wide:

ONE OF THE BEST SHOPPING CENTRES IN MIDLANDS

Although the face of Northampton has altered a great deal in post-war years, nowhere in the town has there been a greater change than in Abington Street.

In many places smart contemporary shop fronts have replaced old and dingy frontages.

Over the past two or three years the changes have been rapid. There has been the demolition of the New Theatre to make way for a super market.

The last two houses in Abington Street were sold in March and site is awaiting demolition and redevelopment.

A site just above Fish Street has been redeveloped and is almost completed and work is in progress to make a roadway from the street through to the Market Square via the Peacock Inn site.

The whole of the area now claims to be the most important shopping area in the town and one of the foremost centres in the East Midlands.

More recently it has become even more noticeable that customers come from many miles around the town to do their shopping.

Mr K.G. Harland, an original sponsor of the scheme and now vice chairman of the Association, said that Northampton served a very wide area. Customers regularly travelled 20 or 30 miles to the town and the traders understood from the customers that the facilities for shopping in Abington Street were just as good as in the larger towns in the East Midlands.

Last year the lights proved to have a big 'pulling power' and attracted many people because the scheme was unique in the Provinces.

From the time the lights are switched on until Christmas there will be

47. Mrs Dilworth and her pram (1950s)

extra facilities for people to do their shopping. It has been left to individual shops to choose their own day to remain open until 8 p.m. and in most cases Friday has been selected.

The ambitious and colourful lighting display will draw the crowds but it well also serve another purpose.

It will advertise to the crowds that Abington Street can offer everything as a shopping centre and will advertise it in such a manner that it must be of advantage to trader and shoppers alike.

The Abington Street lights will again achieve fame through the medium of television.

The BBC have stated that they will be making reference to the decorations on a Midland news bulletin and Independent Television has hinted that it will be sending cameras to cover the event.

One thing is obvious – the lights play a big part in boosting Christmas trade. After last year's switch-on one large store was so crowded it had to employ a person at the entrance to let 20 people in as 20 people left.

Traders all agreed that last year's Christmas trade had been better than ever before and because of the lights people passing through the town stopped to look at them. Then they started looking in shop windows and afterwards they left with their vehicles considerably heavier and their pockets a lot lighter.

One example was of a family who were journeying from Hull to Bristol. The children in the car saw the lights, persuaded Dad to stop, and they spent two hours in the town. (*C & E* 22/11/60)

The energy which Kenneth put into his business was coupled with a caring concern for his staff which contributed to the relaxed atmosphere of this family firm. It is remarkable then that this man found the time and the will to participate in innumerable voluntary activities. A staunch Methodist and member of Queens Road church, his faith and strength of character led him to take part in many aspects of Northampton life.

His name has already been mentioned frequently in connection with the Queens Road Guild of Friendship and the amalgamation of the two Methodist circuits in 1959. He helped Fred Watts start up the luncheon club which was to bring together Methodists from the two different circuits, and became its chairman for a year. At the time, he was Circuit Steward for the Gold Street Methodist church. On a national level Kenneth also served as a member of the Central Finance Board of the church.

Back in the 1920s local Methodists had founded a residence for old people called the Methodist Homestead. Kenneth became a trustee and also the vice-chairman. It is a home situated off Kingsley Road, where residents are sponsored by their family and pay only what rent they can afford. (Next door is the Bethany Homestead, a Baptist home, which provides nursing care as well.)

Kenneth's interest in young people led to his involvement with the NAYC (Northamptonshire Association of Youth Clubs) for nearly twenty years. This was founded around 1959 when the idea of providing clubs for young people was becoming an important part of social planning. The instigator was the late Harry Whittaker – a great friend of Kenneth. He brought together several wealthy people of the town to form an organisation which would sponsor activities for young people. Among them were Sir Hereward Wake of Courteenhall, the High Sheriff of Northampton, Cyril Darby (a builder and property developer and also a Methodist lay preacher), members of the Benham Trust (a charitable trust set up by British Timken), and also Kenneth Harland himself.

In its early days the number and size of the NAYC's projects were quite small. Nowadays there are several major projects on the go, such as the development of the Benham Sports Centre in Moulton Park which is going to be enlarged to provide an indoor tennis complex.

While working on the NAYC council and in the Queens Road Guild of Friendship, Kenneth helped the young people with whom he came in contact practically as well as spiritually. When a young person was seeking a job or career, for example, Kenneth would help them put together references and give them advice, or even a job. Two of the young men known to Kenneth actually went on to become Methodist ministers. Brian Lewis was the son of the publican of the Fish Inn in Fish Street. After a period of time at the Guild of Friendship he and his friend, Tony Smith, went on to the ministry.

Of Kenneth's two sons, Roy and Alan, it is mostly Alan who has carried on the family tradition of social work, whether it be Ewart's leadership in the Queens Road Guild of Fellowship or Kenneth's larger scale involvement in NAYC. Roy spent several years leading youth clubs in London and at his church, Trinity, in Northampton, but it was Alan who actually decided to follow a career in social work. Since the late 1970s he has been involved in the family business in the capacity of Chairman of the board of directors, but his energies have also been put into serving in another, completely different environment.

It is fitting to include here a brief summary of Alan's work, reflecting as it does his Christian commitment to the cause of helping those less fortunate than himself, in the most practical and caring of ways.

Although Alan came to work for his father shortly after leaving school, he left within a year to become a social worker. He had become involved with working in the Queensgrove Methodist Youth Club in his spare time. In fact the club Kenneth had run with his wife, Joyce, had declined and was re-started by Alan when he was only 19 years old. Two years later Alan moved on to Oxford where he worked in a remand home and then qualified in residential childcare, finally returning to Northampton to work in the Children's Department of the Borough Council.

In 1974 the old hostel for homeless young men, situated on Newlands (beyond the Market Square) had to move to make way for the Grosvenor Centre. Alan organised the move to an old Victorian house on the corner of Billing Road and Alfred Street. This house became known as Newlands Hostel; (it now stands empty), and the top floor flat was to be Alan's home for the next five years while he served as warden.

It was an extremely demanding, spiritually exhausting job. The residents did not have to be local people. They could come from anywhere and may have been on the run from the police or just have no roots, wandering from town to town, known to no-one. At the time, he still helped out with Queensgrove youth club, and can now recall with some amusement encountering the youngsters from the club stealing tiles off the roof of his own hostel! Sometimes the home acted as a bail hostel for the courts.

Alan was short-staffed, worked an eighty hour week, and only in the latter part of his time there was he able to employ a deputy warden. It is no surprise, therefore, that after five years he decided he could no longer carry on.

At about this time the MAYC (Methodist Association of Youth Clubs) was founded. Alan became involved with this group and also with a new charity called Women's Aid, based at Queensgrove. He worked on one of the subgroups concerned with violence against women, until some of the more strident feminists of the group decided to ban men from the committee.

However, his work in this connection led to his being asked to help set up another Women's Aid group in the Eastern District in 1981. It was this group which led to the foundation of Nene Valley Christian Family Refuge, of which Alan is still chairman. The Refuge has two houses in town, providing a place of safety for up to twelve women and their families – safety from violence, and away from verbal and emotional abuse from those they have lived with.

The group's annual review of 1995 provides a neat description of the work which the Refuge hopes to accomplish:

> During the time in our care it is hoped that they [the families] will be given the opportunity to recover some of the inner strength and resources necessary in order to make a decision about their future.
>
> By working with the children who are themselves suffering abuse and/ or neglect, or who are in distress because other members of their family are suffering, we aim to break the cycle of family violence being passed on from one generation to the next or at least to mitigate the effect of traumatic experiences on these children.

The two refuges take in about one hundred families a year, although the number of referrals may be over double that amount, and in 1995 about 100 families were also referred for aftercare.

Although it was in the mid 80s that Alan returned to the retail trade again to work for Watts when help was needed in Kettering, he decided that what he really wanted to do was to earn his living from doing the kind of voluntary work which he had been doing for the NVCF Refuge. Combining both his business acumen and Christian commitment, Alan decided to become a self-employed professional organiser of projects concerned with setting up hostels. Later he would be known as a professional fund-raiser or 'project development consultant'. His work today is wide-ranging, and covers such aspects as setting up new charities, finding suitable premises for hostels, and fund-raising.

48. The Directors of A Watts & Sons (1978) – left to right – Roy Harland, Kenneth Harland, Joyce Harland, Maureen Watts and Aubrey Watts.

Alongside this work he still finds time to be involved in the running of the family business as Chairman of the board. Shortly after Kenneth's death it became clear that Roy could not take on the workload of Managing Director *and* Chairman, and so in this capacity Alan has since taken a more active role in the shop, especially in relation to premises and leases and the extension of the use of computers in the shop.

The dual career of Alan Harland carries on the dual interests of his father. Kenneth may have earned his money from the retail trade, but as has been mentioned already, he was also a keen voluntary worker. His membership of the Rotary Club naturally led to much involvement in local charitable work. One of the projects for which Kenneth is most remembered took place in the late 70s in connection with the arrival of Vietnamese refugees in this country. The Northampton branch of the Save the Children Fund was the co-ordinating body for the reception of the refugees in the town, but the Rotary Club arranged the furnishing of the houses allocated to the families.

At the time the Derngate cafe was standing empty above the disused bus station (on the site later developed into the present Derngate theatre). Ken turned the whole of the cafe into a furniture storehouse. He had the whole Rotary Club going round the town in lorries collecting second-hand furniture and carpets. At weekends and evenings the silent cafe became a hive of activity.

A local newspaper report of the time related the experience of the refugees:
Another Vietnamese family have been settled into a permanent Northampton home after months of travel and worry.

Mr Trinh Luong Sanh and his family, who have lived a life of uncertainty since they fled Vietnam last Spring moved into a house in Alcombe Road yesterday. . . .

The freshly decorated house belongs to Queensgrove Methodist Church who were able to brighten it up and furnish it because of the generosity of local residents and friends.

"We are very grateful for all the loving care that has gone into the preparation of the home by members of Queensgrove Church, led by the minister, the Reverend Deyck Adams and Mrs. Adams", said Mrs Christine Cochran, chairman of the Northampton branch of the Save the Children Fund.

"We are also indebted to the Rotary Club of Northampton which has co-ordinated the arrangements for furnishing the house and others which well be occupied by refugee families moving to Northampton in the near future."

Kenneth was well-known locally for his work as a magistrate and in the Chamber of Trade. He was chairman of the Probation and Aftercare Committee for the county, and also served on the National Treatment of Offenders Committee, an advisory body for the government. (It was he who had the initial idea for the programme that became known as Community Service Orders.) His friend, Philip Saunderson (of Saundersons the Outfitters) remembers with affection and amazement the conversation he had with Kenneth one day.

'We counted up how many committees we were on – I was on 27 – Kenneth on 72! . . . . He was involved in all of them too, and he did a full day's work.'

His colleagues and friends remember him as a quiet and serious man, a very caring person who just got on with doing a great deal of good. A Methodist friend, Philip Harradine, sums him up: 'If something could be done in the name of Christ, without shouting it from the roof tops, he would just do it.'

During the 1970s Kenneth chose to organise two anniversary celebrations for his business. The first was in the 75th year of trading – 1971, and the second in 1976, the 80th anniversary. It would seem that A. Watts & Sons Ltd. loved to celebrate. In actual fact it had been decided to commemorate the 80th year of business so soon after the 75th in order to be able to include many older people connected with the firm who might not live to see the centenary.

As far as the 75th anniversary was concerned, Kenneth was in a very optimistic frame of mind as he saw 'the opportunites offered to this company by the continuing expansion of Northampton and Milton Keynes'. Northampton had become by 1971 a developing New Town. The face of the town centre was beginning to change, but Kenneth saw nothing to fear, only challenges to meet.

He retired in 1978. Unlike Ewart Kenneth was in the fortunate position of having a son, Roy, willing to work in the furniture trade and to take over from his father. From the firm's point of view it was fitting that the position of managing director should once again be occupied by a direct descendant of Arthur Watts. Roy Harland is Arthur's great-grandson.

The story of Kenneth cannot be concluded without more detailed mention of what was going on in the town centre in relation to its effect on local shops. No business exists in isolation, and when a town like Northampton is chosen to be a developing New Town, the pace of change is inevitably accelerated. Local shopkeepers cannot remain unaffected.

Chapter VIII
The Changing Town Centre 1961-1978

When the Town Hall clock at midnight sounded the 1st stroke of twelve, Northampton ceased to be a second rate provincial town, and became in the instant one of the 'Great Towns' of England. With an area thrice as large as before, with a population of something like 100,000 people.

And, one would fain believe, with a future even more bright and prosperous, and more important than its glorious past.

Every resident of Northampton was the inheritor of traditions so noble, so glorious and so important that no town in England can in this respect compare with Northampton of today.

No borough, no city, no community outside of London, can boast of so important and lasting influence in the happy destinies of this England of ours, or of the world-wide empire of the British Crown, or indeed of the English speaking peoples of the universe, as can Northampton; geographically the central pivot of England, and historically the home of patriots, reformers, and statesmen in bewildering numbers. (Mercury 1900)

What a positive welcoming response to the expansion of Northampton. In 1900 Northampton had become 'Greater Northampton' taking in Kingsthorpe, St James End, Far Cotton and Abington. What a contrast the Mercury report presents with the response encountered in the 1960s.

In 1961 the Town and Country Planning Association had selected Northampton as a town suitable for rapid expansion. Duston, Weston Favell and other areas such as Whitehills and Boothville were to become part of the borough as a preliminary to the growth of the town. Far from welcoming the situation, the residents affected protested, even making a last minute appeal in the House of Commons – all to no avail. Nothing could be done to turn back the tide of Development.

Wilson & Womersley were named as the planning consultants in 1962 and three years later they unveiled their plan: Northampton was eventually to cover 35 square miles, with a population 220,000, by 1981. (At that time the population was only about 129,000.)

In 1967 a compromise plan was approved after consultations with the County Council. A Development Corporation was to be set up. Wilson & Womersley gave in order of priority:– a shopping area to the north of Abington street and

49. An aerial view of Northampton town centre (1947), showing the Market Square with All Saints' Church on the far right.

the Notre Dame site and around the Emporium Arcade, an office area around Memorial Square (on the site of St Katherines Church behind Debenhams), residential areas to the north of Marefair, parking areas to the south of Ladys Lane, a bus station to the north of the Emporium Arcade.

The aim was to provide town centre services for a total urban population of 227,000, by 1981 rising to 260,000, by 1991, and able also to serve a general hinterland of about 600,000, by 1981. (This target population figure should be remembered when the more recent developments are considered in the next chapter.)

The central area of the town was defined as following the circuit of roads on the approximate line of the old town walls (Regent Square, the Mounts, York Road, Cheyne Walk, Victoria Promenade, St Peters Way, St Andrews Road, and Grafton Street).

The decision was made to retain the existing shopping and business centre as the major commercial centre in the expanded town. That decision was taken on the basis that the existing centre had considerable character and interest, was located at the focus of a web of communications, was already a major service centre and administrative county town of some importance, and had a well established and flourishing commercial district.

The power and responsibility of planning consultants seems awesome, verging on the arrogant. To be able to choose the fate of a town centre over 800 years old – to decide whether it is to be allowed to continue serving its community, to determine whether family businesses occupying a site for decades or more, are in the right place for future development, or whether they are to be cast aside – power indeed. Power authorised admittedly by democratically elected councillors, but still a power that recalls the vast scope of influence of feudal lords of the manor.

The consultants gave Gold Street traders little hope for the future. Its future was described as 'dubious', but the street might serve the useful function of providing lower rental accommodation for some traders. With its steep gradient Bridge Street was not considered to have any future as a shopping area. As far as transport was concerned there was to be parking for 24,000 cars. The town centre was to be traffic-free, with pedestrian access from car parks, bus stops and the town footpath system.

This compromise plan of 1967 was far-reaching, involving massive change to the community of Northampton, but it must be pointed out that as early as 1960 the Borough Council had started sweeping away the old to make way for the new.

In 1960 the New Theatre was demolished to make way for a supermarket (now Primark). The building erected in place of the Edwardian theatre must be a contender for the ugliest, most boring piece of 60s architecture anywhere. The theatre had only existed for 50 years, and although its standard of entertainment had deteriorated in later years, it was still an elegant building, complimenting the Public Library and Notre Dame Convent at the eastern end of Abington Street, and for which a purpose could surely one day have been found.

In 1962 the Peacock Hotel was pulled down. This fronted on the Market Square, the site now being occupied by the entrance to Peacock Place. It was built in the latter part of the seventeenth century after the Great Fire of Northampton of 1675. Its demolition stands out in the memory of old Northamptonians, for it was part of the many lovely Georgian facades that surrounded the old square, and it was replaced by a particularly dull shopping arcade called Peacock Way (since replaced by Peacock Place). Again it must be remembered that the hotel had closed in 1956 and no-one knew what it could be used for. In those days the Council was not able or prepared to wait and see what enterprising developer might come along with proposals for the old hotel. However, it is also true that in those days the Council did not seem to place much value on preserving the past. The loss of the Peacock Hotel seems to have meant little to them.

In the same year they pulled down the 99 year old fountain in the middle of the market square (albeit ostensibly for safety reasons). Money could be spent in better ways than on preserving an historic local landmark.

As the local population realized the attitude of their borough council, they took action and in 1962 a Civic Society was formed, whose prime motive was to ensure the preservation of worthwhile old buildings.

Apart from the negative attitude of the Council towards what is now called 'its heritage', the second factor which must be mentioned in order to set the Development Plan for Northampton in context, is the changing trends in transport. In the 1960s the use of buses had started to decline. The 'two-car family' was still uncommon, but people were relying more and more on their own cars. Many old Northamptonians recall the liveliness of the town centre right through the 1960s when there was a long row of town bus stops round All Saints Church and along Abington Street. Derngate was alive too with the comings and goings of the green country buses based at the Derngate bus station (on the site of the Derngate theatre). Shoppers entering town on the buses dispersed in all different directions to visit the variety of family businesses of which A. Watts & Sons Ltd. was but one. (This point is worth remembering when considering the impact of the Grosvenor Centre and the siting of the new bus station, feeding as it does directly into the shopping malls.)

The third factor in the background to the Development Plan is that despite the booming economy of the 60s there was still a sizeable area of the town centre that presented a picture of 'depressing desolation'(*C & E* 21/10/66). The town was described as having 'many seedy areas', in particular Marefair and Horsemarket. The whole south-central area (south of the Marefair-Gold Street-Derngate axis) was regarded as run-down and neglected.

The beginning of the development should be seen in the light of the three factors mentioned above – the Council's attitude to old buildings, the declining use of the buses, and the dereliction within the centre of town.

As the Sixties closed, many felt uneasy about the proposals – not least the local shopkeepers. A. Watts & Sons Ltd could feel secure in the White House and in the prospect of a growing town population but retailers such as Churchs China were not so fortunate. The following article by Vivian Church written in the summer of 1969 makes a powerful case for the value of local family-run shops. It appeared in the *Bulletin of the Chamber of Trade*:

A BRAVE NEW NORTHAMPTON FOR THE PRIVATE RETAILER?
What is to be the future for the privately owned shop in the new Northampton precinct of the planners? Is it to be strangulation by indecisive planning? ruthless exclusion from town centre positions? or a brave new future? Examining these alternatives it would seem that indecisive and dilatory planning could have a disastrous effect. Those of us who suffer under the threat of demolition are unlikely to have much enthusiasm for improving or even maintaining the condition of our premises. Fixtures and fittings will not be renewed or improved. We shall be chary of buying new stock and extending our range of goods, lest we have difficulty in disposing of stock before removal. Without a forward looking policy it is very difficult to avoid a feeling of stagnation and frustration which is sure to be transmitted to both staff and customers with disastrous effects.

Careless planning, involving the wholesale and uncontrolled disposal of valuable town centre sites to large development companies, can lead to the virtual exclusion of local retailers from the premier shopping areas of a new town. It is well known that developers will frequently discriminate that the small local firm may be quoted an unrealistic rent far in excess of that to

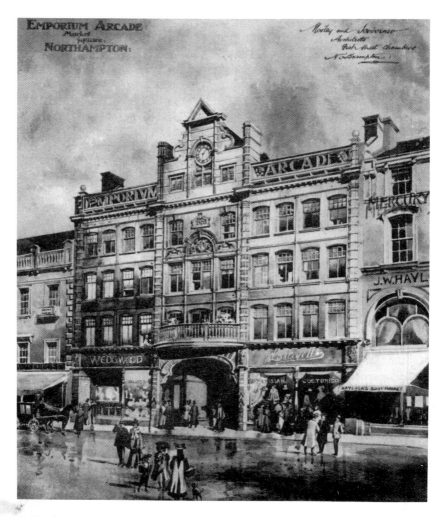

50. The Emporium Arcade (1901) – a watercolour by the architects Madeys and Scrivener.

which a property may let to a chain store. Thus we may be left with the ghastly prospect of a town centre – similar to many to be seen throughout the country – comprising multiple stores, supermarkets, chain-shops, interspersed with innumerable building societies and banks. A gruesome picture of dull uniformity.

A Northampton shopping precinct without privately owned shops is unthinkable. If one wants the best in service, choice and quality one patronises a local specialist, whether it be for jewellery, furniture, clothing, books, shoes, tobacco, sports goods or anything where a specialist knowledge of goods and customer are required. Town centre retailers know well that many of their customers travel many miles from Coventry, Bedford, Rugby and even London to patronise the specialist shops of Northampton. If these shops are excluded from the New Northampton their distant customers will not bother to travel to a shopping precinct that contains the same shops and stores that they have in their own town. Thus Northampton will lose trade that has been built up over many years.

The prospects for a shopping precinct in Northampton can be very exciting. I like to visualise an area of this precinct devoted to local shopkeepers. I know that my best customers are the same people who patronise the other specialist shops of the town. If our shops could be situated in the same area the drawing potential would be tremendous, not only to the people of Northamptonshire, but from much further afield. This area would add a cachet to Northampton that no other shopping precinct in the country has. We have to realise that participation in such a scheme is bound to entail both risk and money, but I am convinced that an exciting future awaits those willing to expand with Northampton. Good personal management and specialist knowledge will always provide a better and more profitable service than group management, no matter how well computerised. However, before this exciting prospect can be realised our planners must make decisions. It is essential that those of us under notice to quit should be given precise details of alternative premises that are to become available. We cannot be fobbed off with vague platitudes indefinitely. We retailers and our customers need and deserve to know what we can expect in the future. Prolongation of our agony by the granting of short leases on existing premises is no good – this will only lead to despair and decay. If development is to be delayed, we must know **now** and be granted new leases for a reasonable term – at least five years so that we may refurbish and improve our shops. With this in mind the planners should meet us individually to discuss our hopes and fears.

My most sanguine thoughts are of a fine new Northampton retaining its ancient individuality and at the same time incorporating a vigorous new shopping centre unlike, and much better than, any other in the country.

His stance is by no means totally against development, merely against disregard for the concerns of the already existing family businesses. In the end Churchs China was able to move into the elegant reconstructed Welsh House, one of the few buildings which survived the Great Fire, and they occupied a position in which they opened on to the top floor of the new shopping centre as well as on to the old market square.

Now Mr Church's shop is once again going through a dramatic change, this time led by Vivian's son, Stephen. In the summer of 1996 Churchs China moved out of the Grosvenor Centre, back to a more traditional shop in St Giles Street. The heady days of enthusiasm for what the new complex could offer both the independent retailer and the large multiples, did not last long. About a dozen independent shops went into the gleaming new precincts of the Grosvenor Centre. During the first fifteen years the cost of the rent, rates and service charges rose very dramatically.

There is now only one independent store remaining in the Centre – Michael Jones the Jeweller. In fact it is not only independent businesses that have closed down or moved out – even large multiples have not been able to survive there.

Churchs moved out of Welsh House because the shop could no longer sustain

51. An aerial view of Northampton town centre (1973), showing the Market Square with All Saints' Church below it , and a scene of destruction to the north and east. (Compare this with the previous aerial view of 1947).

the costs of the Grosvenor Centre. The expenses involved in running their new premises on St Giles Street are *one fifth* of what they were in the Centre.

Stephen accepts that the move may lose them some customers, but he is very positive about the new location. Firstly the shop is on a single storey, having a traditional lay-out with proper shop windows, and secondly, some customers have already said that the access will be easier for them – St Giles Street is a good side of town; with the short-stay parking near by, another asset.

The presence of Churchs China will no doubt enhance St Giles Street and the Ridings arcade, and the shop itself will surely benefit from the more traditional atmosphere of its surroundings.

Back in the early 70s, however, the town centre was all dust and confusion, in more ways than one. In February 1970 democracy had been put into action and a public inquiry held into the Northampton Master Plan. In the following year a further inquiry heard the proposals for the central area, including the Grosvenor Centre and the bus station. In the light of all the objections and protests which are voiced later in the decade, it is quite remarkable, or else a sign of sheer apathy, that only twenty four out of sixty thousand possible people objected. And at the eleventh hour, eleven of these withdrew.

At this time the West was seriously affected by events in the Middle East which led to a serious oil shortage. A few far-sighted people pointed out in the inquiry that the expressway round the edge of the town centre was not a good idea and that the investment ought to be put into public transport. Others suggested that it was stupid speculation to build central offices to employ 40,000 workers with a bus station having a maximum capacity of 5,000, people per hour, and to concentrate shopping facilities in an enclosed area at the expense of five other rate-producing trading thoroughfares. (*C & E* 20/1/78 letters)

The inquiry closed. In 1971 work began on Northampton House (the office block beside the Grosvenor Centre). It was a sign of the times that the Council's Planning Committee required the new building (and any new town centre office scheme) to have car parks on the lower floors. (Over twenty years later, in the 'Green Nineties' local government in London is now *preventing* new office developments from providing car parks in an effort to encourage people to leave their cars at home.)

1972 saw the demolition of one of the most controversial buildings in the town. It was 'a shabby complex of seedy shops'. . . . It was 'an amazing example of Edwardian architecture'. It was the Emporium Arcade, and its demolition led to a protest march into town starting along the Wellingborough road. Few doubted its need to be smartened up, but there seemed to be few who wanted it to make way for a modern shopping centre. It had stood on the north side of the market square and included two floors of little shops, the upper floor looking down on the covered pathway over a balcony. Once again, twenty years later one suspects that today it would have been preserved and called Market Square Mews. In 1972 it became one more building to add to the dust.

Beyond the Horsemarket St Andrews Church was also pulled down, along with streets of terraced houses. Now tower blocks were planned, two to seven storeys high. The residents had expressed a wish to remain near the town centre, despite the fact that they would now be cut off by the new expressway. Their new homes were called the Cooper Street housing scheme.

The population target for the town was now 250,000. Construction work had begun on the Grosvenor Centre and to the north of it, the new bus station. The Centre finally opened in July 1975, having taken six years to complete. It was a momentous time for the town – for the Council as well as the local people and the newspapers were full of speeches and opinions on the development.

Councillor Roger Winter, leader of the Borough Council, said "The centre can be seen as giving a new heart to the town." Three years afterwards, as shall be described later, his adverse comments on the planning of Northampton show that these words were probably carefully chosen for their ambivalence – did the town want a new heart?

The journalist, Jennifer Richardson, heralded the opening as not before time:
Looking ahead to when the whole centre is in full operation, it's hard to imagine that there will be much point in people travelling to other towns and cities like Leicester or Birmingham to shop.

Indeed the reverse may prove the case, with Northampton once again becoming the shopping centre of a very wide area.

But whether other town centre shopping streets will benefit or be overshadowed by the new centre, remains to be seen.

One thing is certain, however, this transition to high choice shopping is not before time. We've all made do, or gone elsewhere, for far too long.

Shopkeepers soon felt the impact of the Grosvenor Centre. The opening of the new precinct was coupled with a new one-way street system and the banning of much on-street parking. The Borough Council was even accused of secret deals with the Grosvenor Shopping centre. David Miles of Jefferys furniture shop on Gold street (the preserved Victorian facade of which is now to be the entrance to another new shopping centre) was quoted in the *Chronicle & Echo* (10/10/75) as saying;

> While it must be admitted that the Grosvenor Centre has taken trade from Gold Street, we are not worried about that because we welcome competition. But what is causing deep concern is the Council's crazy street system and the difficulties caused by street alterations. . . .What we want is equal parking facilities.

Shopkeepers felt so strongly that there were no less than four groups voicing their protests – the Gold Street Traders Association, the Abington Street Traders Association, the Chamber of Trade and the Save Northampton Campaign. At the end of October the latter wrote a letter to the Minister of the Environment complaining about the reduction of trade caused by the Grosvenor Centre, the banning of car parking on the Market Square and the closing of the Drapery and Gold Street to traffic.

> It would appear that the whole of the local authority's activities have been engineered in favouring the new Grosvenor Centre. . . . We want compensation from the Council for all affected parties and a reduction in rates. . . . The Council seems intent on channelling all the traffic to the Grosvenor Centre.
>
> We don't mind fair competition, but this seems so unfair. We feel that three quarters of the traders in the Grosvenor Centre have so far contributed very little to the rates.

Interestingly enough as soon as the major demolition work was behind them, in September, the Council set up 'Conservation Areas'. The largest one covered the area round All Saints – the Market Square, Drapery and Sheep Street, George Row, Bridge Street, Gold Street and St Giles Square. In total the areas covered 151 acres and contained two hundred listed buildings. The Council's announcement was rather overshadowed by the continuing voice of protest against change.

A year later more considered, long-term evaluations of the changes to the town centre were being presented. In 1976 Sidgwick & Jackson published a book by Tony Aldous entitled *Goodbye Britain?* The idea was suggested that 'townscapes' are just as important as buildings of architectural interest. The preserving of Welsh House in a corner of the Grosvenor Centre and of Hazelrigg House on Marefair, opposite Barclaycard, were cited as insufficient steps in preserving the heritage of Northampton.

Mr Aldous describes the Barclaycard headquarters as a 'slab-cake', having nothing to do with the traditional townscape of central Northampton. If towns can be said to have a character, then he concludes that the Barclaycard building is 'one of the nastiest pieces of character assassination' he has ever come across.

The new chairman of the Northampton Civic Society, Gerald Kendall, gave an interesting interview to the *Chronicle & Echo* on 7/6/76:

'The tragedy of it (the Grosvenor Centre) is that all or most of these new shops would have come into the expanding town in any case, bringing new vitality and colour to existing shopping areas. The older businesses in the town would have no reason whatever to complain of an expansion which brought increasing competition. They have **every** reason to be bitter about the Grosvenor development which is forcibly fed through parking grounds and bus station and which shows a brutal indifference to their longer established interests and services to the local community.

To my mind these developments illustrate the pitfalls which seem to attend all large-scale and long-term planning. The hazards seem to be integral to the whole idea of planning as conceived at present. We are no longer satisfied to let anything evolve. We are not prepared to allow the multiplicity of human interests to create, under their own momentum an environment which reflects the diversity and complexity of human needs.

Planning fails because there are too many imponderables at the outset.'

Mr Kendall's opinions express the views of many shopkeepers who had begun to suffer a loss of trade, unlike the boom that town expansion had promised. Philip Saunderson of Saundersons outfitters on the Kettering Road (and at that time on St Giles Street) remembers taking part in a protest on Abington Street, when this street was also partially closed in the interests of pedestrianisation.

'We had a picnic out on Abington Street one day. We rolled some carpet outside the Wedgwood Cafe and put some umbrellas out. We gave out leaflets. We had a tea party in the middle of the road because it was so dead. It was half-pedestrianised and had been partly blocked off. My brother Roger got cautioned for causing an obstruction and I got the television interview. We stopped it then, because the Council hadn't got the money and they wouldn't do it properly. This is what we always said.

At that time we were losing 20-30% of turnover in St Giles Street. We said "You can't do it unless you've got the money and you haven't got the money. You're not prepared to put in the infrastructure and the carparking. You've got to keep the town centre lively."'

Mr Saunderson's experience is valuable because he was chairman of the joint committee of the Chambers of Trade and Commerce in the mid-1970s. The Council approached the committee when they wanted to partly pedestrianise the Drapery. Government money was available and the Council presented an enthusiastic picture of their plans to narrow the carriageway on the Drapery, plant trees, put in street furniture, and reduce the scale of the lamps. For a trial period they proposed to see what happened to the traffic flow.

Mr Saunderson recalls:

'The street went as dead as a dodo because you took out the activity. It made it unexciting and the trade dropped off between 10 and 20%. The shopkeepers were all frightened and shutting down. Eventually we got the Council to open it up again. But while they were doing so, they were proposing that they should do the same thing on Abington Street!'

Just as the Drapery revived somewhat, so did Gold Street, but for a different reason. The Council eventually allowed on-street parking there again and life is said to have come back to the street.

52. Princes Street (1970) – the site of the present Grosvenor Centre showing the Masonic Hall (centre) and the Temperance hall cinema (far right). The Baptist Church has already been demolished across the road.

It is interesting that people like Philip Saunderson are not totally against pedestrianisation. His views will be considered again on this subject in chapter 10, on more recent trends in town centre shopping.

The attitude continued to grow among leading people that 'planning' in itself was a mistake. Councillor Roger Winter wrote a letter to the *Chronicle & Echo* on 25/1/78. (It was he who had made the ambivalent remark in 1975 on the Grosvenor Centre providing 'a new heart' for the town.) He wrote:

> Few people would argue that even before expansion parts of our town centre were in need of modernisation; indeed much of it was still Victorian, hardly suitable for the needs of our townsfolk. However, I believe as strongly now as I did at the start that the whole concept that was 'planned' was wrong, and the central area proposals that were accepted as if they were the oracle were years out of date.
>
> Once the areas declined, opposition faded, on the assumption that anything was better than dereliction. The question is: Could the town have got the Saxon Hotel, the Grosvenor Centre and the bus station etc. without it costing us the enormous sums it does?
>
> The answer is most definitely yes. Other towns have achieved far more with far less to commend them than Northampton.

R.F. Swindall, Chairman of Northampton Ratepayers, presents a voice of protest based on the way in which local ratepayers have had to pay indirectly for the changes introduced by the government-funded Development Corporation:

> It needs to be said that despite the NDC's euphoric, though self-opinionated, assessment of its own worth, it is highly probable that Northampton would

not have the area of dereliction it now suffers if the Corporation had not descended upon the town.

It is also true to say that notwithstanding inflation and government aid cutbacks, our community's rate bill would not have been as large as it now is, nor would the various public services be as stretched as they now are, had we been spared the Development Corporation's visitation. As it is, the elected representatives of the town have, since 1970, been forced to encompass a heavier and heavier burden over which they had no control whatever.

With the more than welcome constraint now placed upon the NDC activity, it is almost amusing to note their sudden interest in the plight of original Northampton. No one will deny that having now been saddled with the aftermath of progressive pestilence, the only approach is a rebuilding programme.

Ratepayers cannot influence NDC, so the rebuilding plan should be in the hands of elected councillors. (*C & E* 22/9/77)

The dereliction to which Mr Swindall refers is dealt with more fully in the Civic Society's report on Northampton's town centre which appeared in the *Chronicle & Echo* on 26/3//77. The report points out that in the booming Sixties there was an inevitable pressure on space and resources, leading to problems of congestion. The population was increasing, and with an expanding economy, land and property values were rocketing beyond the reach of most small businesses and individuals. Also car ownership was spreading.

This was the situation that led to the planned dispersal of people and resources – in other words, the creation of 'overspill towns'. Northampton was to grow in order to accommodate thousands of Londoners.

With no definite future ahead, town centre properties that may have already been neglected, became more and more derelict. Many decent residential terraces that had been converted into offices, remained untenanted. The report cites in particular streets such as Marefair, Bridge Street, Sheep Street and Derngate (where, for instance, the High School for Girls had bought up many houses for future development). The houses on Derngate were pronounced unsafe, the tenants departed, the rot accelerated. The Civic society expressed fear for the entire south-central area south of the Marefair-Gold Street-Derngate axis.

We believe that the only hope for the south-central area lies in a reversal of planning obsessions of recent times and an attempt to reconnect with the more evolutionary patterns of growth of the pre-Development era.

In other words, a return to much more local, small-scale and homespun notions of development. . . small businesses and factories, workshops – possibly selling their own artefacts, restaurants, bars and boutiques etc., and all of this integrated with a strong mixed residential sector.

The programme, we believe, implies a policy of maximum conservation, a determination to preserve and make the best active use of all existing buildings of value in the area, and a readiness to spend the minimum amount necessary to prevent deterioration until positive development becomes possible. . . . The area bounded by Marefair-Derngate-Victoria Promenade-St Peters Way could be renamed the Austin Friars District of Northampton.

Every possible help and encouragement should be given to property owners in the area, but after a period rates should be imposed on empty and neglected buildings. Property owners should be made to accept that they do not hold some automatic title to long-term financial gains regardless of the town's interests. They should be pressed to accept realistic values and rents or leave.

Opinions therefore abounded as to the way in which the town centre should have been developed. At no. 80 Abington Street, apart from a fleeting experience of pedestrianisation in the mid 70s, A. Watts & Sons Ltd. was not obviously affected by the development; it was never in any danger of being demolished or moved. Yet the pull of the Grosvenor Centre and the siting of the bus station north of it with the consequent absence of bus passengers alighting on Abington Street – all this led to a drop in trade. The growth in the population helped of course to compensate for this setback, with an increasing number of houses needing to be furnished.

Perhaps the most significant fact with which to conclude this chapter concerns the population targets set for Northampton. In 1961 124,000, people lived in the town. In 1971 the number had only grown by about 9,500. During that decade the plans for the future town involved setting a target of 200,000 residents or more. The Grosvenor Centre was designed to cater for a population of that size.

By 1981 the population had still only risen to 157,217. Regardless of recessions that may have come and gone, regardless of the success or failure that individual shops may have experienced, one fact is inescapable – Northampton had too many shops.

Chapter IX
Roy Harland and the Present Times

Roy Harland is the fourth generation of the Watts family. During his management of the shop Northampton has been expanding just as it was in his great-grandfather's time. Four generations ago an enterprising Victorian shopkeeper was set fair to benefit from trade in a growing town. Today expansion has brought with it as many problems as benefits.

Spencer Gunn is an old family friend and businessman who has provided some interesting reflections on the changing face of the retail trade in the town.

'I would say the nature of the town changed in 1935. The old businesses were getting old-fashioned. Everybody was thinking futuristic. It was the end of the first generation [of shopkeepers]. Then the war came about and that altered the face completely. There were different standards again after the war.'

Perhaps Arthur would not have agreed about being 'old-fashioned'. Perhaps he would have claimed that he was just as keen on modernising his business as any retailer in the 1920s – after all, he bought a telephone and sold his horse and cart. It is only natural, however, that the second generation, taking over from their fathers, wants to bring new ideas into a business. Ewart moved the firm into the brand new White House. Kenneth overturned some of Ewart's old-fashioned book-keeping practices and introduced new departments. How did Roy react to his new position of authority on taking over from his father? As shall be seen later, it was not in the manner that might be expected.

Kenneth had had to work hard to build up the business in the 1950s and enjoyed considerable success in the following two decades. However, the expansion of the town in the 1970s and the inflationary economy of that period were storing up problems for the shop.

Expansion would lead to a great deal more competition for a family furnishing business such as Watts, and the inflationary economy was considered by some to be a disaster waiting to happen. Roy looks back on what it was like for a shopkeeper to cope with rising inflation:

'Gradually through the 70s we were learning to live with rising inflation. As the decade went on, inflation became more and more of a problem. The country was used to having double figure inflation and interest rates. From

53. *The new double frontage, including 82 Abington Street (1978).*

a retailer's point of view that was good if you could control your costs; the stock you were carrying was a good asset (unless it was highly fashionable and therefore short-lived). Certainly the factories at that time were very busy – they weren't as technically advanced as they are now and used a lot of hand labour. In some cases furniture had to be ordered more than 12-18 months in advance. It wasn't such a worry to us the retailer, as we knew we had rising inflation. If it wasn't 20% it was going to be 15%.'

In the early 80s came the first recession of recent times, followed by the present one which has existed throughout the early 90s. Roy makes the interesting point that to some extent the state of trade today is normal, not in fact recessionary.

'It was an unreal situation in the late 70s and late 80s because of the easiness of money and the 'explosion' of house prices.

My father used to say "In a ten year cycle you get two or three bad years and 7 or 8 good ones", but now you're lucky to get five good ones. I think the difference is – when people used to start in business, they would definitely own their own property. Watts has been compromised into having to lease property more so than we own it. And that is when you have overheads which you can't keep up with.

We could have rebuilt 80 Abington Street if we'd been allowed to buy the Council property at the back. In 1972 it would have been a quarter of a million pounds for a four storey building. In those days we might have been able to finance it. Today we couldn't.'

The problems of leasing a commercial property are amply illustrated by the situation in the late 70s. In 1977 Watts had decided to lease the property next door, no. 82, to provide a better site for their toy department, release more space for furniture and to double the frontage on to Abington Street. (The lease had 18 years left to run.) In 1981 shortly afterwards they were faced with a rent review – their rent went up fivefold from £6,000 to £31,000. It was apparently a very unusual lease, with 14 year review and a steep rise each time.

At about this time fresh blood was introduced into the business. Ewart's son, Aubrey, lived in Kent, but his side of the family still owned 50% of the business. Aubrey had two sons – Patrick was involved in motor racing, but the older son, Graham, decided to leave the Health Service Administration and come and join the management side of the shop in Northampton. It was during

Graham's time at Watts that the major transfer of shares took place between the older and younger generation. Graham and Roy became the effective owners of the business between them, both representing their 50% family interests.

Roy got on well with his cousin, but disagreed with Graham's radical view of the shop. Graham had the predictable spirit of a new generation seeking to do better than the previous one. When he arrived on the scene, all he saw was a family firm from which it was difficult to earn a living. Naturally enough he wanted to make money out of the business and favoured cutting back on senior staff. He had not seen the prosperous growth of the shop during the 60s and 70s and did not see, as Roy did, that the image of Watts depended on its staff. Roy has commented

'I feel that I inherited the company and the staff. Part of our image is our staff.'
Roy was a son of whom Kenneth could be proud, in the sense that he wished to continue the supposedly old-fashioned tradition of loyalty to ones staff and in return the consequent loyalty of the staff to the shop and its customers.

It was unfortunate that Graham's arrival coincided with the recession of the early 80s. The problems must have seemed enormous to him, for on top of the recession came the advent of new competition from major national stores and the deterioration of the Watts business in Kettering. Nevertheless Roy refused 'to bring the knife out' and take action as his cousin would have wished.

Another member of the family rallied round – Roy's brother, Alan, decided to attempt to help the Kettering store overcome its difficulties. Nothing could be done, however, and the Kettering branch was sadly closed. The lease of Dalkeith Place was assigned to a kitchen business and F.A. Watts closed as a company. The closure came just in time, for the kitchen business eventually went bankrupt and the leaseholder demanded rent from F.A. Watts. Fortunately for A Watts & Sons Ltd., F.A. Watts no longer existed.

To bring to an end the story of the link between Roy and Graham, or to be more precise the link between the families of Ewart's son and younger daughter, Aubrey and Joyce:– in 1989 Aubrey's side of the family decided that they wanted to sell their share in the business. This was a golden opportunity for the Harlands to buy out the Watts. Roy has said

'You only get one chance in a generation to do it. My father had struggled for years with a 50-50 holding. He couldn't do anything without their permission and they weren't local; they only had meetings 3-4 times a year. There was a problem in getting the wider family agreement to any decisions, and new investment was difficult without the full involvement of the rest of the family. You never miss an opportunity to reduce the range of shareholders in a family business.'

In 1996 Joyce retired from the board of directors after 44 years, so the present board is made up of just Roy, his wife Tricia, who is now company secretary, and his brother Alan, the chairman. The Harlands have at last completed paying off the Watts family, but at a tremendous cost. Attention must now be turned to reducing the level of borrowing and the possibility is recognized that no. 80 may not be a suitable premises in the long term. The building that was designed with so much enthusiasm and enterprise in 1930 as the White House – one of the major furniture stores in town, might now be considered unsuitable for the furniture trade and sadly past its prime.

So the firm of A. Watts & Sons Ltd. is now in the odd position of not actually having anyone of that surname in the firm. Nevertheless the strong Methodist commitment still remains. Just as Kenneth resembled Ewart and Fred in his involvement with the social, pastoral and administrative aspects of his local Methodist church and in his work in municipal affairs, so does Roy resemble *his* father.

In 1960 Roy left Kingswood School in Bath to study at the College for the Distributive Trades in London while he worked at Heals Furniture Store. When staying in the London Methodist hostel he helped in running youth clubs for his local church and eventually felt called to become a lay preacher. Four years later, on returning to Northampton, he was trained in preaching by Ted Taylor, the father of Derek Taylor of the soft furnishing shop Carnival Taylor. Then in 1967 he married Tricia Bird, daughter of the Kingsley Park minister.

Kenneth had urged Roy to come and join the family business in 1964, but in spite of his furniture experience gained at Heals, Roy was placed in the toy department at first. He also worked alongside his father in many areas and became a director in 1968, rising to managing director in 1976, two years before his father retired.

Lay preaching takes up much of Roy's time, but in the shop it is not only Roy who is so involved in work in the local community. Many of his staff are active in various capacities in the town, and Roy has always been prepared to encourage them by allowing them to have time off to pursue their chosen field of work.

In particular, John Kightley is closely involved with the Restoration Trust of the Church of the Holy Sepulchre; his wife, Pat, makes the costumes required for Holy Sepulchre's pageants and flower festivals; Roy Horner (now retired) is a well-known singer in the local Gilbert and Sullivan group; Dave Parish and David Corrie are active members of the Territorial Army. David Parish even had the honour of being awarded the MBE in 1996 for his services in that field. In the area of voluntary activities Roy is not only busy as a lay preacher in the Methodist Church; he also works with enthusiasm in the Northampton Chamber of Trade. In 1992 he followed in the footsteps of his grandfather Ewart and became President of the Chamber. The new vice-president working with Roy was Gordon McKinnon, then manager of Marks & Spencers. Roy expressed pleasure at the fact that the new leadership combined representatives of both local and national businesses. He also admitted that the Chamber had gradually declined over the last few years, but he himself planned an administrative shake-up to re-invigorate the Chamber's work.

'The Chamber has good representation in the town centre, but not much from other areas and from the owner-occupier businesses.

We would like to see more of the smaller people coming forward and offering their services.'

He is pleased that yet again, in 1996, a local businessman, Colin Richardson, is president of the Chamber of Trade.

Roy of course had decidedly different problems to address from his grandfather, for instance the provision of car parking was a major problem, but the Chamber enjoyed good links with the Borough Council and were discussing the issue with them.

'What we want to see is Northampton promoted as a strong shopping town, which it undoubtedly is.'

A few years previously, in 1989, the Chamber of Trade had celebrated its 75th anniversary. The *Chronicle & Echo* published an interesting article by the Chamber's secretary, Jack Dunkley, looking back on its 75 years. In connection with the subject matter of this book it is worth including as an interesting snippet of history:

OLD AND NEW

It was on February 25, 1914 that 38 of the town's leading businessmen met at Franklins Hotel in Guildhall Road to form the Northampton Chamber of Trade.

Since then, for the past 75 years, the Chamber has watched the interests of the local retailers and assisted them with their problems.

Seventy five years ago virtually all the shops were local family businesses with the owner or a member of staff living on the premises, a good example being Adnitts in the Drapery with many members of staff living in dormitories on the top floor.

Over the years problems faced by retailers have been similar yet very, very different. In the early years, there was the problem of petty theft from shops – the theft of sweets, fruit etc – and today there is organised shop theft and violence.

In 1915 members stressed the need for pedal cycle 'parks' and complained of the nuisance caused by mud splashing and dust from buses and other vehicles. Today car parks and pedestrianisation are the main topics.

In the early years members complained about alleged unfair trading by street traders and under-age newsboys. Today there are the arguments about Sunday trading.

Two World Wars brought many headaches with ever changing Emergency Regulations. During the First World War members complained that market stalls were permitted 'bright' lighting whilst shops were only permitted 'dim' window lights.

In 1917 no man between 18 and 61 could be taken into employment unless he was a serviceman discharged on medical grounds. Following the Second World war, complex Regulations and Restrictions continued into the 1950s. (*C & E* 7/3/89)

The Chamber of Trade in the 1960s has done a great deal to promote the retailers' views on the ever-changing town centre. Although the Borough Council has stopped pulling down buildings as readily as it used to, new ideas are often being put forward for improvements to the town centre 'environment' – one of the key words in the 90s. This aspect of change is considered in the following chapter as it is such a major issue, and in the meantime there are other features of Roy's time as managing director which are worth considering.

On April 1980, four years after Roy became head of the firm, the country was hit by a recession which was to last for over four years. Retailers coped as best they could, and one idea was especially useful to the furniture trade: Watts decided to start offering part-exchange in order to encourage people to keep buying new items. Their second-hand trade thus became re-established in 1980, although it had been present to a minor degree before this date. Having started on the top floor of Abington Street, the storage area moved to a warehouse on St Michaels Road.

At about this time Gary Morris had become warehouse manager for Watts. He is a familiar face in the second-hand/pine department, and he remembers how much second-hand furniture had to be thrown away before a market grew up for it.

'When we delivered new furniture to a customer, we used to take the old furniture away and store it until we had enough to fill a van and take it to the dump. It used to be stored at the end of a passageway out in the open. I can remember loading up drop arm Chesterfield sofas to be taken away to the tip – people just weren't interested in them then.'

The warehouse eventually moved to a spacious site on Christchurch Road near Abington Park, where it was large enough to accommodate the workshops from Connaught Street as well. Through the wide doors goods were visible to the general public and unofficial sales began to be made. The local residents around the Park quite naturally objected and so the trade was moved to an old shop on St Andrews Street (off Mayorhold). The premises here were cold and dingy, but the second-hand sales were a steady business during the next decade; Gary even began buying in second-hand items as well.

When the boom arrived in the mid 80s the St Andrews shop seemed too down-market. The former Knights furniture shop was available, not far away on Sheep Street, although it was to be sold to developers. Watts decided to rent it temporarily and on the last Saturday at St Andrews Street Roy, his wife, Tricia, and Gary took £1100, in £5 per item sales. (Even so they still had to take a few van loads down to the tip.) Watts occupied the shop for nine months until they were given short notice to leave in July 1989.

The trade now had to be found a suitable spacious site, for sales had expanded to include pine furniture and beds. With only one month to arrange the move, Roy's attention was drawn to a large Gold Street shop that was standing derelict. This was the premises of Watts' former rival – Jefferys. The elegant Victorian facade still stands today, preserved as a listed building, a gaunt reminder of the days when Gold Street was so prestigious it was called the Regent Street of Northampton.

Behind this somewhat derelict facade was a huge shop. Jefferys the furniture shop closed after 104 years of trading and was sold to developers in the 1970s. The building was eventually taken over by Courts in about 1980. This was the era just prior to the massive retail warehouses that Courts and many other furniture retailers now favour. For about eight years Courts occupied the shop, letting off the attractive first floor as a restaurant. Then they decided to move to an 'edge of centre' site and the premises became semi-derelict before Watts decided to move in on the 29 July, 1989.

Gary remembers how the move had to take place on a Saturday. Business was so good that while they were moving items in, people were already walking into the shop to have a look round. Although second-hand items were still stocked, three quarters of the shop was devoted to new items of high quality pine furniture and imported lines for which there was no room at Abington Street, concentrating as it did on British manufacturers. For this 20,000 square feet of shop floor Watts had to pay an enormous fourfold increase from the previous rent at Sheep Street. In 1989 business was still quite good. Roy increased the staff at Gold Street from two to three and confidently expected a larger turnover in order to pay for the new premises. Unfortunately it was in 1990 that another recession arrived, triggered in part by the 2½% rise in VAT in April. The boom changed to despondency. In Northampton housebuilding suddenly came to a halt as builders found they could not sell their houses. Roy was presented with a major problem.

'In Gold Street we were getting two thirds the turnover we needed to survive.
We suddenly were forced to accept that we weren't going to increase turnover
year on year as we had in the 80s. We had to start cutting back.'

One of the ways in which Roy cut back was in reducing the Gold Street frontage, thereby helping to save on rates and rent.

The future of Watts in these premises had never been very secure in the long-term. At first they negotiated a three year lease. Then it was shortened to 18 months, but a 28 days notice clause was always built in to the leases because of the prospect of major re-development to the south of Gold Street.

This area to the south had long been somewhat derelict and ripe for development. Several planning proposals had been made for a superstore, and as the changes came closer, Roy found that he actually lost the rear part of his shop. Bulldozers moved in to pull down the back. (Rows of nineteenth century terraced houses were discovered beneath the rear of the shop.)

Stock had to be swiftly reduced in order to fit into the smaller space left. History seemed almost to have come full circle when in an effort to promote the Big Sale Roy went out on the pavement shouting "Clearance! Second-hand clearance! £15 a time!" This style of selling proved very effective and very little had to be taken to the tip this time.

A few years ago new fire retardant legislation on furniture made it impossible to sell second-hand soft furnishings (which would not meet the new standard). The second-hand trade was therefore curtailed. In fact it virtually halved overnight. There is still a useful trade in recycled furniture such as Ercol, G-Plan and Stag. In this field the same customers who buy new will also buy second-hand, and in 1996 gradually increased second-hand sales are being achieved again.

The motive behind buying in second-hand items was always to obtain a new sale. This policy has proved particularly useful with regard to Ercol and other brands like G-Plan, Nathan and Stag. There are customers who want to replace furniture, but do not want to sell privately or to a house clearer.

'We have people who want to sell Ercol furniture who ring us up from as far
away as Bedfordshire and Hertfordshire because there are retailers there

who tell them we buy second-hand. There are only four or five places in the country who offer this service. The Ercol factory itself puts people on to us.

It's a bit of an indulgence as it's only a very small percentage of our trade.'

Despite the dwindling of one side of the Gold Street trade, the popularity of the good quality pine items has increased.

When a final notice to quit Gold Street was received in Autumn 1995, Roy knew that the pine furniture was a line worth continuing and believed that although he could not afford to house it in a prime retail site such as a retail park or Abington Street, he might find a low-cost secondary shopping site (such as Kingsthorpe). Although the retail parks are attractive to retailers, Roy is realistic about their pitfalls:

'I don't think you can afford to pay prime rates for furniture. The retail parks are filled by big multiples, some of whom succeed, some don't. There have been many changes of occupancy on the Towcester Road in the last ten years and there are always empty units at the Weston Favell Centre and now at the Grosvenor Centre. Although the Riverside Park retail park is now fully let, after 12 months not all the original tenants are still there.

Of course retail parks are where the public go and where we should be, but we don't have the capital or the finance to take that sort of risk. We have had colleagues who have done so and gone bust very quickly.'

On the furniture trade in retail parks in general Roy believes that the public are beginning to realize that what is available there is much of a muchness and sold at very high prices. 'When they want something a little bit different and at a good cash price, they come to us.' Also in so far as the pine trade is concerned, quality varies enormously, ranging from very cheaply made items to the specialist made-to-order pine. Watts has focused on the decent middle of the market range.

In 1995 it was a stroke of good luck that Roy was able to move into a site extremely close to the White House. The Co-op virtually next door had recently been rebuilt, combining with C & A into the upper arcade between the Ridings and Abington Street. The shops in the lower arcade, however, between the Ridings and St Giles Street had been closed by the Co-op. This site is the very place where the early Methodist meetings were held in the eighteenth century Regimental Riding School. The Methodist connection was thus revived when Roy decided to take a lease from the Co-op on this lower arcade, thereby replacing all the space lost at Gold Street. Unfortunately a two week gap was involved which necessitated warehousing of the stock – all 23 van loads! Watts have now re-opened all of the Ridings arcade, giving superb showrooms for the pine furniture and good windows and showrooms for a large range of other furniture, chairs, sofabeds etc., plus the second-hand operation. Exposure in the centre of town can be of enormous value and perhaps more and more shoppers will appreciate the convenience of being able to visit a good furniture shop right in the heart of town.

Many people assume that for major items such as furniture it is cheaper to buy from a retail warehouse out on a retail park. They imagine that the prices in an independent retailer such as Watts are bound to be higher than in a nationally owned store. They are in fact wrong, for since the 1970s there has grown up the phenomenon of the buying group to replace wholesalers and to protect the independent retailer from the competition provided by the growing multiples.

Without a buying group a shop such as Watts would have to buy an item for a higher price than a firm owning one hundred shops all around the country. Such firms can buy in bulk and are thus able to negotiate approximately 20% discount. Consequently they could sell at a significantly lower price than a family firm owning one shop.

The advent of catalogue shops such as Argos, and supermarkets in about 1970 precipitated the independent retailers' 'counter-manoeuvre'. Customers were obviously becoming more price-conscious as they saw the discounted prices available. Independent retailers such as Watts became reluctant to buy from wholesalers (as opposed to the manufacturers). Manufacturers in their turn became frustrated dealing with wholesalers and grew more flexible. A group of independent retailers got together to deal directly with the manufacturer, thus becoming a 'buying group'. One of the first in furniture was called Floreat, with a distinctive brown and cream colour scheme which Watts adopted when it joined in the early 1970s. (The now familiar yellow and brown scheme was adopted in 1983.) The group proved especially helpful in the flooring department. With regard to toys Watts joined a group called Snowfold and then pioneered another group called Centre Toys.

To their 80th anniversary dinner in 1976 Roy invited one of the directors of Floreat, Peter Lebosquet. His speech was recorded and it still rings with an almost revolutionary fervour, extolling the virtues of the little man banding together with others against the big impersonal giants:

'Another wonderful thing about Floreat is the friendship that exists between ourselves as an organisation. I know that if Watts of Northampton have a problem, they can phone up a Floreat member nearby who will do their damnedest to assist that particular retailer with their problem.'

Floreat at that time was an amalgamation of some 200 furniture retailers throughout the UK who were all established family businesses.

'What is particularly nice about Floreat is that it gives to the independent furniture retailer the chance of competing alongside the rather boring mass multiples that we see throughout the UK. It gives you considerable buying power. This year it will total £30 million at retail prices, which is a phenomenal figure and places Floreat fourth in the league table of British furniture retailers. It means that companies like Watts can give to their customers the preferential prices that we are able to negotiate.'

Floreat later merged with AIS (Associated Independent Stores). For toys Watts continued to belong to Snowfold and later the Centre Toy Group, where Roy served as a director for six years and chairman for two. Centretoys recently closed in 1994, leading to Watts' decision to go in with Toymaster, whose head offices are in fact in Northampton. It is possible to become a branded shop displaying the Toymaster sign and holding all the stock advertised in the Toymaster catalogue, but Roy has chosen to maintain the Watts name on the frontage for the present time, retaining greater control of the stock selection.

This sacrifice of a certain amount of decision-making on stock-holding is

54. Together at the Derngate Theatre in 1995. Left to right – Leader of the Northampton Borough, Councillor Mr John Dickie and his wife Councillor Marie Dickie, Chief Constable and Mrs Ted Crewe, the Chief Executive of the Northamptonshire County Council Mr Geoffery Greenwell and his wife Mrs Margaret Greenwell, the Managing Director of A Watts & Sons Ltd. Mr Roy Harland and his wife Mrs Patricia Harland.

the drawback entailed by belonging to a buying group. It is quite a significant sacrifice for the family firms who have enjoyed their own independence for so many decades. Nevertheless both Roy and his senior staff feel a great debt of gratitude to their buying group. Roy has said 'AIS is Watts' saviour. We probably wouldn't have survived without them.'

AIS have an annual conference which Roy attends and where he can benefit from hearing about the latest technological developments to help the retailer.

In the 1996 conference Sheila Cooper of AIS presented her listeners with a forceful challenge:

'Whilst outlook is improving, consumer spending is not rising fast enough to support retailers with the wrong trading formats, the wrong cost structures or both. New ideas, fresh approaches and the willingness to adapt are now the only guarantees for success. Businesses need to focus on how they can create that experience which is comprised of many more elements than price alone.' ('Winning Through', AGM and Conference of AIS Ltd. 28/4/96)

One of the technological advances which is referred to is EDICAT, a computerised ordering system for retailers, whose software is supported and developed by BT. Multi-media versions of the catalogue will be introduced in 1997 which will include product photographs, diagrams and even videos to promote product ordering. This technology enables retailers to view products in sufficient detail to make buying decisions without leaving their shop.

In future such catalogues can also be used for in-store promotions or direct customer ordering. It is clear that a competitive shop must take on the new technology or lose out by not being able to provide the same services as its rivals. If and when consumer demand justifies the investment, BT will review making EDICAT available via the Internet. This development would then offer round-the-clock shopping from home.

In his recent book, *The Road Ahead*, Bill Gates described 'a shopper's heaven':

All the goods for sale in the world will be available for you to examine, compare and often customise. When you want to buy something, you will be able to tell your computer to find it for you, at the best price offered by any acceptable source or ask your computer to haggle with computers of various sellers!

Of course it is not known for sure how realistic are these predictions. Home shopping will not replace the social experience of the High Street or shopping centre, but it does provide an opportunity for retailers to reach their customers in a home shopping environment.

Not all products lend themselves to home buying. It has been suggested that the least suitable are shoes, used cars and fresh food, while the most suitable are books, videos, computers and toys. In this respect Roy is very much aware of the need to keep up with computer technology, so that Watts can play a part in this new development.

In talking to the staff at Watts it is clear that one of the major changes over the last few decades has been the method of buying stock through a buying group. Another change which is of interest is the changing attitude of customers.

With the growth of the consumer protection movement it is generally accepted that it has been good to redress the balance in favour of the customer, so that he does not have to suffer for faults in manufacture etc. Nevertheless Roy has noticed that the balance seems to have tipped too much against the retailer. For instance, in the furniture trade technicalities have to be explained at the point of sale. An incident remembered by John Kightley illustrates the point.

'A couple had plain carpets put in and wouldn't pay their bill because of different shading in the pile. Now I knew we had to give the customer all the information necessary according to British Standard regulations, and I had told them about the possibility of shading, pile reversal, pile compression.

The judge wouldn't believe me and the case cost the company thousands of pounds. We have disclaimer boards up and the judge would not accept they were in the right place.'

Roy admits that legislative technicalities have led to many difficulties when not everything is explained at the point of sale. A number of court cases have led to his concluding: 'In this Age of Consumerism judges side with the consumer.'

Miss Swan also has experienced the difficulties of consumerism in the toy and nursery department. As she explains:

'When they started this "customers' rights", people used to bring buggies back which had been misused, and they wanted another one. We would offer to lend them a pram while we sent it back, but sometimes that was not good enough. They wanted a new pram – now. We'd ask McLaren or Silver Cross, but they wouldn't allow it. They insist that you've got to be sure that the item has not been misused. Of course it's a matter of opinion, and the customer can be very unpleasant.'

Selling prams and buggies had become an awkward trade which Watts found hard to deal with. Then when nursery goods began to be offered cut-price at stores such as Argos and Toys R Us, Watts decided that the trade was not worth it. It was too difficult to make a profit; the sale could cause too much trouble, and the large amount of display space required could be filled more profitably with toys.

Roy expresses regret at the way times have changed in respect of customer relations:

'We would like to be able to trade in the manner in which we want to trade – to be allowed to have time to smile, to help those you really think need the help, to be discretionary in who you give discount to. But these days you have an unpleasant element among customers – the louder they shout, the more they think they can get. We don't get so many of them nowadays; our attitudes have been hardened by the last two recessions.'

Having described how awkward some customers have become with the advent of the Age of Consumerism, it is worth mentioning the good 'old-fashioned' customer relations that can still exist. Gordon Hardy, who moved to Abington Street when the Kettering shop closed, takes great pride in Watts' service to customers:

'We care about the customers and make sure we answer all their questions and find out the answers if we're unsure. It's being a family firm that does that.

A lot of our customers are the sort who expect personal service – they expect you to remember not only their name, but the piece of furniture or carpet they bought twenty years ago!'

In this respect computers have helped staff, for it is possible now to have a readily accessible database of customers and their purchases.

Early on in his career at Watts in about 1970 John Kightley was given responsibility for following through the progress of orders, so that customer service could be given a personal touch. His title became Service Manager and in those days the idea was new and progressive; Watts was an enlightened company. Nowadays the idea has caught on and Customer Service Departments are the norm in big companies.

Mr Kightley explains the way in which experienced staff can benefit a family firm relying on its customer service reputation:

'Furnishing is one of the most complex retail establishments that you will come across. For instance, people want to know if two pieces of teak will be the same, or how a curtain will hang from a particular pole or track; what is the difference between all the different types of spring unit in a sofa, or between the construction of a Wilton or an Axminster and a tufted carpet; what is the tensile strength of a fabric, and so on.

If only more people knew what we can offer. Some other shops have 16 year olds on the staff who know very little about furniture. They know the price and that's all. . . and some of our customers have had horrible experiences of carpet fitting by other furnishers. People have their carpets from us because they know they're going to be well fitted. That does make a lot of difference.'

He recognizes that many people today are what he calls 'Americanised', i.e.

'We buy today. We don't pay a lot for it, and in five years time we throw it away.' It is usually the younger generation who are likely to go for the cheapest price and not worry about quality.

As a new generation of customers come along, there can be the occasional heartening incident such as Vernon Nicholls relates:

'I was shocked recently – it made me realize I was getting older. A very nice young lady came in with a young man and she asked to see me. She said "Mum and Dad asked me to come and see you, Mr Nicholls , because you did their furnishing scheme for them when **they** set up home."'

Whatever the change, there is a sad fact behind the comments of many of the staff. Gary Morris sums it up: 'The problem nowadays is that everything revolves round money, whereas years ago it was quality and service.'

The only way forward for any firm, especially an independent family business such as Watts, is not just to keep matching prices but to keep offering the best service. Gary Morris illustrates the importance of this with one of his anecdotes about a customer at the old Gold Street shop.

'This evening I'm going out to one of my customers to deliver some Ducal, the balance of his order. So far I've sold him about £6,000 worth of Ducal furniture. When he first came in here he was shopping around and had been offered a 20% discount at two other places. I offered him 20% as well. He couldn't make up his mind on the pieces, so that evening I took a brochure and pattern swatch out to his house. I wasn't pushing him for the order, but he gave it to me the next day.

He said "The only reason I gave Watts the order was because you put yourself out to come and see me. I could have got up to 25% discount elsewhere, but they weren't really bothered."'

Gary is lucky. He can still say 'I love furniture. I love meeting people. And that's what it's all about.'

Buying groups, a new kind of customer – these are changes that independent retailers can learn to live with, but throughout this whole chapter there has been discernible the background threat of the new multiples moving into town.

Of course in the late 70s multiples were nothing new. As early as 1961 Sainsburys had a supermarket on Abington Street. It caused quite a stir, providing the American style of self-service shopping that was new to the British public.

The Green Shield stamp shops of the 1960s, followed by Argos, were dramatically new and a very important retail development. What they failed to offer in the way of personal advice and service was made up for in price and the convenience of shopping from a catalogue. However, the value placed on personal service is obviously still high. Shops such as Watts toy department notice that they are used by potential customers in the selection of an item, but then the same customers go to a catalogue shop actually to buy the product. If this habit continues, shops offering personal service will have to close and the high street will consist of catalogue shops or we will all stay at home buying on our computers. It is to be hoped that the people following this trend realize what they are doing and will feel a personal sense of responsibility for the consequences of their actions. Trends are not anonymous, but the result of the efforts of *individuals*. Something *can* be done to reverse the decline of the family-

55. In the nursery department. Left to right – Freda Riches, Pauline Swan and Ivy Hudson.

run high street shops.

Still on the subject of the toy trade, in the late 70s and early 80s Watts had to face increasing competition from chain stores opening new toy departments, such as W.H. Smiths, Boots and Woolworths. Taylor & McKenna occupied a niche in the Grosvenor Centre. Roy looked back with nostalgia to the days when his only toy competitors were Pooles (of Abington Street), Marks (of the Drapery) and the Co-op.

Another great bombshell happened when Toys R Us moved into Northampton. This again was a revolution in retailing, offering the atmosphere, size and choice of a wholesale warehouse, but coupled with this an absence of personal service and advice. Toys R Us was one of the first occupants of the new 'retail park' created on the wasteland beyond Gold Street and St Peters Way. The idea of this retail park was to create an 'edge-of-centre' shopping site, housing the new warehouse retail units and offering free car parking. The Borough Council did not at first support the idea of new shopping centres outside existing ones, and from 1975 to 1985 rejected planning proposals for such development. However, by 1986 the Council bowed to the growing popular trend. Their decision had an inevitable effect on the town centre shops, but the story of the overall development of retailing in Northampton is dealt with in more detail in the following chapter, continuing as it does the story begun in chapter 8.

Roy reflects on the shock of the new retail trends:

'All this meant that during the 80s we couldn't be sure that we were always going to get bigger each year. During the 60s and 70s you were brought up with the belief that things were going to grow. In the early 80s we had warning shots – we began to have figures that were not as good . We had to adjust our thinking and it's been difficult ever since.'

As far as competition in the furniture trade is concerned: prior to the opening of the Grosvenor Centre Roy considers Watts was reasonably fortunate in the amount of competition it had to face. Although there have long been several family firms such as Caves, Jones, (both in the Kettering Road) and Parsonsons (on the Wellingborough Road), there was only one department store dealing with furniture – the Co-op. It was thought that the demolition of Notre Dame convent would lead to a new department store occupying the prestigious site (and incidentally providing a great advantage to the shops on this eastern end of Abington Street), but the first major multiple that provided Watts with stiff competition on the furniture front was Waring & Gillows in the Grosvenor Centre. This particular firm was the first multiple aiming at the good, middle-of-the-road standard of furniture supplied by Watts.

'History tells us, [says Roy], that Waring & Gillows' move to the Grosvenor Centre was doomed, but we weren't to know that at the time. It is interesting because we were offered a really large unit in the Grosvenor Centre when it first opened – a 20,000 sq.ft. unit with a rent of £32,000 a year plus rates of £10-20,000 a year. We thought long and hard about taking it. It would have meant selling up Abington Street. We discussed it as a family, but turned it down. It just seemed too risky.'

Two different furniture businesses have occupied this unit and both have closed and moved out – the unit now stands empty.

On the edge-of-centre retail park site on Towcester Road more furniture multiples moved in during the 80s. These firms had enormous national advertising budgets. DFS, for instance, can afford to advertise fortnightly on the television and with double-page spreads in the local paper.

Roy has noticed that over the last thirty years, since advertising has become such a powerful medium, people's shopping habits have changed. We no longer automatically return to the same shop but realize that there are other stores with varying prices.

Customers can be attracted to a large chain store by the offer of 'interest-free' credit, but Roy points out the actual truth behind these offers. The product is overpriced in the first place to include the cost of the loan to the potential customer.

'If you look at the adverts, they're all based on so much a month. It's not the furniture they're selling – it's the **finance** they're selling. The public is being conned in a sense, because they're paying more than they should for the product they're buying. But they know they can afford it per week, so. . . .'

This service seems to be what the retailer has always provided. It is no different from the days when Watts salesmen travelled around on their bikes collecting weekly payments on HP agreements.

Although increasing competition is a problem for both the furniture and toy departments of Watts, both departments enjoy the advantage of offering something a little different to the general public. On the furniture side, the quality and selection is very good, and on the toy side, as has been mentioned before, there is a wide range of traditional toys, collectable items and hobby and craft items.

In 1989 Tom Hebblewhite was appointed the new manager of the toy department. Apart from the traditional toys, he built up a new range of products call 'role-playing' or 'fantasy' games. The first of these was 'Dungeons and Dragons', invented back in 1974. They are not 'traditional' toys as such, but now have a firm following of customers, mostly men, and are not subject to the vagaries of fashion toys. Hundreds of characters can be collected, some resembling Tolkien-type figures, and not all are linked with warfare. (In their early days the Methodist stand-point of the Watts family meant that Roy did not want to sell games that might encourage aggression, such as Dungeons and Dragons.) Tom describes the advantage of the hobby:

> 'These fantasy games are **social**, needing more than one person. It's so different from the lone child in front of a computer, and you have to really use your imagination, not just your reflexes.'

The obvious traditional toy which Watts specializes in is the teddy bear. They are one of the best bear stockists in the country, with prices ranging from £1.50 to £400. The expensive teddies are in fact collectors' items that keep their value, even having their own collectors' clubs. Doll's prams can be similarly expensive, with Watts' top range being a luxurious Silver Cross.

Watts has never gone in for electronic toys. They had suffered a loss in the late 70s and early 80s when they attempted to stock Spectrum computer games. As Roy says:

> 'The problem with computers and videos is that you need a lot of demonstration space, a lot of know how, and a lot of surveillance, apart from the fact that they create the wrong sort of ambience in a traditional toy shop.'

Watts toy department has been changing over the years, so that it is now aiming at more of a specialist market – the adult collector, the hobbyist and those who want crafts and other specialist items. They still sell soft toys, pre-school toys and construction games, but they don't rush to stock all the latest character merchandise.

It is quite interesting that after the great surge of interest in computer games, there is a resurgence of interest in creative activities such as the new construction toy called K'nex and a plastic version of Meccano. Watts are in fact one of K'nex's top accounts and have been able to display in their window a large K'nex windmill provided by the firm.

Tom had to carry out a major change in his department in 1994 when the recession forced Roy to make cut-backs. The size of the toy department was to be reduced to one floor in order to save on stock and on staff, and make it all more efficient. The exercise proved valuable because despite a 40% reduction in stock, turnover only went down by 10%.

Coupled with this condensing of the toy department Roy experimented with putting a toy concession in Bookscene, an out-of-centre unit on the Weedon Road. This involved renting space in the large warehouse unit run by Bookscene and paying the firm commission on whatever Watts toys they sold. This action did not prove profitable, however, and Watts withdrew in July 1995.

The exercise had been an interesting experiment for Watts, testing the water, as it were, for out-of-town retailing. However, a 12,000 sq. ft. unit at £7 a sq. ft. would cost them £84,000, plus rates, and such an undertaking was out of the question at the time.

In the face of increasing competition both the toy and furniture department were surviving on the basis of the quality and specialisation which they offered. However, it has not just been prices and advertising with which Watts has had to compete. In 1987 the arrival of Toys R Us in the town brought with it the controversy surrounding Sunday trading.

The new warehouse store flouted the law in the run-up to Christmas 1987 and opened on Sundays and even until 10 pm. The *Chronicle & Echo* were quick to report on the reaction of small competitors such as Watts. Philip Oxley, then manager of the toy department, remarked:

'We don't mind competing. That's what business is about, but when it's a case of competing unfairly, it really grates a bit. The toy trade concentrates its business towards the end of the year, and if Toys R Us are allowed to operate until January, Council action will have no effect.'

The newspaper saw the potential in the story and reported:

The season of goodwill has gone out of the window at Watts the Furnishers in Abington Street, where Toys Wars has broken out.

Ray guns, pellet bullets and the odd model tank are being lined up in the direction of the invading Superstore Toys R Us.

There followed several years of a concerted campaign between those who wanted freedom to trade on Sunday and those who wanted 'to Keep Sunday Special'.

The background to the situation dates from 1448 when the Sunday Fairs Act came into force. On this act was based the 1936 Shops Act, which in turn formed the basis for the 1950 Shops Act which largely prohibited trading on a Sunday.

In the decades after the Second World War life changed. England was no longer a nation of small shopkeepers. The big multiples began to rule the roost.

In 1988 the Northampton Keep Sunday Special Campaign was begun with the Rev. Ted Hale as its acting chairman. He was quoted as saying :

'In the new parliamentary session the government is almost certain to try again to allow commercial interests to overrule wider interests in a life of real value. Unless people are vigilant and active, another socially desirable aspect of our lives will be taken away.'

For those older residents of the town there must have resounded echoes of the campaigns in 1946 to keep cinemas closed on Sunday and games banned in the parks. Fred Watts had presided over the earlier debate forty odd years before, but Roy felt a helpless bystander in the face of the power of the giant multiples who could afford to pay any fines levied to punish them, and also in the face of the increasingly secularised general public.

In 1993 Sunday trading became legal. It is a sign of the hard recessionary times that the Methodist principles of a firm such as Watts had to be sacrificed in order to compete for trade. Watts began to open on Sundays in the pre-Christmas period.

Sunday trading hits the small firms harder than the large multiples. There are two reasons: An independent shop usually employs only 3-4 staff, compared with a pool of 20 staff which might be found in a large multiple store. It is therefore less likely that there will be a sufficient proportion of the staff willing to work on Sundays. Secondly, independent shops are usually situated in parades of high street businesses to which shoppers are not attracted on a Sunday. Sunday shoppers enjoy the shopping outing as a chance to browse and wander round large stores. Small independent stores are not part of the complexes which provide this facility, and so it is not worth their opening on Sundays. The custom is just not sufficient (except perhaps prior to Christmas). Nevertheless, the Sunday trade carried on in the big stores inevitably reduces the potential trade of the smaller shop.

The battle over Sunday trading in general may have been lost, but Roy is always optimistic about Watts' future ability to face competition, and apart from Christmas time is able to close his shop on Sundays.

The battle over prices has not been as hard as might be expected, for belonging to a buying group has made it possible for Watts to buy in cheaply. Toys, for instance, can be bought in at the same price as at Argos or Woolworths. It is the failure in efficiency of the business that prevents Watts from always *selling* the toys as cheaply as Argos or Woolworths. Roy believes that Watts must be computerised to improve its efficiency and thus help reduce its prices even further. The toy shop will in fact be computerised by Toymaster by 1997.

Computerisation in the retail trade is just one small part of 'the Computer Revolution'. It has been suggested that the spread of the personal computer heralds a new industrial revolution to compare with the one which saw the introduction of machines into manufacturing in the 18th century.

Computers even play a part in new advertising techniques. 'Talking Pages' is a free method of listening to the Yellow Pages via the telephone, and Watts have recently started participating in the scheme. At the present time, however, the most efficient advertising medium for them remains the Yellow Pages.

In contrast it might seem very old-fashioned, but Vernon Nicholls still finds a good detailed listing of products in a sale a very effective method of advertising. It is a method which he first introduced in Kenneth's time:

'I still do a sale list in the paper. When I first did it, we suddenly had a tremendous response. In fact I put my head on the block when I took out that first listing page. I can remember Mr Kenneth was shocked that I was contemplating spending so much of the firm's money on an advert. Prior to that we'd normally had an 8" double or triple column saying 'Watts Sale Now On' and listing half a dozen examples. Anyway we did get the response and I've stuck to it ever since.

I got quite carried away one year. I thought I would see what the public's reaction is to a list in line. I put the manufacturer's name, then the item, then a price (not a reduced price) and 'Stock Take Clearance', and carried it on like a continual reading. Do you know, that was fantastic. It worked. You wouldn't think people would read all through those things, but it worked. They'd phone up and say "Can I see the Alson's suite or whatever." So we knew people did read it.'

Another tradition in Watts that might be considered old-fashioned, but is favoured for its effectiveness is the layout of the furniture display. Many modern stores have their items arranged in room settings, but here again Mr Nicholls believes the public prefer more of a casual arrangement.

' I've heard stories – we've had two companies who decided they would completely renovate their building. They put it into room-sets and showed less stock. One company had to reverse the decision because sales dropped dramatically, and the other went out of business.

I think it's foolish if you're well-established suddenly to change course. It's still true that many people like a lot of furniture pushed together. They like hunting through it.'

People still enjoy the jumble of items pushed together in the White House and in the Ridings arcade shop, just as they enjoyed looking through the pieces of furniture that spilled out on to the pavement in the Kettering Road days.

Likewise people still appreciate the service and trust that is built up over long years of doing business with a family firm such as Watts.

Unlike Kenneth, Roy cannot yet be certain who will be willing to take over his business when he retires in about ten years time. For all the clashes of opinion between Kenneth and his son, at least Kenneth knew that he would be handing over the shop to a willing and committed member of the family. Roy's two children, Susan and Adrian, are now in their twenties; Susan is a teacher and Adrian runs his own music business. As shareholders, together with the present directors they will have to help reach the decisions on the long-term future of the business – will this mean bringing in a new Managing Director, or selling the business, or finding somebody in the family to carry it on?

This chapter has described the changes in the retail situation since the mid-70's, from inflation leading to recession, from the competition with huge multiples to the growth of the buying group, from deferential customers to the boldness induced by a new consumerism, from half-day closing to Sunday trading, from HP ledgers to credit cards and computer technology.

Roy Harland has had to face much that would have taken his father by surprise, but he has reacted with the same positive attitude and the same support for traditional values with which Kenneth would have responded.

At the beginning of this chapter it was suggested that Roy did not react to his new position of authority in the manner that might have been expected. He did not sweep away the old, as a son might have done, faced with taking the shop into the twentyfirst century. Perhaps that was no surprise. In a world where the big multiples and modern advertising were bringing in sweeping changes to the retail trade, Roy saw that the old-fashioned values of his father were not only worth standing by, but could be used to make A. Watts & Sons Ltd. special in the eyes of the consumer.

Who knows if one day Watts will beat a retreat from the high street and occupy a warehouse unit 'edge-of-centre'? Perhaps one day that will be the only way forward, but if so, the tradition of personal service and expert advice will no doubt remain.

As in the case of the story of Kenneth's time as managing director, the picture is not complete without recalling the developments that have been taking place in the town and their effects on the local shops. In 1976 when Roy took over, Northampton was still expanding and the Borough Council's attitude to the town centre was still evolving and changing. The final chapter of this tale will therefore be the story of this same town centre and the discussions and arguments about its fate in the last two decades up to the present day.

This is the setting in which Watts has evolved and whose influence has been felt throughout Roy's time as managing director.

Chapter X
The Changing Town Centre
1976-1996

At the end of chapter 8 it was clear that whatever the plans for the future of Northampton, in 1976 there were too many shops for the existing population of about 145,000. The Grosvenor Centre had been built in 1975 for a population of 200,000, and in 1977 the population target was slashed to 180,000. As it happened, Watts' trade in furniture, curtains and carpets benefited from the residential building development taking place to the east of the town, but no shop exists in isolation, and the changes that would eventually take place in the immediate vicinity of Abington Street and in the wider area of the whole town would have an inevitable effect. In this respect Roy was to face problems that his father probably never dreamed of.

To set the scene for the late 1970s there is an article by Ian Nairn of the *Sunday Times* as part of a series on *Towns in Trouble*:

Three hundred years ago, in 1675, Northampton had a disastrous fire. It was rebuilt and given public buildings and a market place as grand as any in Britain.

It stayed intact until 10 years ago, with little war damage and few slums. Now it is a dump. Two comments overheard last weekend were "like a morgue on Sundays" and "bloody ghost town now, isn't it!"

What happened? The key decision was to double the town's size, taken in 1969: a crazy thing to do to a place that was already happily in balance. Even then, it could have been done successfully – albeit with difficulty.

In fact the result is deplorable and probably irremediable, short of another – selective – fire. The whole north side of the market place was taken out for the Grosvenor Centre and the product is a gruesome combination of gentility and brutality.

Gentility in the lacklustre facades around the market place; brutality in the multi-storey car park which rears above them, dominating everything. And sheer terror – I'm not being melodramatic – in the blank, man-hating passageways that run through to the new bus station, at the back of it all.

Yes, the other three sides of that market place are intact, and the market still functions in a dispirited kind of way. But instead of shops there are building society offices, estate agents, the headquarters of the Development Corporation. All fine in their way, sprinkled through the town. But not en masse, in the very place where vitality and diversity should be at its strongest.

And yes, the Grosvenor Centre did preserve the Welsh House, a tudor building of 1595, in the north-east corner: there is a self-congratulatory plaque there to record the fact. What it **doesn't** say is that permission to demolish was refused in 1972.

Disaster on disaster. The first thing to hit you in the eye on the way up from the station is the juggernaut of Barclaycard House. And though the new brewery down by the river is a dramatic and impressive building by Ove Arup and Partners, all that it brews is Carlsberg lager, which ain't quite the same animal as it is in Copenhagen.

The old brewery belonged to Phipps – a local family so involved in the town that there is a Victorian suburb called Phippsville.

Ten miles south of Northampton you are in Milton Keynes, which could have taken all the new development and made it into something truly modern and truly worthwhile. Milton Keynes is on the main line (at Bletchley); Northampton is on a loop with no fast trains to London. It all adds up.

It all adds up to a mountain of misery, and the human consequences are only just beginning to show. It must never happen again. We now know all about the evils of tower blocks, indiscriminately used; we must learn from Northampton the worst evil of town expansion inadequately carried out. In the Angel Hotel, where I stayed – a cheerful place against the odds – the juke box stuck, forever, on the Beatles record of "You can't do that". You can say that again, squire. (*Sunday Times* 26/11/78) (Copyright Times Newspapers Ltd., 1978)

By 1978 the economy showed signs of entering a recession and the Borough Council had to have a serious re-think over the town centre 'to overcome major problems'. (*C & E* 12/4/78) The amount of office space was to be cut and there was to be more multi-storey car parks. Private housing could be planned for on the sites initially set aside for offices. Nevertheless it was decided to leave some options open on office space in readiness for a national economic recovery.

The dilemma over an uncertain future use of land demonstrates the difficulties faced by councils all over the country, whose responsibilities for town planning had increased so dramatically since the 1960s. The scale of development had grown. Expectations were so much higher. The sophisticated tools of market research forecasts and planned targets were now becoming available and had to be used to plan the way a town would grow. In the case of a town chosen to expand to accommodate London overspill and to become a New Town, the responsibility was all the greater.

The business slump was becoming so bad in 1978 that the move towards pedestrianisation was reversed in order to generate more traffic. The Council thereby implicitly recognized that loss of passing traffic causes loss of trade.

Abington Street had been closed at the Abington Square end. (Philip Saunderson's story of the protest against pedestrianisation has already been mentioned in chapter 8.) It was decided to re-open it, thus allowing motorists direct access to Abington Square and the Mounts. The *Chronicle & Echo* reported on how much the news pleased town centre traders, many of whom had argued that business was bad because of the restrictions on access for cars.

> While the present restrictions on traffic have successfully removed through-traffic from main shopping streets, resulting in great safety for pedestrians and reduced traffic noise and pollution – they have presented exit problems to motorists, particularly visitors to the town. (*C & E* 1978)

Traders were no doubt also to benefit from this lifting of motoring restrictions. The *Chronicle & Echo* article was headed '*Kiss of Life for the Centre*'.

Pedestrianisation was only one of the Council's policies which were to cause difficulties for local shopkeepers. During the early 1980s. the new phenomena of retail warehouses outside town centres was beginning to emerge. Fortunately for Northampton traders in the late 70s and right up to 1986 the Borough Council opposed retail development outside existing shopping areas, just as Kettering Borough Council opposed it.

A hint of change came in 1979 when the Council made an application for a change of use for the area of wasteland known as Baulmesholme. This was the land, part of which had been the town gas works. It was situated between Carlsberg Brewery, the river Nene and St Peters Way. The land had been idle for many years because it had been landlocked by the railway and the river. The change of use application was necessary as it was part of one of Northampton's common grazing lands decreed by Royal Charter to be made available in perpetuity as grazing land for people who lived in the old walled town. An alternative site of the same size had to be found as close to the original as possible.

The Council's plan in 1979 was not for a retail development, but for an estate of small businesses. Sixty plots were to be created for industrial or warehouse use. The Borough Councillors at least had no plans for a 'Nene Valley Retail Park', although Council officials were to express growing concern over the Council's refusal during the early 80s to grant planning permission for retail development outside existing shopping areas.

However, the Council's attitude had its drawbacks for lovers of old Northampton. Along with the Council's opposition to edge-of-centre or out-of-centre retailing went support for new shopping developments *within* the town centre itself. In this respect the eastern end of Abington Street looked old-fashioned. To be sure the New Theatre had gone, but on the northern side there still stood the Convent of Notre Dame. Behind its graceful Victorian facade were beautiful panelled rooms, a chapel, a lovely garden with mature trees – an oasis in the heart of town.

In April 1979 the announcement was made that Notre Dame was to be demolished to make way for a new shopping centre. Its demolition was to be another major landmark in the development of Northampton for many old Northamptonians, starting with demolition of the Peacock Hotel. Even the old trees were cut down and the nuns' cemetery concreted over.

It was hoped to find a large nationally known retailer to occupy the vacant site, but in the end a row of small retail units was built. Watts had hoped to see a major store open to provide a counter-balance to the pull of the Grosvenor

Centre. John Kightley comments sadly:

'If you go down Abington Street, turn about in front of Marks & Spencer and look back up this street, it's no more than suburbia – it's building societies, it's banks, travel agents, a cafe – we haven't got anything such as a John Lewis to give us the draw.'

This mention of John Lewis is a reminder of the presence of Milton Keynes and of the growing fear of competition from a rival town. The new president of Northampton's Chamber of Trade, Tony Wilson, made a speech at the annual meeting in April 1980 emphasising the special merits of Northampton's shops:

Service and courtesy are the things that count. Let us work hard at this and make shopping a pleasure for people. Customers wish to discuss the merits of the goods they are purchasing with someone who knows what they are talking about and takes an interest.'

He emphasizes the abundance of excellent specialist shops of all shapes and sizes that attract people from outside the town.

The Conservative leader of the Borough Council, Cyril Benton, was quoted as saying "We have nothing to fear from Milton Keynes. We have far more character" (*C & E* 2/7/80). British Rail reported that their sale of Awayday tickets indicated that people were coming to Northampton purely to shop. The town was said to attract shoppers regularly from London, Oxford, Cambridge, Luton, the West Midlands, even Milton Keynes.

The Council decided to raise car park charges from 20p to 30p in August of that year, but this led to a drop in the use of the car parks. The fear still existed among councillors and of course traders that Northampton was losing customers to Milton Keynes with its free car parks and Wellingborough's Arndale Centre, where there were also no car park charges.

A few months later double yellow lines were put down in the Drapery. Traders such as Roger Saunderson (whose protests at pedestrianisation have already been mentioned) protested, advocating more on-street parking in the town centre. The campaign ran for several years, for the protesters believed that shoppers had come to expect to park as close as possible to the shops they wished to visit. Retail parks with their free parking close by had changed people's expectations. Town centres must change accordingly.

The following year, 1981, the recession of the early 80s began to take its toll. In December headlines announced that the town was seeing the worst trade for ten years.

Traffic congestion was still a problem despite the fall in business, and the Council decided to introduce a new scheme to help ease the problem. They called it Park 'n Ride. Cars could be parked for free outside the centre of town at the Council offices, and passengers would be ferried into town by bus for a nominal fee. The idea was so new and so much against the public's expectations that the scheme failed to start with. In 1982 roads in the town centre during Christmas were said to be chaotic, but it was not until 1987 that the *Chronicle & Echo* reported that Park 'n Ride was a success. In the mid 90s it is now an established way of shopping on Saturday throughout the year, but the idea took a long time to become accepted.

Also in 1981 the Development Corporation announced that they would close in 1984. This was of course no surprise, as their job had been essentially a temporary one, their work to be taken over by the Commission for New Towns. What was a surprise was that in 1984 the maximum population would be only 170,000. As has been mentioned before, the Grosvenor Centre was designed for a population of 200,000. Businesses had even been extending on the basis that the town would grow to 230,000 by the mid 80s! *(C & E* 22/12/81)

The recession continued and unemployment grew. In 1983 in an effort to fight the competition from Milton Keynes car park fees were reduced to 10p for the first hour and 20p for two hours. Later that year in the run-up to Christmas late night shopping on Thursdays was introduced as an experiment. The secretary of the Northampton Chamber of Trade, Jack Dunkley, hailed the idea as a great success. Traders were said to be jubilant over the new spending spree. The general manager of Debenhams was quoted as saying that "Loyal shoppers in Northampton have had enough of the big out-of-town centres and are returning in droves to the stores on their doorstep" *(C & E* 23/12/83).

In the light of this remark it must be remembered that the Borough Council was still resisting retail development that would compete with existing centres. Any loss of custom referred to would have been to places some distance away such as Milton Keynes.

In 1984 the Council refused planning permission for a shopping development at Weedon Road, saying that it was outside Northampton's designated shopping area and would result in loss of trade for established shops. Also it would jeopardise the future of a shopping precinct in Northampton's Southern District (Danes Camp). It is interesting to note that the government had turned down the proposal for the shops in the Southern District because there were "already too many shops in the town" *(C & E* 15/3/84).

As trade began to improve in the town centre, the Council felt able to raise car parking charges once again, leading to a heated discussion about the rights and wrongs of the cost to potential customers. It was pointed out that towns such as Nottingham, Ipswich and Cirencester had adopted a scheme where car park tickets could be presented at shops in exchange for a discount on goods purchased. (In those days, prior to the green revolution, did anyone ever think of the unfairness to bus users?)

That same year pedestrianisation made its first major mark on the image of the town centre when the Fish Street to Wellington Street section of Abington Street was closed to traffic. British Home Stores and Marks and Spencer expressed their delight at the increase in their trade. 'People can actually walk down Abington Street, whereas before they had to fight their way down,' said the manager of BHS, Richard MacKenzie. The Co-op, however, disagreed, presumably regretting the decrease in passing traffic. That year they closed their food department.

In a persuasive speech that should once and for all have put paid to the continuing jealousy about Milton Keynes' 'free' car parks, Councillor Ron Liddington, chairman of the Council's traffic committee, argued that free car parking did not exist.

'Someone has to pay for the upkeep and cleaning of car parks. Ratepayers with no car should not have to pay for something which benefits traders. In Milton Keynes the cost of 'free' parking is reflected in the rents paid by traders and the costs passed on to the customers.'

He supported a rise of 40p to 60p and explained that even this 50% increase would not cover the cost of maintaining Northampton's car parks.

His argument failed to convince people such as the lady who wrote to the *Chronicle & Echo* on 15/11/85. She described how one Saturday lunchtime she had taken 40 minutes to get out of the Grosvenor Centre from the top floor, and declared that next time she would rather spend 40 minutes driving to a nearby town where the parking was easier and cheaper.

Roy Harland also participated in the debate, but the traffic problem to which he objected was concerned with traffic flow, down Abington Street. 'We've had drivers say they had trouble finding our store after negotiating the one-way system,' he remarked (*C & E* 15/11/85). He pointed out that the Ridings car park was a particular problem, as anyone leaving who wanted to go south had to go miles around the north side of town before they could head for home. 'The time people spend trying to park is time they could be spending in our shops. We compete with Milton Keynes for shopping, and they just don't have hassles. It's very frustrating for people who are new to the town, and if it goes on any longer, they will just shop elsewhere.'

The Northampton Chamber of Trade expressed their concerns about traffic to the NBC and the NCC, who insisted that traders had been consulted. The flow was made the way it was to make access to car parks easier. The NCC claimed that traders had originally been in favour of the scheme.

For all the furious debating over keeping Northampton's town centre attractive to shoppers, the fact remained that by 1985 Northampton had rocketed upwards in Britains's Top Thirty in the shopping centre charts. It now ranked number 26 – a dramatic improvement on being number 53 in 1971. (Milton Keynes was number 87).

1985 was the last year in which the Borough Council held out against pressure for out-of-centre shopping developments. Signs of change were already visible and Watts was given a taste of the competition to come. In April Queensway opened on the Weedon Road and MFI expanded its retail showroom in Brackmills. The *Chronicle & Echo* were quick to describe the development as 'the battle of the Furniture Giants'.

In June there was a meeting of the Planning Committee to discuss the Borough Council's continuing discouragement of shopping developments outside established areas. The last report on retail patterns in and around the town centre was ten years previously and since then there had been radical changes in shopping habits, including the revolution of pedestrianisation in town. The Development Control Officer, Roy Talbot, said 'Over ten years ago retail warehouses were something of a novelty. Now they are more a part of the retail scene' (*C & E* 27/6/85). He voiced the opinion of Council officials that the Borough's policy was against that of the County Council and that it was time for it to be reviewed.

In response to the debate the Northampton Chamber of Trade along with Debenhams urged Council planners not to reverse their decision to refuse planning permission for out-of-town hypermarkets. They feared 'the life-blood of the town would ebb away if the green light were given to such schemes.'

However, the following year, 1986, saw the decisive change in the Borough Council's policy and they began to approve planning applications for major edge-of-centre and out-of-centre retail developments. They were being bombarded with planning applications for five major retail sites. Even the town centre was in danger of changing its image in the face of the great competition for spaces from businesses such as betting offices, amusement arcades and estate agents. In the end, in February the Council proposed a 'shops only core area' for the town centre, to include most of the Grosvenor Centre, much of Abington Street and some of the Market Square. This was an important and effective way of helping the viability of the town as a shopping centre.

The Commission for New Towns had by now taken over from the Development Corporation and had to start fulfilling its task of executing the proposals for the use of land in its possession. They announced plans to build a non-food retail warehouse next to Lings Forum (eventually to be Great Mills) and caused a storm of protest.

A few months later even more controversial plans were publicised for the riverside site between Billing Aquadrome and Weston Mill. In this green unfrequented corner of the Nene Valley there were to be non-food retail warehouses and 'leisure facilities'. Many local people protested at the devastating change this proposal would make to this precious piece of natural environment.

The Council were divided on the issue. One Labour Councillor was reported as saying:

'If it goes ahead there will be jobs lost in the town centre. One of the members (of the Commission for New Towns) was talking about changing the nature of the town centre to specialised shopping – that **did** alarm us.'

On the other side a Conservative Councillor explained

'Our immediate reaction is that we have spent so much on the town centre to make it viable, we don't want to lose retailers who have stuck by us. [These remarks were then followed by the] But. . . we have to take into account new shopping trends' (C & E 31/10/86).

In order to support their case and provide guidance for the future, the Council commissioned a report to be called the Northampton Shopping Impact Study.

In the meantime Mr Woodhall of the Commission for New Towns was quoted as saying:

'I would like to stress that in no way is the Commission seeking to dilute or in any way undermine the trading pattern of the town centre. We believe that this scheme is one which is complimentary to existing traders of the town. It is a concept which is essentially one which is going to happen by virtue of market forces somewhere in this area.'

Mr Woodhall's view could be countered by pointing out that fortunately market forces cannot be the sole dictators on the use of land. Planning permission still has to be granted. In this case, however, the Borough Council succumbed.

Riverside Park, as it came to be called, is an out-of-town development. The term 'out-of-town shopping development' needs some clarification. It is a retail site built outside the urban boundary, i.e. on a greenfield site. The majority of shopping developments which the Council has to consider are 'out-of-centre' or 'edge-of-centre' developments, i.e. they are outside or on the edge of the boundaries of the existing town centre and district shopping centres, but not 'out-of-town' as such. There are eight of these district shopping centres in town: St James, Far Cotton, Kingsthorpe, Kingsley, Kettering Road, Wellingborough Road, Hunsbury and Weston Favell.

One of the first of these edge-of-centre sites was at St James End and also the Towcester Road site, now called Nene Valley Retail Park. The original plans for industrial use were changed to allow for retail expansion.

Even Sainsburys, one of the mainstays of the Grosvenor Centre, wanted to move out to the edge of town and build on the Weedon Road at Duston. They were only allowed to build their new store when they promised to remain in the Grosvenor Centre for at least another five years.

The other major supermarket in the town centre was Tesco on Gold Street. In 1986 they moved out, leaving a great gap in the town centre's selection of shops. Traders on Gold Street were seriously affected, and were quoted as saying that 'the street died' when Tesco moved out. Even traders on the Drapery noticed a difference in the level of business. It was with great pleasure therefore that these same traders heard of the proposals for a new shopping development on the six acre site between St Peters Way and Woolmonger Street. This area was very dilapidated and the new plans would bring life back to Gold Street and Bridge Street. Initially the plans were for a food store, car park and leisure facility.

The boom was well underway in 1986 and Christmas trade proved very successful. It was suggested that late-night shopping and traffic-free streets helped to increase business, but it is never easy to find a clear reason for a changing trend. The boom had arrived and everyone benefited to a certain extent, at least in the short-term.

Despite being in the middle of a boom, in 1987 the town centre retailers expressed their sense of insecurity. The chairman of the Chamber of Trade, Jack Dunkley, was quoted as saying that he believed the Planning Committee of the Borough Council would not approve any big edge-of-centre complexes likely to threaten established traders (*C & E* 7/3/87). The current proposal that sparked off Mr Dunkley's statement was the shopping complex to be combined with the new sports stadium at Sixfields. (In the event this development did not include shops.)

Other traders expressed their worries. One town centre retailer wrote a letter to the *Northants Post*:

> With the mushrooming of out-of-town shopping areas with their huge free car parks, will the town centre of Northampton become a white elephant? It seems to be that the attitude of some council officials is anti-car, and with the chaotic parking and one-way street systems in Northampton, will succeed

in driving the shopping public away from the town centre.' (*Northants Post* 21/10/87)

The Chairman of the Borough Planning Committee, Councillor Stan James, presented a different view of the town centre:

'We have struggled for years to retain small traders in the town centre.

I am thrilled with the way the town centre has retained the small trader and absorbed the tremendous pressure for large retail units... Peacock Place is for the little man ... It has been uppermost in my mind and the mind of the Planning Committee to retain the viability of the town centre, and I feel we have done just that.' (*M & H* 18/9/87)

Perhaps the major event of that year as far as the future of the town centre was concerned was the publication of the Northampton Shopping Impact Study. As has been mentioned, it had been commissioned by the Borough Council from a firm of London specialists to guide the Planning Committee for the next 15 years (to the year 2002).

The *Chronicle & Echo* reporter, Chris Hilsden, made a lively assessment of the report:

Weighing in at 1lb 1oz. and stretching to 92 pages the Northampton Shopping Impact Study is quite a weighty document in several senses.

It sets out to provide guidelines for the development of retail shopping in the town for the next 15 years or so.

Developers and retailers quite naturally want to establish new stores where they will bring in most customers and make the biggest profit. And at the moment fringe-of-town developments like Weston Favell and Mereway are the biggest attraction with their easy car parking and access to the high speed road network.

The job of councillors is to take into consideration the interests of everyone in the community – both the general public and the retail community

It is no good allowing a lot of out-of-town development if it means we end up with too many shops chasing too little money, a town centre which is half dead and decaying, too much traffic drawn to unsuitable roads and major stores based where they are inconvenient for a substantial portion of the population.

The report underlines the widespread move across the country in the last few years towards out-of-town shopping centres, a process fueled by town centre congestion, car parking restrictions, growth of car ownership and the huge increase in the sale of 'leisure' goods such as DIY, gardening etc.

It is good to see that the general tone of the report is one of caution and that this seems acceptable to councillors on the planning committee.

Planning chairman, Councillor Stan James, told me: 'It is a very worthwhile report and will help us tremendously in making up our minds about applications. We need to establish a firm policy for the future of shopping in our town.'

The need to set out a firm policy and to stick to it is extremely important as it gives the council more chance of fighting off appeals from disgruntled developers who might have their planning applications turned down.

While for most of the people who have ready access to cars out-of-town shopping may be a wonderful thing, the move in that direction does have disturbing social and commercial implications.

The more that fringe shopping centres become established, the more town centre retailers will want to join the trend.

Not long ago there were four supermarkets in the centre of Northampton. Now there is just one. It is obviously easier for someone with a car to get their groceries at Weston Favell or Mereway, but it is probably easier for many people without a car to get to town than it is to get to other areas.

And according to the latest census results, it is the elderly section of the population – those least likely to own a car – which is increasing fastest.

In fact the 1981 census showed that only 37% of local households contained children under 16, indicating that this 'elderly' trend is going to increase even more.' (*C & E* 26/2/87)

One of the conclusions of the report was that the town could only support two major non-food superstores over the next four years. Also it did not favour proposed developments on St Peters Way, the old Cattle Market site or the Abington Lock River Village.

So far applications for shopping developments totalled 1.4 million sq. ft., i.e. 57% of the existing town shopping area.

To help them assess the needs of Northampton the consultants looked at the potential spending power in the town's catchment area up to the year 2001. They concluded that over the next 15 years total retail expenditure could increase by 45% at current levels, and a total increase in floorspace of 33% was acceptable (*M & H* 27/2/87).

The words 'at current levels' are very significant. Predicting human behaviour is not an exact science and predicting the amount of shopping that will be done by the population of Northampton is certainly not a science. Market research, with all its forecasts and targets, can be very misleading. It seems unwise to allow the predictions of specialists to influence what is built and where in Northampton. The boom has now been followed by one of the longest recessions of recent times, and so the value of any forecasts and targets made in 1987 is immediately brought into question. In fact the over-expansion during the boom may have increased the severity of the recession.

By the end of 1989 the *Chronicle & Echo* was reporting that shopkeepers were facing a bleak Christmas as sales slumped in the wake of high interest rates.

'Some businesses are predicting a cut in staff and possible bankruptcy, because most High Street traders rely on the Christmas period for 25% of their total income' (*C & E* 6/11/89).

Yet despite fears of an imminent recession, major retail firms were still queueing up for premises in the town, and dozens of office and industrial firms were also setting up business after relocating to Northampton.

As the recession got underway some shopkeepers were faced with increasing difficulties. The Chamber of Trade did a survey and found that some were faced with rent rises of over 400%, with the average increase being 70%.

Even the prime retail area of Abington Street felt the recession, with 8 units standing empty in 1991. The *Chronicle & Echo* described the centre very gloomily: 'A ghost town of empty shops, offices and factories has sprung up in Northampton as businesses feel the chill wind of the recession.' (*C & E* 4/11/91) People decided to use their money to pay off debts, wishing they had never 'bought now and paid later' back in the 1980s. It became fashionable to be quite open about not being able to afford expensive items and to have to pay on tick. Debt used to be the ultimate shame. It was now an acceptable part of life.

It was unfortunate for town centre traders that at the height of the recession, in 1993, the Sunday Trading laws were altered, enabling big stores, especially those on edge-of-centre or out-of-town sites to cream off the business on Sundays. Smaller stores with their correspondingly smaller number of staff were more reluctant to burden themselves with seven day opening. Buses did not alter their schedules to cater for possible shopping trips into town on Sundays. More and more people started to get in their cars on Sunday and drive to retail parks.

Another blow to town centre traders was the pedestrianisation programme. The Borough Council decided to pedestrianise virtually all of Abington Street. Staff in A. Watts & Sons Ltd. watched in dismay as the life went out of the street. No longer were old people able to drive up and park outside. The buses had been gone for some time already; the banning of cars was the final straw. It is remarkable therefore that there were only two objectors to pedestrianisation at the inquiry – Spin-a-Disc and Roger Saunderson (who does not even own a shop in the street). The other shopkeepers were either apathetic or believing that pedestrianisation was what the public wanted.

The words of Philip Saunderson of Saundersons the Outfitters are worth quoting here:

'With pedestrianisation Abington Street went dead as the Drapery went dead, and trade dropped off.

Really the danger is that we end up with estate agents, solicitors, banks, building societies – everything that doesn't have to carry stock. If you add the investment in stock on to a shop premises, you can hardly make a living out of it.

If you've just got staff and you're a service industry, you can probably just about survive. The only way you can survive is if the landlords drop the rent, which some of them are doing. Otherwise a property can stand empty and go derelict.

The town centre wants to be an exciting place to go into, and to do that you've got to spend a lot of money. One statement comes to mind at a recent meeting of the Council – "We've got to make it safe for people to walk about in the town centre." Well you can make it so safe for people to walk about that you kill off the businesses in there and there's nothing for them to walk about and look at. So it's self-defeating . I think this is what the Council is in danger of doing. People are being molly-coddled too much.

As soon as we got car parking back into Gold Street, as soon as we got traffic up and down the Drapery again, life came back in. The cars went up and down.

Kenneth Harland would look on the town centre now with great concern.'

The following year, in 1994, Riverside Park opened – out-of-town. It was said by the councillors who supported it that the shops were not competing with existing town shops; they were offering something new. Few were convinced. The names and size of shop may have been new, but some of the names were duplicated on the western side of town. The Borough Council saw it as providing a balance to the central and western concentration of retail warehouses in town. Watts saw no need for 'a balance'. In the early 90s Abington Street had not been aware of any 'even balance' between retail warehouses on the west of town and town centre shops that could be spread eastwards across the town. To continue the metaphor: central and west-of-town retail warehouses were decidedly riding high on the seesaw of market forces. Independent town traders felt that *they* could well do with a balancing out of the share of trade.

Riverside Park seems, however, to have been a foregone conclusion because of decisions made in the past. The spokesman for the Commission for New Towns, who owned the land, could simply say that retail and leisure purposes were what the land had been designated for when it had been taken over by the Development Corporation, and later the Commission for New Towns. This statement cleverly crushed any counter-arguments or democratic involvement. The decision had been made, 'full stop'.

Regarding the shopping developments proposed during the first part of the 90s, the Borough Council has been working to several documents, one of which is guidelines provided by the Department of the Environment in 1993 called Planning Policy Guidance: Town Centres and Retail Developments. One of the key statements here runs as follows:

> A cautious approach to out-of-town retailing is justified where significant long-term impact is likely – for example in contributing to urban decay resulting from significant increases in vacant shop floorspace and reduced levels of investment in neighbouring town centres. . . . Prime considerations in planning for new retail development should be to enable the community to benefit from increased retail competition, to ensure the effects of proposals upon the vitality and viability of existing town centres are properly weighed and to ensure that a choice of transport mode is available. (PPG 6 Revised, para 27)

As far as the choice of transport mode is concerned, where are the bus stops outside Nene Valley Retail Park or Riverside Park?

Further guidance on retailing is provided in Planning Policy Guidance: Transport, published in March 1994. This lends even more support to developments within existing centre or edge-of-centre sites:

> In local plans authorities should enable development within central and suburban shopping centres, encourage local convenience shopping by promoting the location of facilities in local centres, where suitable central locations are not available seek edge-of-centre sites for larger retail development and avoid sporadic siting of comparison goods shopping units out-of-centres or along road corridors. (PPG 13, para 3.10)

In its Local Plan the Borough Council points out that these guidelines were published *after* they had prepared the Local Plan Deposit Draft, thus implicitly indicating that retail sites such as Riverside Park would not be allowable under strict observance of the national guidelines (with reference to the 'siting along road corridors').

The Northampton Local Plan produced by the NBC in 1994 is of interest to anyone concerned with the way in which Northampton is changing. The background paper on Retail Policy gives an overview of recent shopping developments and possible plans for the future. It was influenced of course by the Northampton Shopping Study produced by DTZ Debenham Thorpe in 1986 and which has since been updated in 1988, 1990 and 1994. (The very fact that the study has been updated so frequently shows the drawbacks of relying on forecasts made by a 'Shopping Study'.) It is impossible to make accurate forecasts of how much shop floorspace a town can sustain per head of population.

The Local Plan states that Northampton has now a well distributed foodstore provision on all the major routes into town – Tesco at Hunsbury, the Co-op in Far Cotton, Sainsburys on the Weedon Road, Aldi/Iceland on the Harlestone Road, Safeway and Waitrose at Kingsthorpe, Safeway on the Kettering Road, and Tesco at Weston Favell.

The Plan pinpoints the initiatives taken to improve the town centre environment – pedestrianisation, the appointment of a town centre manager, the installation of CCTV, street entertainment, the refurbishment of the outdoor market, plus the opening of Peacock Place in 1988 and the renovation of the Co-op in 1993.

Concerning the plans for the immediate future, there are several sites mentioned which could be developed for retail purposes. When these have been described, it will be interesting to see how they fit in with the national, regional and county guidelines.

The Shopping Study is understandably full of figures and percentages and so the following assessment may seem very dry. However, a brief summary of the study is included here for its relevance to the impact of town planning on an independent retailer such as Watts. The following two pages can easily be skipped by a reader more interested in local developments than local statistics and an assessment of the Northampton Borough Council's planning policy.

THE SHOPPING STUDY

First of all it is necessary to appreciate that there is a formula to work out how many shops can be sustained by a certain number of residents, i.e. as the total spending power of Northamptonians increases, so can the number of shops.

The Shopping Study forecast in 1990 that up to the year 2000 there was a remaining capacity for 30-67,000, sq. ft. of large food stores, 201-418,000, sq. ft. of 'bulky goods' stores and 278-355,000, sq.ft. of residual comparison goods stores. (It might be helpful to note that a store such as Tescos, Mereway or Sainsburys, Weedon Road comprises about 65,000, sq. ft.; Waitrose – 21,000, sq. ft.) This meant the suggestion was being made that the town could sustain no less than 840,000, more square feet of shop floorspace (on top of Sainsburys at Weedon Road, Riverside Park and a development at Woolmonger Street which were all expected to take place).

In June 1991 as the recession hit the country, the forecasts were considerably reduced to 23,000 sq. ft. for large food stores, 191,000 sq. ft. for bulky goods stores and 412,000 sq.ft. for comparison goods stores – i.e. 626,000 sq. ft. in total.

Following the deposit of the Local Plan in 1994 it became clear that the 1990 forecasts were dated and another statistical update was commissioned.

In order to take into consideration the needs of existing stores within the town centre and other shopping centres, two forecasts were produced – one assuming that existing shops increased their share in the market (the upper range forecast) and another assuming that existing stores did not expand their share of the market. This seems to be a first recognition that existing stores were struggling and affected by the building of new stores.

For large food stores the upper range forecast indicated that whilst there would be over-capacity of 34,000 sq. ft. by 1996, this would be balanced by a capacity for 39,000 sq. ft. by 2006. The lower range forecast calculated that there was *no* additional capacity for new food stores in the whole period to 2006.

The forecast of immediate concern to a shop such as Watts is that for bulky goods. The upper range forecast capacity was for 280,000 sq. ft. by 2006. The lower range forecast claimed 120,000 sq. ft. more floorspace could be sustained.

For residual comparison goods stores it was estimated in the upper range that 340,000 more square feet could be sustained by 2006, and even 300,000 sq. ft. in the lower range.

SITES FOR DEVELOPMENT IN THE LOCAL PLAN
With these huge statistical forecasts behind them the Council identified in its Local Plan sites which could be developed for retailing. The locations considered suitable for non-food retailing comprise: Bridge Street/Angel Street, the Cattlemarket, Weedon Road (near Sainsburys), Mereway (adjoining the Hunsbury Shopping Centre), Little Billing Way (for which outline planning permission already exists), the former power station at Nunn Mills (opposite Avon Cosmetics, the development would also include other uses), Towcester Road (the British Gas site adjoining Nene Valley Retail Park), and the St Peters Way/Woolmonger Street site behind Gold Street which has already been mentioned.

This then is the crux of the Local Plan for future retailing developments. How do the plans fit in with the national, regional and county guidelines?

NATIONAL, REGIONAL AND COUNTY GUIDELINES
As far as the national guidelines on transport are concerned, it has already been mentioned that they advise councils to enable development within central and suburban shopping centres, and where suitable central locations are not available, to seek *edge-of-centre* sites for larger retail developments and to *avoid* sporadic siting of comparison goods shops *out-of-centre* and *along road corridors.*

The Regional Planning Guidance for the East Midlands (published in 1994, again after the Deposit Draft Plan had been prepared), follows similar lines in supporting town centre or district centre locations for new stores: 'Out-of-centre developments may be acceptable, but only where the scope for in-centre developments is very limited.' (Regional Planning Guidance for the East Midlands Region PPG 8, para 4.16)

The Northamptonshire County Structure Plan (approved by the Secretary of State in 1989) likewise advocates protecting the vitality and viability of a town centre where planning applications for large-scale shopping developments are under consideration. Planning permission for such developments should only be given provided certain criteria are met – for instance, if 'by reason of its size, servicing and access requirements (it) cannot be satisfactorily accommodated in association with established areas'; secondly, if it 'does not adversely affect the environment and amenities of a locality'; thirdly, if 'the access, car parking and public transport facilities are able satisfactorily to cater for such development.'

The national and regional guidelines were published after the Deposit Local Plan was drawn up, but it is still a worthwhile exercise to see how far the Borough Council's policy fits in with them. In any case the County Structure Plan was in existence already by 1989 and should therefore have been conformed to.

The retail development of Riverside Park is an out-of-town site and would not have been allowed if all the various guidelines were followed. It could have been satisfactorily accommodated in association with established shopping areas. There are several sites on the edge of the town centre – the Cattlemarket, Towcester Road, Woolmonger Street – that are now proposed for development and were not considered. Riverside Park adversely affects the environment. It generates more traffic and spoils a green space.

The proposed location on Little Billing Way 'reflects the outline planning permission which exists at the site'. Here again this is not an existing shopping centre and its development for retail purposes would not conform with national, regional or county guidelines. The Commission for New Towns arranged for the planning permission and it may well be that, as in the case of Riverside Park, the Borough Council is unable to reverse, only slightly amend the decision. It would seem totally unfair and undemocratic if plans made prior to the early 90s could not be changed. In 1987 central government began to convey the message that out-of-town or out-of-centre developments needed to be curtailed. Opinions are now changing in this direction as we become more environmentally concerned in the 1990s. Are we to be saddled with outdated proposals made by the Commission for New Towns?

The site for Safeway on the Kettering Road was another area of green space in an area that would suit residential and parkland development. It certainly does not seem to be 'an established shopping development', unless it could be classed as on the edge of the Kingsley shopping centre.

Concerning public transport provision, there are no bus stops outside Riverside Park and no regular bus service to Nene Valley Retail Park. Public transport facilities do not therefore cater satisfactorily for them.

Here is the statement of the general planning strategy in the Local Plan :
to promote the role of Northampton as a sub-regional shopping centre

through a planned expansion of an appropriate range of shopping and associated uses for the benefit of the town. The intention of the Local Plan policies is to **concentrate major shopping development primarily in the town centre and district centres,** to strengthen and enhance the range of shopping facilities to meet the needs of the town and **to accommodate new forms of retailing to meet the needs of both customers and retailers.** (Northampton Local Plan Deposit Draft Para 6.5)

Most of the statement is heartening, but then comes the vague phrase 'to accommodate new forms of retailing to meet the needs of both customers and retailers'. The door seems left wide open to retail developments as and where the Borough Council pleases. If the Council meet the needs of *retailers*, there would be retail warehouses all over the town, and beyond.

According to the Local Plan the criteria which have to be met for retail developments outside existing centres are firstly 'if the development would be inappropriate within an existing centre'; secondly, if there is no undermining of existing centres as a result; thirdly, if the impact on traffic and the immediate environment is acceptable. (Northampton Local Plan Background Paper No. 4, p.23)

It is the second criteria which stands out as being disregarded. Existing centres are struggling. In a recession how can there possibly be 'no undermining' of existing businesses if more shops are built? To be sure the population of Northampton is still increasing, but by only another few thousand.

Another disturbing factor in the Local Plan is the Council's belief that 'it is reasonable for retail proposals to be assessed in relation to forecasts of shopping requirements.' These forecasts keep changing, and who knows when a decision is taken that very soon becomes out-of-date through a change in the economic climate and because out-of-date forecasts have been followed? Furthermore the Council also states that 'forecasts are not regarded as rigid floorspace limits' (Northampton Local Plan Background Paper No. 4, p.24-5). These few words seem to devalue all the preceding paragraphs about forecast capacity. It sounds as though there need be *no* limit imposed on retail development.

CURRENT DEVELOPMENTS

To bring this chapter up-to-date: 1995 and 1996 have seen a possible beginning of the end of the recession, and the Council has been eager to promote the success of its policies in safeguarding the viability of the town centre.

In September 1995 the local press announced that the Council was delighted with the success of late night Thursday opening, which was celebrating its first six months.

In October the Chamber of Trade presented the Council with a manifesto designed to revitalise and upgrade the town centre. The Council agreed to consider the proposals – items such as better on- and off-street parking, more park and ride, more big stores such as John Lewis, more restaurants, an alcohol and begging ban, and of course shopping to be concentrated in the town centre.

In the same year Northampton secured almost £10 million over the next five years from the government's Single Regeneration budget to help improve derelict urban areas. Then in March 1996 the Borough Council produced a report painting a very positive picture of the town centre. '*Myth that town is dying is dispelled*' was the headline in the *Chronicle & Echo* (14/3/96). According to the figures 71 retail organisations had registered an interest in moving into Northampton town centre and only 4 of the town's shops were listed as vacant. (This would only apply to the main streets of the centre.)

It remains to be seen how robust the town centre really is and whether the background policy of building more and more shops elsewhere in town can co-exist with this new 'vital' town centre of which the Borough Council is so proud.

Before concluding this chapter on the changing town centre there is one other aspect which has to be considered apart from retail developments.

One hundred years ago shopkeepers only had to think about attracting customers into their shops. Since the 1960s the number of cars on the road has increased so dramatically, causing such congestion that shopkeepers now become involved in the debate on how their customers should actually get to their shops – are there bus stops outside? can people park outside? can they park cheaply enough in a nearby car park?

Watts has seen the road outside the White House change – first came restricted one hour parking, then part pedestrianisation and no bus stops, and then complete pedestrianisation. They have noticed a reduction in trade whenever access to their shop is made more difficult.

Maybe as the environmental concern of the 1990s grows, an even more dramatic change might occur to Abington Street. The Northamptonshire County Council has a very progressive attitude towards transport, as is evident in their Transport Policies and Programme 1996-97 (published July 1995). The plan is to reduce the number of private cars in town by traffic management. This would be done in several ways.

First of all, improvement to public transport is necessary, coupled with more cycle routes. Secondly, the number of short stay parking spaces will be increased to stimulate shopping and the tourist trade. Thirdly, there will be a reduction in long-stay parking spaces. Long-stay is to be encouraged on the edge of town with more park 'n ride schemes available – possibly at Sixfields, Boughton Crossing, Thorplands roundabout, Riverside Park, Eagle Drive (near Delapre Golf Complex) and a possible area to the north on the present Althorp estate. Long-stay in town will also be made more difficult by allowing more Residents Only parking schemes in the side streets close to the centre.

The most exciting proposal, however, and the one that could transform Abington Street again is the policy for a rapid transit tram system. Under-used and disused railway lines are to be protected from development so that they can one day be used as part of a public transport plan. This would include the line to Boughton Crossing and the old line by the River Nene out to Brackmills. Both the Borough Council and the County Council have backed the idea for a network of electronically powered trams in Northampton, developed by a Northampton-based company, Rapid Transport International plc (RTI). The town is said to be a suitable location for this revolutionary mode of transport which has already helped to regenerate a number of European cities.

The rapid transit system would come through Abington Street. Perhaps Watts will once again have a tram stop outside the White House. It would be a strange turn of events if the scene outside the shop came to resemble the 1930s again, with a tram moving slowly along the centre of the street.

This chapter has described a background of enormous and rapid change affecting town centre shopkeepers. The thought is an appealing one that 'traffic management' might one day render the central streets more peaceful and reminiscent of the good old days enjoyed by Arthur and Ewart. Along with this development is of course the tense situation where the small central shops are competing with large warehouse units on the edge of town. It would seem that this situation is the most important problem that has ever faced Watts the Furnishers. It is a difficulty the scale of which Kenneth barely dreamt of, but which his son, Roy, has had to meet almost throughout his time as managing director. A determination to survive and take his firm into its second century has helped him find a way to continue providing Northampton people with a good traditional furniture and toy shop right in the heart of town.

A Conclusion

For all the uncertainties about the future, one thing is sure, that Arthur little imagined a book would be written on his family and his shop when he set up business in Adnitt Road in September 1896, nor that the lives of his sons, grandchildren and great grandchildren would be closely involved with so many aspects of Northampton life.

Some of the older members of the Watts family fear what might happen in the years ahead. Francis has said 'I think the town centre will be a graveyard if they don't watch out. This policy of out-of-town shopping centres has got to stop.'

On the other hand, Roy Harland faces the future with determination and confidence. Modernisation and an upholding of the traditional values of personal service and good value quality products are the way to help his business survive into the twentyfirst century. With a loyal staff behind him and the loyalty of customers both old and new, it might just be true that Watts the Furnishers will continue for a long time to come to be a part of the town centre scene, and to share the view . . . from behind the counter.

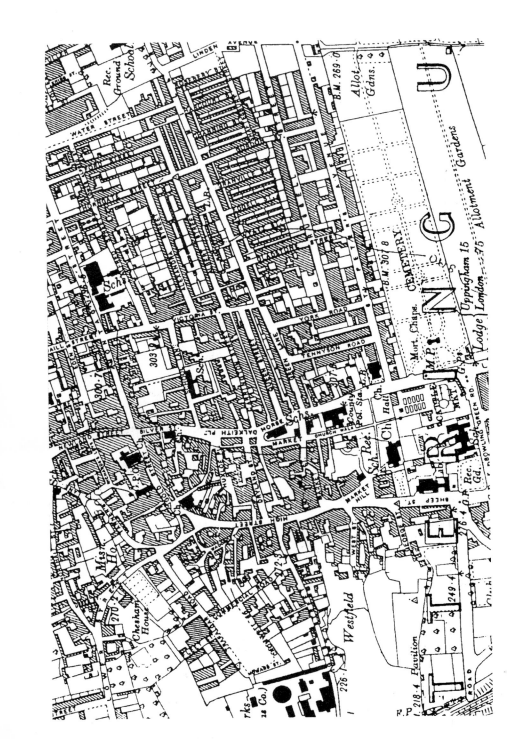

Index